IT'S SO EASY

{AND OTHER LIES}

IT'S SO EASY {AND OTHER LIES}

The Autobiography

DUFF MCKAGAN

First published in Great Britain in 2011
by Orion Books

1 3 5 7 9 10 8 6 4 2

© Duff McKagan 2011

A CIP catalogue record for this book is available from the British Library.

ISBN: 978 1 4091 3163 2 (Hardback)
ISBN: 978 1 4091 3164 9 (Export Paperback)

Typeset by Input Data Services Ltd, Bridgwater, Somerset
Printed and bound by CPI Group (UK) Ltd, Croydon, CR0 4YY

The Orion Publishing Group's policy is to use papers that are natural,
renewable and recyclable and made from wood grown in sustainable forests.
The logging and manufacturing processes are expected to conform
to environmental regulations of the country of origin.

Orion Books

Orion Publishing Group Ltd
Orion House
5 Upper Saint Martin's Lane
London, WC2H 9EA

An Hachette UK Company

www.orionbooks.co.uk

For Marie Alice McKagan

He went on and on down the road, finally coming to a black woods, where he hid and wept as if his heart would break. Ah, what agony was that, what despair, when the tomb of memory was rent open and the ghosts of his old life came forth to scourge him!

—Upton Sinclair, *The Jungle*

✛ CONTENTS ✛

AUTHOR'S NOTE

My friends and old band members may remember some of the stories I recount differently than I do, but I have found that all stories have many sides. These are my stories. These are my perspectives. This is my truth.

PROLOGUE

✦ ✦ ✦

August 2010

DJ Morty is standing behind a table in the backyard. The anemic last rays of a late-afternoon California sun stream over the adobe roof tiles of the single-story house I share with my wife, Susan, and our two girls, Grace and Mae. In front of the DJ table is a small patch of polished wood planking—a portable dancefloor we rented along with a few little tables and chairs.

Morty scans the tracks on his laptop, fiddles with his MP3 console, and double-checks the cords connecting it all to the amp and speakers. He's getting ready for the party. I've met Morty a few times at other events around town; I often end up feeling like the middle-aged dork at hipster shindigs, and sometimes the most comfortable thing to do is chat about music with the DJ.

Today, though, as the afternoon fades to evening in Los Angeles, I'm even more out of place than usual. Or at least less welcome. Grace is turning thirteen today and we're throwing a party. Grace has already told me and her mom to stay completely invisible. Her exact words: "You're *not* invited."

Ah, the joys of parenthood.

Still, Susan and I are going all out for the party. Birthdays at this age are a big deal. I remember when turning eighteen was considered a milestone, but even at that age my celebration had been limited to a few good friends and family members. Partly it's to do with socio-economic differences between my childhood and my children's. These days we live in a far more affluent area than the one where I grew up. When you can afford more, you do more, and the kids in a neighborhood like this develop a set of expectations. So in addition to the DJ, there's a photo booth and a henna tattoo station.

Another reason we've gone all out is that we suspect this could be the last time Grace, the older of our two girls, will want to celebrate at home. Oh well.

Planning this party was bewildering at times. When I called the photo-booth rental company, the first question they asked me was, "What will the theme of the photo paper be?"

Huh?

"Yeah, the machine spits out strips—four little passport style photos on each strip. You can have writing along the side."

I got up to speed fast. The strips of passport photos will read *Grace's 13th Birthday Party*.

Now the day of the party has arrived and I'm making sure everything is ready. The woman at the henna tattoo table has her book of patterns set out and is comfortably settled into a chair. I take her a glass of water. I hungrily eye the food table, where the makings of a delicious Mexican feast are being laid out. The caterer is even dredging up tortillas, made from scratch, out of a kettle of oil. There's also an ice-cream bar. I love ice cream. This is going to be a kick-ass party.

DJ Morty puts on Prince's "Controversy" and cranks the amp up to party volume. I yell to Susan. When she joins me in the backyard, I drag her out onto the little dancefloor and start to shimmy. Little known fact about the original members of Guns N' Roses: we dance. Everyone knows Axl's serpentine slither, of course. Far fewer people know that Slash is also a world-class Russian crouch-down-and-kick-your-legs-out dancer. And me, well . . .

"Dad!" Grace yells.

I stop in the middle of a move and turn to look at her.

"People are going to start arriving any minute!"

She's mortified. Already.

Yes, yes, yes, I can deal with this. She's just growing up.

As Grace's friends start to show up, Grace again makes it clear that she has forbidden us from coming out to the backyard during the party. Apparently parents are an embarrassment at this age. Whatever. Peeking out the back door as the party gets into gear, I see little packs of boys and girls hanging out, smiling, and laughing shyly. Some of these kids are starting to look like adults—one of the boys is almost my height.

An hour or so later I'm thinking I should *really* take a glass of water to the guy running the photo booth and see how things are going for the henna tattoo artist and make sure everyone is behaving. I'm responsible for these kids, after all. Hell, the DJ is a friend of mine, so I have to visit a little bit with him. And, well, the food looks really good, too, and I should probably get a plate for Susan. And while I'm at it, might as well get one for myself.

I'm not snooping, I tell myself as I push open the back door and step out. By no means. I am just being a responsible dad. Yep.

Should I go for ice cream now, or come back for it later?

As I round a blind corner of the house I stop cold, stunned: a boy and a girl are kissing.

Oh shit.

I freeze, not sure what to say or do.

I wasn't expecting *this*.

My mind rushes through a checklist I didn't even realize I had in my head. It's a checklist of things I was doing at this same age—and it doubles as a checklist of things that as a parent I do not want a group of kids in my charge doing in my backyard.

Are they boozing?

No.

Smoking pot?

No.

Dropping acid?

No.

I started smoking pot at a really young age: fourth grade, to be exact.

I took my first drink in the fifth grade and tasted LSD for the first time in sixth grade when I was offered blotter acid by an eighth grader on my way to Eckstein Middle School in Seattle. In the Northwest, mushrooms grew everywhere—on parking strips and in people's backyards and just about everywhere else—and I soon learned which ones got you high. By the seventh grade, I was an expert at distinguishing liberty-cap mushrooms from all the ones that didn't get you high. I first snorted coke in seventh grade, too. I also tried codeine, quaaludes, and Valium in middle school. There wasn't a huge stigma attached to child drug use in the 1970s, and there weren't warnings blaring everywhere about the dangers.

Then I got into music. The early punk-rock movement in Seattle was pretty minuscule, so we all knew one another and played in one another's bands. I was only fourteen when I started playing drums, bass, and guitar in various bands, and I went on tour with the Fastbacks at a time when other kids in my class were eating cotton candy and dreaming of the day they'd be old enough to get their driver's licenses. I continued to drink a ton of beer and to experiment with LSD, mushrooms, and coke.

Are these kids taking mushrooms?

No.

Cocaine?

No.

Then, sometime in 1982, as the music scene became bigger and a recession hit Seattle, we all noticed a huge influx of heroin and pills. Addiction suddenly skyrocketed within my circle of friends, and death by overdose became almost commonplace. I witnessed my first overdose when I was eighteen. I saw the first love of my life wither away because of smack and one of my bands implode because of it. By the time I was twenty-three, two of my best friends had died from heroin overdoses.

Heroin?

No.

Thank God.

These kids aren't doing drugs or drinking. No telltale scents or dilated pupils out here.

My mind races on to other activities I had gotten into by Grace's age.

My best friends and I started hot-wiring cars in middle school. Car theft led to breaking and entering. I remember breaking into a church one night in hopes of getting some microphones for my band. My liquid courage at that age had no conscience. When I couldn't find any microphones, I swiped the Communion chalices to use as pimp cups for my cocktails. That crime made the papers.

Any of these kids stealing cars?

No.

I saw all these kids arrive. Their parents dropped them off. None of them arrived on their own.

Oh, God, what about . . . ?

I was introduced to sex in ninth grade. The girl was older—I was playing music among an older set of people. The thing about that first time, though, is that I got the clap. Of course, I couldn't just stroll up to my mom at thirteen and announce that I had something wrong with my penis. Luckily for me, somebody in this older group of friends steered me to a free clinic run by Catholic nuns. The experience was not cool at all. Nope. It scared the hell out of me. Still, after a three-day dose of low-grade antibiotics, I was gonorrhea-free.

But these kids are not having sex. In fact, these kids' hands aren't even wandering. No, these kids are just kissing.

Sex?

No.

This reverie—the run through my mental checklist—takes less than five seconds, but the boy and girl have stopped kissing and are now standing there frozen, their shoulders pulled awkwardly up toward their necks as if to withstand the bluster they expect to come their way.

I take a deep breath.

"Sorry," I say.

I nod and quickly retreat back into the house.

+ PART ONE +

KNOCKIN' ON HEAVEN'S DOOR

CHAPTER ONE

+ + +

I've known a lot of junkies. Many of these addicts have either died or continue to live a pitiful existence to this day. With many of these same people, I personally witnessed a wonderful lust for life as we played music together as kids and looked toward the future. Of course, no one sets out to be a junkie or an alcoholic.

Some people can experiment in their youth and move on. Others cannot.

When Guns N' Roses began to break into the public consciousness, I was known as a *big* drinker. In 1988, MTV aired a concert in which Axl introduced me—as usual—as Duff "the King of Beers" McKagan. Soon after this, a production company working on a new animated series called me to ask if they could use the name "Duff" for a brand of beer in the show. I laughed and said of course, no problem. The whole thing sounded like a low-rent art project or something—I mean, who made cartoons for adults? Little did I know that the show would become *The Simpsons* and that within a few years I would start to see Duff beer glasses and gear everywhere we toured.

Still, given what I'd seen, a reputation for drinking didn't seem like a big deal. But by the time Guns N' Roses spent twenty-eight months from 1991 to 1993 touring the *Use Your Illusion* albums, my intake had reached epic proportions. For the round-the-world *Illusion* tour, Guns leased a private plane. It wasn't an executive jet; it was a full-on 727 we leased from MGM casino, with lounges and individual bedroom suites for the band members. Slash and I christened the plane on our maiden journey by smoking crack together. Before the wheels had left the ground. (Not something I recommend, incidentally—the smell gets into everything.) I don't even remember playing Czechoslovakia; we played a stadium show in one of the most beautiful cities in East Europe not long after the fall of the Berlin Wall, and the only way I knew I'd even been in the country was because of the stamp I found in my passport.

It wasn't clear anymore whether or not I would be one of those who could experiment in his youth and move on.

Every day I made sure I had a vodka bottle sitting next to my bed when I woke up. I tried to quit drinking in 1992, but started again with a vengeance after only a few weeks. I just could not stop. I was too far gone. My hair began falling out in clumps and my kidneys ached when I pissed. My body couldn't take the full assault of the alcohol without bitching back at me. My septum had burned through from coke and my nose ran continuously like a leaky faucet in a neglected men's room urinal. The skin on my hands and feet cracked, and I had boils on my face and neck. I had to wear bandages under my gloves in order to be able to play my bass.

There are many different ways to come out of a funk like that. Some people go straight to rehab, some go to church. Others go to AA, and many more end up in a pine box, which is where I felt headed.

By early 1993, my cocaine use had gotten so bad that friends—some of whom did blow or smoked crack with me—actually started tentatively talking to me about it and trying their best to keep my dealers out of my life when I arrived back home for a break between legs of the tour. Ah, but I had my ways to circumvent all the do-gooders. There was always a way in L.A.

One of the lies that I told myself was that I wasn't really a cocaine addict. After all, I didn't go to coke parties and never did cocaine by itself. As a matter of fact, I hated the idea that I was doing coke. My use was strictly utilitarian: I used its stimulant effects to stave off drunkenness and to allow me to drink for much longer—often days on end. Actually, mostly days on end.

Because I was adamant about not becoming the stereotypical "coke guy," I didn't have any of the fancy grinders that made coke a lot easier to snort. I would just get my package, open it, break a rock into a few smaller pieces in a half-assed way, and shove one of the pieces up my nose. Of course I could tell that my primitive process was taking a toll. The inside of my nose was always on fire; sometimes it flared so badly that I would double over in pain.

Then the wife of my main coke dealer, Josh, got pregnant. I started to worry that she had not given up her own coke habit. One thing that never seeped from my otherwise porous ethical system: almost anything could be deemed fun and games when it was your life and your life alone that you were toying with, but endangering someone else was unacceptable. I was not going to participate in any situation where an innocent third party was being harmed. This was not just basic human decency. I came from a huge family, and by this point in my life I had something like twenty-three nephews and nieces, all of whom I had known since they were infants. No, I was going to put my foot down here with Josh and his wife, Yvette, and insist that she quit. I didn't yet have the capacity to lead by example, but I did offer to pay for her to go to rehab.

Both Josh and Yvette swore to me that, Geez, of course she had stopped and that there was absolutely no fucking way she would do that while the baby was in utero. I was suspicious.

One weekend they came to stay with me and some other friends at a cabin I had bought on Lake Arrowhead, up in the mountains east of L.A. Josh had of course brought drugs, and I had given him and Yvette one of the downstairs bedrooms. I could tell Yvette was high. To check on my suspicions, I quietly entered their downstairs bedroom and found her bent over, snorting a line of coke. Seeing this for myself made me realize that I had sunk to an all-time low in my life. I lost it. I kicked them out of my house and told them that I never wanted to see them again. I was seething—at them, and at myself.

I quit coke that day and drank myself through two brutal weeks of serious depression.

Even though the effects of my drinking were more noticeable without the coke, drinking proved harder to rein in, much less kick. These days I know what having the "DTs" actually means. The clinical definition of *delirium tremens* is a severe psychotic condition occurring in some persons with chronic alcoholism, characterized by uncontrollable trembling, vivid hallucinations, severe anxiety, sweating, and sudden feelings of terror. All I knew then was that it wasn't cool. I felt really sick. My body was falling apart so badly that I looked like I was getting radiation treatment.

Throughout the *Use Your Illusion* tour I had recorded songs on my own, ducking into studios here and there. This project had served largely as a way to kill time I would otherwise have spent drinking, and I didn't know what the demos were for, really. One of them—my version of Johnny Thunders' "You Can't Put Your Arms Around a Memory"— ended up on GN'R's *Spaghetti Incident,* the album of cover songs issued just after the end of the *Use Your Illusion* tour.

I played a bit of everything over the course of the sessions—drums, guitar, bass. I sang, too, and if you listen to the album, it's clear I wasn't able to breathe through my nose on some songs. Then at some point during the tour, a record label employee who was out on the road with us asked where I kept disappearing to on off days. I told him. When Tom Zutaut, who had signed Guns to Geffen records, caught wind of the demos, he asked me if I would like a solo deal. Geffen, he said, could release the tracks as an album. I knew he was probably being mercenary about it—by this time Nirvana and Pearl Jam had broken, and Zutaut probably figured leveraging my Seattle roots and punk connections could help the label reposition GN'R.

But I didn't care. To me it was a chance to realize a dream. I had grown up idolizing Prince, who played over twenty instruments on his debut album, which featured the amazing credit line "written, composed, performed, and recorded by Prince."

Cool, my own record done the way Prince did it—largely on my own— getting distributed around the world.

Geffen rushed it out as *Believe in Me* in the summer of 1993, just as the *Illusion* tour was wrapping. Axl talked it up on stage during the last few gigs. And I even started to promote it while Guns was still in

Europe—at a signing in Spain, so many people showed up that the street outside the record store had to be shut down by police in riot gear.

I had scheduled a solo tour that would start immediately after GN'R's last shows—two final gigs in Buenos Aires, Argentina, in July 1993. My solo tour would send me first to play showcases in San Francisco, L.A., and New York, and then to open the Scorpions' arena tour around Europe and the UK. Returning to L.A. from Argentina, I joined the group of friends and acquaintances I'd arranged to back me on the tour. They had already started rehearsing before I got home. Together we did whirlwind preparations for the tour.

Axl heard I was planning to go back out on tour. He called me.

"Are you fucking crazy? You should *not* go back out on the road right now. You are insane even to think about it."

"It's the only thing I know how to do," I told him. "I play music."

I also knew that if I stayed at home, it would probably devolve into more drug insanity. I didn't have any illusions about getting sober, but at least out on the road—with a band made up of old Seattle punk-rock friends—I figured I had some chance of toning things down. And of staying off coke. If I stayed in L.A., the temptation of readily available cocaine would likely be too much for me to resist. GN'R management sent Rick "Truck" Beaman, who had served as my personal security guard on the *Use Your Illusion* tour, out on the road for my solo tour, too. By this stage his concern for me seemed to extend beyond his professional duties. He had taken a deep personal interest, as a friend, in trying to limit the damage I was doing to myself. Now, finally, our goals had dovetailed—at least as far as cocaine was concerned.

But Axl was right. Before the first gig in San Francisco, my then-wife Linda got into a fistfight backstage with another girl and lost a tooth. Blood spattered everywhere.

Hell's Angels packed the show at Webster Hall in New York, and brawls broke out. I shouted at the crowd to settle down, thinking I could somehow make a difference.

After the show, people tried to come backstage but I wanted to be alone.

"I'm too tired," I told security. "I just can't take it."

Lyrics from "Just Not There," one of the *Believe in Me* songs we were performing, reverberated in my head:

You know I look but just can't find the reasons
To face another day
Cause I feel like crawling up inside,
Just fading away, fading away . . .

I toured the record as planned until December 1993. There was still a fervor for all things Guns, especially in Europe. Audiences knew my songs and sang along. With the exception of keyboardist Teddy Andreadis, who had been out with Guns for *Use Your Illusion* and who had been touring with artists like Carole King since he was barely out of his teens, the band members were fairly inexperienced with arena-scale touring. The band had also been thrown together quickly and lacked cohesion: we had some rough patches, including an intra-band fistfight at an airport somewhere in Europe.

For the most part I did stay off the coke, though it was by no means a clean break. There were slip-ups. I also switched from drinking vodka to wine.

Downshifting to wine was all well and good, but the volume of wine quickly skyrocketed until I was drinking ten bottles a day. I was getting really bad heartburn from all the wine, taking Tums all the time. I wasn't eating but I was badly bloated; my body felt awful.

At the end of the European leg, our lead guitar player pulled a knife on our bus driver in England. I had to fire him—luckily the tour was finished. Back in Los Angeles, I called Paul Solger, an old friend I had played together with as a teenager in Seattle, and asked him to fill in for the next part of the tour. Solger had gotten sober in the ten years since I'd last played with him; needless to say, I had not. Still, he agreed.

My band and I headed to Japan in early 1994. Over there we crossed paths with the Posies, a veteran jangle-pop band from Seattle. They came to our gig and said they thought it was cool that the new version of my band was sort of a Seattle punk-rock all-star band. Good to know: I was still Seattle.

After Japan, we had a few weeks off. I returned to L.A. before the next leg of the tour in Australia.

Back home I felt as sick as I ever had. My hands and feet were bleeding. I had constant nosebleeds. I was shitting blood. Sores on my skin oozed. My L.A. house was awash in the fetid effluvia of my derelict body. I found myself picking up the phone to tell my managers and band that we weren't going to Australia.

I'd bought a house back home in Seattle at that point—a dream house, right on Lake Washington—and I could feel its pull. I had bought it a few years before, sight unseen, in a neighborhood where I used to go to steal cars and boats when I was a kid. In the interim, I had barely had a chance to spend any time there because of the endless *Use Your Illusion* tour. I thought it might be the right place to try to recover, relax, recharge.

On March 31, 1994, I went to LAX to catch a flight from L.A. to Seattle. Kurt Cobain was waiting to take the same flight. We started talking. He had just skipped out of a rehab facility. We were both fucked up. We ended up getting seats next to each other and talking the whole way, but we didn't delve into certain things: I was in my hell and he was in his, and we both seemed to understand.

When we arrived in Seattle and went toward baggage claim, the thought crossed my mind to invite him over to my place. I had a sense that he was lonely and alone that night. So was I. But there was a mad rush of people in the terminal. I was in a big rock band; he was in a big rock band. We cowered next to each other as people gawked. Lots of people. I lost my train of thought for a minute and Kurt slipped out to a waiting limo.

Arriving in front of my house in Seattle, I stopped in the driveway and looked up at the roof. When I'd bought the place, it had been old and leaky, and I had paid to have the cedar shakes replaced. The new roof was rated to last twenty-five years, and looking up at it now I thought it was funny: that roof would surely outlast me. Still, staying in the house gave me the feeling that I had finally made it, able to live in a place like this, in a part of town like this.

A few days later my manager called to tell me Kurt Cobain had been found dead at his Seattle house after putting a gun to his own head. I'm embarrassed to say that upon hearing the news I just felt numb. People in my band had overdosed multiple times. My own addiction had spun out of control and my body was failing. I didn't pick up the phone and call Kurt's bandmates, Dave Grohl and Krist Novoselic. I figured my condolences would be meaningless anyway—a few years prior, I'd gotten into a scrap with Krist backstage at the MTV awards, where Guns and Nirvana both performed. I lost my shit when I thought I heard a slight of my band from the Nirvana camp. In my drunken haze I went after Krist. My means of dealing with any sort of conflict had been reduced to barroom brawling by then. Kim Warnick from the Fastbacks—the first real band I played with as a kid in Seattle—had called me the day after the awards show and scolded me. I had felt so low. Now I felt lower still, staring at the phone, incapable of calling to apologize for the earlier incident and to extend my sympathy for his loss and Dave's.

Not that Kurt's death made any difference in how I dealt with my own funk. I just didn't deal at all. Until one month later.

Even after GN'R became wildly successful and my world spun out of control, my three closest friends from childhood—Andy, Eddy, and Brian—would still call and come down to L.A. By the time the tour was winding down, I didn't want them to see too much. I was playing a game by then. But they saw the pictures in the magazines and the interviews on MTV. And I'd call them on the phone all the time. I called them too fucked up too many times, too late at night. I probably called Andy every second day while I was out on the road. He would defend me back in Seattle. He would tell people they didn't know what my life was like, what I was going through. He was protective. But I knew he was going to have a talk with me—the one my mom couldn't have. I knew now that I was off the road, it was just a matter of time—that either I was going to die or Andy was going to give me the talk. I didn't know what I was going to do when we had the talk. I went to sleep on May 9, 1994, with those thoughts in my head, albeit garbled by the ten bottles of wine I had consumed that day.

The morning of May 10, I woke up in my new bed with sharp pains in my stomach. Pain was nothing new to me, nor was the sickening feeling of things going wrong with my body. But this was different. This pain was unimaginable—like someone taking a dull knife and twisting it in my guts. The pain was so intense I couldn't even make it to the edge of the bed to dial 911. I was frozen in pain and fear, whimpering.

There I was, naked on my bed in my dream home, a home I had bought with the hopes of one day having a family of my own to fill it.

I lay there for what felt like an eternity. The silence of the empty house seemed as loud as my raspy, muffled moans. Never before in my life had I wanted someone to kill me, but I was in such pain I just hoped to be put out of my misery.

Then I heard Andy, my best friend from childhood, come in the back door. He called, "Hey, what's up," just as he had ever since we were kids. *Andy, I'm upstairs,* I wanted to answer. But I wasn't able to. I could only silently sob. I heard him start up the stairs—he must have seen my wallet in the kitchen. He made it upstairs and came down the hall.

"Oh, shit, it's finally happened," he said when he reached my room.

I was thankful to have my friend there. It was comforting to think that I would die in front of Andy. But he had other ideas. He pulled some sweats on me and began to try to move me. He must have felt a jolt of adrenaline—otherwise there is no way Andy could have carried the two hundred pounds of dead weight of my bloated body. As he carried me down the stairs and out to his car, the searing, stabbing pain in my intestines spread farther down to my quadriceps and around to my lower back. I wanted to die.

The doctor I'd had since I was a kid lived just two blocks away, so Andy took me there. Though Dr. Brad Thomas was my longtime physician, I hadn't let him see me very often once I descended into full-blown alcoholism. Together, Andy and Dr. Thomas carried me to his first-floor office. I heard my condition being discussed and I felt the prick of a needle in my ass. Demerol. Nothing. Another shot of Demerol in my ass and again nothing, no relief whatsoever. One more shot. Again nothing. The pain kept on spreading and I was starting to panic. I whimpered as my spirit began to blacken and fade.

They decided to rush me to the emergency room at Northwest Hospital. Dr. Thomas told Andy to drive me, as it would be faster than waiting for an ambulance. He said he would meet us there. Andy drove as fast as he could without jerking the car too much—every little movement made me moan and cry.

As they put an IV drip of morphine into my left arm at the hospital, the staff asked me questions I could not answer.

"Name? Address?"

Andy answered those.

"How much do you drink on a daily basis?"

"Are you on drugs right now?"

I just whimpered.

I was mute from pain. The morphine wasn't working as I knew it should. I knew a thing or two about opiates by that stage in my life. I knew the warm rush they offered, yet I was getting none of it.

They wheeled me into a room next to another guy on a gurney. The motion made me writhe in agony.

"Dude, I broke my back," said the guy in the other bed. "And I'm glad I don't have whatever you have."

Dr. Thomas and an ultrasound technician ran a scanner over my organs and I saw my doctor's face go white. My pancreas, apparently swollen to the size of a football from all the booze, had burst. I had third-degree burns all over the inside of my body from the digestive enzymes released by the damaged pancreas. Only a few parts of the inside of your digestive tract can handle the enzymes, and the outsides of your organs and your stomach muscles are definitely not among them—it just burns all that tissue.

A surgeon with thick glasses explained the surgery. They had to take out the top part of the pancreas—cut it off. Sew me back up. And then I'd have to be on dialysis for the rest of my life.

Suddenly I understood the pleading mouthed by miserable souls back to antiquity, those left breathing after being run through with a rusty sword or scalded with hot oil. I was there.

I summoned all my power to whisper to the ER doctor.

"Kill me."

I begged over and over.

"Please, kill me. Just kill me. Kill me. Please."

CHAPTER TWO

+ + +

It happens in a flash, life does. Only the ever-deepening lines on my face tell me that I have been alive for a while. I don't feel any different. I still have geeky and adolescent thoughts. I still tell the same dumb jokes. I look up at that cedar-shake roof on the house in Seattle—now looking a bit the worse for wear—and think, *Hang on, didn't I just have that redone?*

But then again, the real question is different: How did I manage to outlast that roof? To put it another way, how did I get here from there? And how did I find myself there in the first place? That's what I've tried to figure out through the process of writing this book. Because it certainly wasn't a given that my story would amount to anything more than a lurid cautionary tale. It had all the elements: sex, drugs, and rock and roll, and fame, fortune, and a fall. But instead, the story became—well, it became something *else*.

Here's what I do know, as I set out to answer those questions. I let myself lose track of what I thought was meaningful in life even as Guns N' Roses began to become meaningful to others. Back then—on the few occasions that I thought about it at all—I could think of a million excuses for going off the rails. But in the end it seems to have hinged on a failure to grapple with a few basic definitions—of what it meant to be successful, of what it meant to be an adult, of what it meant to be a man. The way I liked to define myself diverged from the actions that *actually* defined me. And this disconnect proved a nearly fatal level of self-deception.

But I'm getting ahead of myself.

I'm afraid this is one of those stories that takes a long time to unfold. There have never been any easy epiphanies for me; it took a lifetime to start to understand even the slightest goddamn thing. So I'll just have to start at the start.

My dad was a World War II vet who began having children with my mother when he was eighteen and didn't stop until he was thirty-eight. He went straight from the war to working for the Seattle Fire Department, desperately trying to provide for what would become a family of eight children by the time I arrived, born Michael McKagan on February 5, 1964.

There were several Michaels on my block—including one of the kids immediately next door. The Michael next door had a grandfather from Ireland living with him, and his grandpa apparently gave me the nickname Duff to simplify things on our street. Later, once Guns N' Roses took off, my dad liked to claim credit for the name, too. He said he used to call me McDuff. Either way, I was called Duff from before I can remember.

I'm not sure a little boy could ask for much more than having a father whose vocation happens to be working as a fireman. If at times during grade school I was embarrassed that my mom and dad were much older than my friends' and classmates' parents, at least I could find comfort in the fact that my pop was a heroic older guy.

Both my parents had come of age during the Depression, and that experience colored their thinking on money, on work, on life. I remember my mom telling me stories of what it was like growing up in the Depression. Stories of not having enough money to heat the house in the winter, of having to wear sweaters and coats all of the time. Stories of how her mother would fix a broken roller skate or doll and that would be her sole Christmas present.

If you are at any McKagan family gathering (a large crowd to be sure), try muttering "FHB" and see what happens. Well, I'll tell you what will happen: you will suddenly see the eight brothers and sisters each take a minuscule portion at the pot-luck buffet table. "Family Hold Back" is a saying that comes from years of too many kids and not enough to feed us all of the time. One of us would almost always have a friend over for dinner and this is when the secret code of FHB started: make sure the guest had enough to eat, take a small portion, don't say anything. We kids were taught lessons of frugality and thrift by example.

The old man also had a house-painting business on the side, and I'll never forget how happy I felt when I was finally old enough to climb up onto scaffolds and scrape and paint with my older brothers and other firemen who needed extra work.

With the Cascade mountain range practically in our backyard, my dad would take my brother Matt and me—along with our trusted dog, Moo—on backpacking trips up in the Alpine Lakes region to fish and camp under the stars with the bears and the deer. In that setting my dad seemed all-knowing and all-capable. But I started to notice that things around the house were tense when we would come back from a weekend of house painting or camping.

It was becoming painfully apparent to me even at that young age that my parents' marriage was an unhappy one. My dad always seemed agitated. I started to resent his anger and short temper. My mother was a saint in my eyes, and when I recognized pain in hers, I would become enraged.

My dad retired from the fire department when I was seven and soon found work as a fire inspector for an insurance company, a job that frequently sent him on the road. Or so the story went. I just remember being relieved when he was away. Our household returned to normal. All of us kids could stop walking on eggshells and could laugh and joke and play music.

Soon after my dad retired, my mom decided to take some vocational training at North Seattle Community College so that at the age of forty-five and after raising eight kids, she could finally join the workforce outside of the home.

Mom started working when I was nine. One of the first days she was at her new job, I came home from school and found my father—who was home that week—in bed with our next-door neighbor's wife. The mother of my best friend. Oh sure, they pretended nothing unusual was going on, and I am sure they thought I was too young to figure out what was happening. But I figured it out all right: all at once, in that very instant, I understood what sex was, what cheating was, I understood that my dad's seemingly heroic life was a deception, and I understood that I would have to hide all of this from my mom so that she would not get hurt. It was a harsh introduction to grown-up life.

From that day on I stopped talking to my dad. Not a word. Soon he and the woman next-door both left their spouses and moved into an apartment together. My parents got divorced. My best friend and I were put into the strangest of predicaments—was it his mom or my dad's fault that both of our homes were now broken? We began to fight and he began to act out at home. For his father's birthday a few years later, he presented his dad with the severed head of the family cat as a present. Gift-wrapped. He also took an axe to the outside wall of my bedroom one night while I was on the other side in my bed. All of this because my dad couldn't keep his dick in his pants.

At that age I figured I must have had something to do with the problem. That is what we do when we aren't old enough to see the bigger picture. Many of the things I soon grabbed onto in order to muddle through—things I'd call coping mechanisms now—would come back to bite me in the ass. When, a few years later, I started to get acute panic attacks, I learned to self-medicate with alcohol and drugs. Of course, we all have shitty stuff we have to deal with growing up. I cannot with a straight face blame my childhood for the drugs and alcohol that I would ingest later in life. More accurate, perhaps, would be to say that a perfect storm of factors began to whirl around me before I had a chance to address any of them: a predisposition to alcoholism, a family history of panic disorders, the need to hide a secret and protect my mom, and coming of age at a time when experimenting with drugs was much less frowned upon than it is today.

My mom was pretty much left to provide for the household on her own. This meant that she had no choice but to leave me with a lot of responsibility, and I just didn't rise to the occasion right away. I wish I could've been a better son in those difficult transition years for my mother. I still kick myself for some of the hell that I put her through. I was trying to figure out my place in the world without a father to rely on as a role model.

After my dad left, my mom's brother—a doctor—would let us spend summer vacations at a cabin he owned on a lake up in the mountains east of Seattle. While up there, one time between sixth and seventh grade, I went waterskiing with my brother Matt—out of the eight kids, he was closest to me in age, just two and a half years older—and a couple of other kids. Matt and a friend of his were driving the boat, and another kid and I were skiing behind it on a double rope. As we sped along, I lost my balance and the belt attached to the towrope came whipping off.

In the instant I fell forward, the slack in the rope formed a loop in the water and my arm went through it. Then I heard it go *zip*, snapping taut again.

Searing pain jolted my upper arm at the same moment the rope started dragging me.

Shit, the boat isn't stopping.

My brother thinks I'm holding on—joyriding.

Sheer terror took hold as water gushed into my mouth and nose and I struggled for breath.

The rope had cut all the way down to the bone on my right arm and stripped the muscle from my shoulder to the elbow—just taken it all down like a sock.

I'm going to drown.

I'm going to die.

Suddenly it felt as though time had been suspended. Everything started to slow down. I looked intently at the cool green light refracted beneath the surface, particles suspended in the sunbeams, dancing in slow motion. Silence replaced the howl of water rushing past my ears. All I felt was the pale sunlight on me. Then the dim underwater light began to burn brighter until it saturated my field of view. A feeling of warmth and bliss washed over me and I sensed a welcoming presence—it felt as if I were surrounded by family, generations of family, forefathers I'd never met but somehow knew. By the time I resurfaced and everyone started to scream and people gathered along the shore of the lake, I had blacked out.

Someone onshore managed to revive me. I was rushed to a hospital. Doctors were able to roll the muscle back up my arm, but we didn't have enough money to pay for them to reattach it. Obviously we also couldn't afford cosmetic surgery on it either, so to this day my upper arm looks as if someone took a wedge of muscle out of it with a hatchet.

Soon after the accident, my mom had me participate in a study at the University of Washington on near-death experiences. My recollections appeared in the resultant book, *Closer to the Light: Learning from the Near-Death Experiences of Children.* That warm, peaceful embrace removed any fear of death I might ever have had. I felt a sense of exceptionalism after that, but I also now operated under the assumption that I would die young—that this had just been a preview of a death that would come sooner rather than later, and definitely by thirty.

After glimpsing the other side, that seemed just fine.

CHAPTER THREE

+ + +

In September 1984, I pointed the grille of my 1971 Ford Maverick south, with $360 dollars in my pocket. I was twenty years old.

Heading out of town, I had the sensation that I was carrying the weight of Seattle on my shoulders. Obviously that sort of sentiment is overly dramatized when you are barely out of your teens, and it probably also reflected the extent to which, like anyone that age, I maintained a rather more grand sense of my own importance than was warranted by reality. But I had been the boy wonder of the scene, the eighth grader playing in bands with people in their twenties, the kid who could play everything—guitar, bass, drums, none of them particularly well, but all well enough to play in a band. Now, with my sights set on L.A. and the Space Needle in my rearview mirror, I felt as if everyone was counting on me to be "the guy." Some of the pressure was no doubt self-imposed, but people had started talking once I said I was leaving, taking sides about whether I would make it in L.A. or come slinking back home.

My first stop was San Francisco, where I flopped in a punk squat. The intention: to stay overnight. The upshot: I stayed a week. Inevitably, there was a girl. I also knew and liked a lot of the people in the Bay Area punk scene. Still, I wasn't interested in joining a band there and playing the same old kind of stuff.

When I finally left San Francisco, my $360 kitty had dwindled to sixty bucks. The situation looked dire. From a gas station pay phone I called my brother Matt, who was by this point studying at Cal State Northridge, which was in greater Los Angeles.

"Dude, you know I'm coming down there?"

"Yeah, I heard," he said. "Where you going to go?"

"I dunno, Hollywood. Any openings at the Black Angus?" Matt was paying his way through school working as a cook at a steak house out in the valley. He played trombone and wanted to become a music teacher.

"Maybe," he said.

"I have a reference from Lake Union Café," I said. That was the name of the restaurant where I'd been working for the past two years in Seattle.

"I might be able to get you something," Matt said.

"How do I get there?"

"Take 5 to the 405 and get off at the Roscoe Boulevard exit. Go west on Roscoe until you hit Corbin Avenue. Make a right. The restaurant is at 9145 Corbin."

I drove straight there and started a shift as a prep chef that same night, September 14, 1984.

At the end of the shift, I figured I'd go check out my new home: Hollywood. I asked for directions.

"Well, it's about twenty-five miles . . ."

What? Where the hell was I? I thought *this* was Los Angeles?

"You go down to Ventura and make a left. Follow that all the way to Laurel Canyon—you'll need to take that over the mountain . . ."

Huh? A canyon that went *over* a mountain? How could that be?

I set off, keeping an eye out for anything resembling mountains. I saw plenty of hills, but no mountains. Eventually I found Laurel Canyon—a road that went up a hill and then . . . Los Angeles! From the top of the hill, I could see that the downtown was no bigger than Seattle, but that the twinkling lights of densely packed low-rise neighborhoods went on forever—the city stretched as far as I could see.

I stayed with my brother a few nights during the first couple weeks in town. But his place was just so far from Hollywood, which to an outsider like me seemed the center of the L.A. music scene. With the added drive time from all the traffic, my brother's place—and the Black Angus—might as well have been in another city entirely. Besides, I couldn't just show up and take over his apartment.

So on many nights I slept in my car in the Hollywood Hills. The cops didn't cruise the nice tree-lined streets perched up above Franklin Avenue.

The luster of that year's summer Olympics had worn off, and the police presence had virtually vacated central Hollywood since the end of the games, leaving the floodgates wide open for criminals and thugs and general unwatched anarchy. Gang activity was in high gear then, too. Crack was sold all over Hollywood. I landed in the middle of all of that—with a bass I was still learning to play.

Still, I had confidence in my social skills and in the belief that I had a lot to offer. I felt punk rock was basically in its death throes by 1984. The first two waves were done—the original punk bands and then the hardcore bands. Whatever happened next, the people my age—who had been through the punk scene and come out the other end looking for a new direction—were going to be the ones to do it. The future was resting on our shoulders. I was looking to find other guys out there like me, interested in trying to create the next paradigm. I was sure I was going to play an important and vital part in whatever musical innovation would be next. This was not conceit on my part, it was excitement.

With all of this going through my head, an ad in a free local music paper called the *Recycler* caught my eye during that first week in L.A. It was a want ad for a band seeking a bass player. The name to call was Slash. With a name like that, I assumed he must be a punk-rock guy like me. And if we had similar backgrounds, maybe he was also looking toward the horizon musically.

As far as I could tell, there was really no discernible rock scene in Los Angeles in the fall of 1984—only the palpable hangover of a once-thriving punk movement, a thriving but really bad heavy-metal scene, and something called "cow punk." This was basically punk-rock dudes in plaid shirts trying to play Patsy Cline songs with their fat girlfriends singing.

Slash's ad had listed his influences as Alice Cooper, Aerosmith, and Motörhead. This was far preferable to anything else I had encountered that first week. And anyway, I was just trying to meet people.

I called Slash on the phone and talked to him. He had the same soft-spoken voice he has now. When he said the name of his band, I heard *Rodker.* Wow, I thought, that's a really strange name for a band. I arranged to meet him and drummer Steven Adler at a 24-hour deli named Canter's down on Fairfax.

"I'll make sure we have the first booth on the left," he said.

I told him I had blue hair and would be wearing a long black and red leather coat.

"Won't be able to miss you, I guess," he said.

One thing I'd already realized: folks from Seattle just plain looked different in those days. When bands like Black Flag or the Dead Kennedys came through Seattle, they would always comment on how different the crowd looked, but I had never thought much about it. Until now. In L.A., I decided to use this distinctive look to convince people checking IDs at the door to bars that I was not from the United States and thus spoke no English. When asked for ID, I would produce my sunglasses and a puzzled look. They must have thought I was Swedish or something, but, no shit, it worked more often than not. Now I was about to see the other side of the coin.

I headed to Canter's in my pimp coat, as promised. This was a floor-length black leather coat with red trim. Originally it had a big red *A* for "anarchy" on the back, but I had taken a Sharpie marker and blacked it out when a Seattle band I was in disbanded. The band was called the Fartz and our logo included the anarchist *A.*

I walked in, looked at the first booth on the left, and saw all this fucking hair. Somehow I had expected these guys to look like Social Distortion. Instead, even though they appeared about my age, the dudes in Rodker had long hair and rocker chick girlfriends.

If the *sight* of two long-haired rockers from Hollywood was a shock for me, I could hardly imagine having to talk to them. Of course, with my short Day-Glo blue hair and long coat, I must have looked like a Martian to them, too. Both parties were a little surprised and curious when we first met face-to-face.

Slash's long hair, it turned out, hid a shy introvert. He was cool, though. He had a bottle of vodka stashed under the table—he and Steven weren't yet twenty-one, either, and this was as close as they could get to a bar. We drank vodka and ate bowls of Canter's barley-bean soup. I still love that soup.

Club bouncers weren't the only people confused by my Seattle punk look. Slash's girlfriend got kind of smashed and leaned over and said, "Are you gay?"

"No, I'm not gay," I told her, laughing.

"You have short hair—I think you're gay. It's okay, you can tell me. Do you have a girlfriend?"

"No," I said, "I just moved here."

"It's okay, we'll get you one."

Steven Adler was really nice, and expressed himself with an infectious, almost childlike enthusiasm.

He said, "Listen, we're going to be great—going to get the feet stompin' and the hands clappin'."

He still says that to this day when he climbs behind a drum kit and gets excited: going to get the feet stomping and the hands clapping.

We all went back to Slash's place—he was living with his mom. It was obvious even on the acoustic guitar he played that first night that Slash was a special player. I was absolutely stunned by the raw, emotive power he so easily tapped. Slash was already in a league of his own and watching him play guitar was a "holy shit" moment.

Even so, I was afraid he and Steven were coming from a very different place musically than I was. Some of my fears reflected the way things had been in Seattle—long-haired guys there tended to be kind of behind the times. Long hair in Seattle meant kids from the suburbs or farming or logging towns. Long hair meant heavy metal. Those of us in the punk scene called guys like that "heshers." We were city kids. We thought of ourselves as ahead of the curve. Of course, some of my fears about Slash and Steven were more concrete—Anvil's "Metal on Metal" was part of the cover repertoire they played. And it turned out the decidedly less offbeat name of their band was Road Crew, not Rodker.

Still, the more we played and talked about music and listened to music, the more common ground we found. Slash also showed me some of his artwork that night—though I would never have imagined that less than a year later he would be hand-drawing a logo for a band we would be in together, a logo featuring two pistols with thorny rose stems twisting around the barrels.

Slash was an eccentric guy. He had a snake in his room.

"She's really sweet," he told me.

I didn't say anything, but in my mind I was going, *Hmm, a snake, sweet?*

Still, he was cool. If nothing else, I thought, he's a genius guitar player—and I like him. And perhaps most important, I now knew where Slash lived and I knew how to get there. Given the fact that I didn't know anyone else in town, this was key to our remaining friends. I met a lot of people in those first few weeks, but many I never ran into a second time. Now I could find Slash whenever I wanted.

As an added bonus I also liked Slash's mom. She was great to me. She called my mom to let her know I was all right. Later she would call me at the Black Angus to make sure things were going okay. She became a surrogate mother during those initial weeks in L.A. (She ended up continuing in that role for years, in fact.)

Slash, Steven, and I started playing together at a rehearsal space at the corner of Highland and Selma. The space cost five dollars an hour, fifteen if you wanted a PA. I spent a week jamming with them while sleeping in my car.

In the end, though, I was kind of bummed out by the rehearsal sessions. Slash's talent notwithstanding, the way he and Steven were going about it was not my cup of tea. The songs they had, the sound of the guitar, Steven's double-kick drum kit with all those rack toms and cymbals—it was all too conventional. They were working in a pre-existing mold. I was looking for people ready to create a new mold.

There was also no singer. It felt like a high school band, albeit one with an amazing guitar player. Having already been in a dozen bands and played with countless professional musicians, I considered myself a seasoned veteran. I could tell Slash and Steven had real aspirations—that they wanted more—but I didn't move all the way to Los Angeles to play with people who were still trying to figure their shit out.

After about a week, I told them, "I don't want to play with you, but I still want to be friends."

"Oh, okay," they said.

At that age, there wasn't any weirdness—it was fine to be straight like that. I loved the two of them, but Road Crew wasn't what I wanted to do at that point.

We did continue to hang out a lot together. A few weeks later, in October, Slash and Steven took me to an all-ages show at a West Hollywood club called the Troubadour to see L.A. Guns. The two of them had briefly played with the singer, Axl Rose, in a band called Hollywood Rose, which had already happened and died. Now Axl was with this other band, named for the guitar player, Tracii Guns. Tracii, it turned out, was a local hero. He had gone to the same high school as Slash and they had played in rival bands.

The Troubadour was a real rock club, and at this point in my life I had only been to one other rock club. Punk gigs in Seattle took place in completely different types of spaces—squats, basements of private houses, VFW halls rented out for the night. Things were clearly different here in L.A.

CHAPTER FOUR

✦ ✦ ✦

My older brothers and sisters all listened to lots of rock and roll and many of them played guitar and sang. Musical instruments littered the house and the basement and the garage. As early as I can remember, Jimi Hendrix, the Rolling Stones, the Beatles, and the Sonics constantly blasted from our family living-room stereo, a Sanyo system my brother Mark had shipped back from Vietnam after his tour of duty.

I remember being captivated by *Sgt. Pepper's Lonely Hearts Club Band.* The picture on the cover is what got my attention—the marching-band uniforms, all the faces. But then I started listening to the music. I listened to "Lovely Rita" over and over, fascinated with the way the words sounded, the exotic cadence. I was amazed how the lyrics managed to paint a picture in my mind. I listened to that song so many times that I even convinced myself that I had written it—for a girl I had a crush on in my kindergarten class. The music had the ability to conjure images in my head and help me drown out the tension and noise I was trying to avoid at my house.

Another older brother, Bruce, was in a rock band. He had long hair and a sheepskin rug in his room. He drove a convertible. And he had a beautiful Gretsch hollow-body, six-string guitar and a Les Paul Custom left-handed bass. Bruce was always playing gigs and coming home with stories that reinforced my romantic image of rock and roll. He would also take time to let me sit with him and bang on his guitars and ask him questions. It was a big deal for me; he is fourteen years older than me and I am sure I was a pest at times.

One day, Bruce asked me if I would play a gig with him. Me? What? I guess he hadn't noticed I had yet to learn how to play an instrument. I told him sheepishly, thinking with despair as I did that my big chance was about to pass me by.

"Don't worry about it," Bruce said. "I'll teach you how to play bass."

All right!

Bruce and I are both left-handed, so learning to play that way came naturally. (It was only after Bruce moved out with his guitars that I was faced with the dilemma of having to relearn to play on a dusty right-handed guitar I found forgotten in a corner of my mom's garage.) The first song I learned how to play was the Beatles' "Birthday." Your first song always remains a musical touchstone and this one not only taught me finger dexterity, but also included the rudiments of the whole blues major scale, a scale that I would use and use again in my later career in Guns N' Roses.

From that day on, I realized how easy I found it to pick up songs by ear—any songs I wanted to learn. I think if I hadn't been able to learn so quickly back then, I might have practiced a bit more and become a better technical guitar and bass player as a result. I guess we can all look back and see things in our lives that we could or should have done differently—and better—and that's one for me. Still, learning to play other people's music was only satisfying to a point. I felt there was more I could do, but I hadn't the faintest idea how to write a song or start a band.

Then, in seventh grade, I spotted a homemade flyer for an underground punk concert. I didn't really know what it meant to be anti-establishment—and I had no notion of the music industry or what it meant to operate outside it—but it was clear these bands were not part of the same system that produced glossy handbills for shows at the Paramount Theatre or the Kingdome. That same week, I happened to hear Iggy and the Stooges for the first time. Maybe the Stooges' garage-rock simplicity echoed the Sonics and Don and the Goodtimes records I loved to listen to as a little kid; whatever it was, the Stooges hit me like an earthquake—I wasn't moving so much as being moved. The back of my legs felt weak, chills ran from the base of my neck down my spine, the world began to crumble leaving just this pounding music.

I experienced the most memorable dream of my life soon afterward, a dream that seemed to rewind and play over and over again in my mind for years. In the dream, I was singing in a band in a local church basement in front of all of my friends. I was possessed by the music, shrieking, snarling, grunting. There was no separation between the audience and the band, and everyone was jumping around as crazily as I was, dropping beer bottles and glasses, which smashed on the floor. I writhed around on the shards of glass yet felt no pain. I could hear and see exactly how rock should be: raw and fucked up with nothing held back, raw and fucked up with no boundaries left unbroken, raw and fucked up.

When I woke up the next morning, I went straight to the record store and bought my own copy of *Raw Power* by Iggy and the Stooges. My older siblings' music had been supplanted by something all my own. It was called punk rock, and it was my thing now.

CHAPTER FIVE

✦ ✦ ✦

I continued to get a lot of shifts at the Black Angus, the steak house in Northridge where my brother worked. Once I had socked away a few paychecks, I decided to rent an apartment. I headed straight for Hollywood and began my search for the perfect place. Well, the perfect place that I could afford. Okay, so I was looking for a cheap place.

One of the best spots I had found to sleep in my car was on Orchid Street, just up the hill from Franklin. It seemed natural to look in that area—though, of course, anywhere up the hill was out of the question because the higher up you went, the higher the rents were. One morning I woke up, left the Maverick parked in the shade of a wooded hillside block, and walked down toward Franklin in search of a bargain in the skeezy, treeless streets below.

Orchid went through to Hollywood Boulevard then, right behind Grauman's Chinese Theatre—Mann's at the time. That short block of Orchid between Franklin and Hollywood was one of the most drug-infested lanes in the city, visited nightly by dealers, hookers, and cops. The Chinese Theatre was a mess back then, too, full of creeps.

I saw an "apt for rent" sign in a window and ducked into the Amour Arms, an apartment building on that block behind the Chinese Theatre. The place available was a ground-floor studio apartment, one room with a hot plate and a little fridge. The window looked out onto an alley—there were alleys behind all the buildings in this part of Hollywood. The price was $240 per month.

When I told the woman who managed the place that I would take it, she said it was a Section 8 building. I said nothing.

Then she said, "Are you Section 8?"

"I don't know," I told her. These days I know it's the designation for federally subsidized low-income housing. But back then I had no idea what it meant.

"Well, do you go to the music school?"

"No," I said. In fact, not only did I not attend the school, I didn't know about its existence until she mentioned it that very moment. I had to ask Slash about it later. Turned out just around the corner, above the wax museum on Hollywood Boulevard, the Musicians Institute trained shredders like Paul Gilbert of Mr. Big and John Frusciante of the Red Hot Chili Peppers.

"Just say you do," she said. "Say, 'Yes, I do.'"

"Yes, as a matter of fact, I do go to the music school," I said.

I got the apartment.

My first night there, a police chopper buzzed overhead, beaming its searchlight into the alley my window faced. My room was briefly as bright as midday and I heard a lot of rustling, running, and shouting outside. Helicopters—"ghetto birds," as the other residents called them—circled over Hollywood all the time. And those searchlights shined into my window on a nightly basis as the cops chased people around the alleys of my new neighborhood.

The other thing I noticed that first night was an odd sensation when I first turned out the lights and flopped down on the mattress on the floor. It felt as if something were crawling on me. At first it was on one of my legs, then on my back. When I felt it on my face, I jumped up and turned on the lights. My bed—the entire apartment, in fact—was teeming with cockroaches. I went to war with rolled-up newspapers. I say newspapers plural because I had to throw away one after another as they became wet with bug guts after a dozen swats or so. I could never quite win that war, though, and soon I had to reconcile myself to falling asleep with those bugs crawling on me. Ah, the glamorous life of Hollywood.

Still, after living in an unfinished house in Seattle, crashing for a week in a San Francisco squat, and sleeping in my car and showering at my brother's place, I finally had a place to call home. And anyway, cockroaches don't bite.

A mother and her twenty-year-old daughter lived across the hall and they were always really nice to me. On weekends, a line of Marines up from boot camp in San Diego would form in front of their apartment and stream out into the lobby of the building. I was naive; I didn't know to suspect anything. It took several weeks before I deduced that my neighbors had a little family business going as hookers.

Soon I was bringing girls home, cockroaches be damned. Once I even hosted the hostess of the Black Angus. She was definitely not used to vermin-infested apartments. But, as I found with other women who came over, she either didn't notice or pretended not to notice. I guess it was, if not exactly romantic, at least an expected part of the rock-and-roll milieu—and everyone knew I was in L.A. to make music.

I also found a gig playing with the Michael McMahon band, a Tommy Tutone–like pop group with regular club gigs. It gave me a chance to work on my bass chops—and they even paid me. I was playing clubs and meeting people. I was observing, looking for my opening.

Things were going so well, in fact, that I began to have grand illusions of being there in L.A. for a reason. It steeled my resolve to find the right group of musicians with whom to push toward something special.

By then the local punk community knew I was in town, too. One day I picked up the phone at my apartment and the guitar player from the Mentors was on the line.

"Hey, Duff, it's Sickie Wifebeater. El Duce wants you to join the Mentors."

The Mentors called their music "rape rock." El Duce was the drummer and sang. He played with dildos. Every song was about sodomy.

"I'm here to offer you a welcome call," Sickie continued. And I was thinking, *How do I get out of this?*

Chuck Biscuits, the drummer from D.O.A., Black Flag, and the Circle Jerks (and later Danzig and Social Distortion) called me, too. He'd been my favorite drummer since I was a kid. He and the guitar player from

M.I.A. had me come down to Long Beach so the three of us could play together.

Fuck, I'm playing with Chuck Biscuits!

But I soon learned that what they were doing wasn't anything special. I wasn't going to join a band with Chuck Biscuits just to play with Chuck Biscuits, even though I idolized him. Just as I wasn't going to be in a band with Slash and Steven just to do it—it was all too comfortable.

CHAPTER SIX

+ + +

Early in high school, I embraced the exciting new punk-rock scene that had recently hit Seattle. Together with my friend Andy, I started going to shows and slam-dancing among the other scruffy kids in basements, garages, and nearly derelict downtown buildings. Andy and I practiced our instruments, listened to albums that got passed around the scene, and tried to put together bands. In the daylight hours, I would take the bus anywhere and everywhere that I had to be for band practices or various jobs I held. But the buses stopped running at midnight—and it being Seattle and all, it was always raining and usually cold. There had to be a better way to get home than trudging along on foot for miles.

Andy and I had heard of a simple and easy way to trip the ignition on pre-1964 VW Bugs. It was typical of the stuff middle-school boys talked about and dreamed about. One night Andy and I decided to put that knowledge to the test. It was 2 a.m., and we were stuck without a ride home at a punk-rock party deep in the Ballard section of town. It was raining. Andy and I got only about ten blocks into our seven-mile walk when we came across a 1963 Bug.

Hmm, what do you say we, um, borrow *this Bug and drive ourselves the rest of the way home?*

It all seemed innocent enough at first. We clumsily broke in a window with one of our boots. The hot-wiring trick worked. But once we got the car started, we realized that neither one of us knew how to drive a car, let alone one with a clutch. We found out that first gear can indeed get you from point A to point B, seven miles away, albeit slowly.

Andy and I had a dangerous new piece of information: we no longer had to wait until we were sixteen years old to have access to a car. We began to hone our tactics and skills as car thieves—even studying ways to hot-wire exotic cars like Peugeots and Audis. As time went on, we held on to certain cars for a week or more, parking them in rich neighborhoods where the police would be less likely to look for a stolen vehicle. On top of this, things we found inside these cars would on occasion lead us into further criminal activities. One time we found a large set of keys that had an address attached to them, written on a piece of tape. The address turned out to be a large coin-op laundromat, and the keys were to the lockboxes of each machine. By that point our exploits began to garner attention from older, savvier criminals.

I knew my mom would be disappointed to learn about all of this, and I didn't want to let her down. In fact, if anything, I wanted to take up the slack in the house and make things easier for her. But I was trying to figure out manhood—and I had a lot of anger.

Still, when the newspaper began to run stories about things we were involved in, I began to see a dire fate for myself—jail or worse. It was time to get out. Besides, my music career was beginning to get more serious.

There was an older kid in my neighborhood who was way ahead of the rest of us when it came to punk rock. His name was Chris Crass and he already had a Mohawk and skinny jeans. In 1978, no one in Seattle had seen fashion or attitude like that yet. One day Chris came up to me at school and told me that he had heard I could play bass. I nodded in the affirmative, totally tongue-tied and nervous.

"I'm starting a band called the Thankless Dogs, and I need a bass player and a drummer," he said.

The person I spent by far the most time playing music with was Andy. He played drums.

"I know a drummer!" I blurted.

Chris wrote down an address and told me to show up for a trial rehearsal the next day.

I quickly called Andy. We were both really excited and nervous. A band! A real band! The rehearsal spot was in the industrial outskirts south of downtown, near the current site of Safeco Field.

I'll plead ignorance on the details of how Andy and I got our gear down there for that first rehearsal. We were only fourteen and a momentous opportunity like this didn't present itself every day; a car may have been borrowed.

When we got there, an older dude with a leather jacket and droopy eyelids answered the door. Up to then I had never met anyone who was actually high on heroin, but I was certain that I just had then and there. His name was Stan and he seemed pretty affable—and also a little amused to see two stubble-free teens coming to audition to be the rhythm section.

What Chris hadn't told me—or I was too nervous to hear the day before—was that the other guitar player and main singer was Seattle punk legend Mike Refuzor. I had seen Refuzor flyers up around town and instantly recognized him when he said hello as we walked into the room. To me, this was like meeting someone from Led Zeppelin. The loft space where we rehearsed was also where Mike and a few other people lived. I got a crash-course on how to act cool in a situation that was completely beyond the scope of my experience.

Andy and I got the gig, and as the weeks progressed the thing that struck me most about Mike Refuzor was his ability to write great songs with real choruses. He made songwriting seem effortless.

All of the guys in the band were in their early twenties, and from where I stood they were not only much older and wiser but also seemed to have lived hard and interesting lives. Mike turned out to be a great mentor; he took an interest in what I thought and would brag to his friends about me and Andy. The key thing for me was that nobody in that circle was critical of me. It became a comfortable place to hang out and make mistakes in front of other people.

Back at my mom's house at night, I was busy writing my first song. I was nervous and had nothing at all to gauge my little opus against. No, I would have to play it in front of my newfound friends to see if this song was any good or not. The nurturing atmosphere of that first band made me feel safe sharing my first ever attempt at songwriting, a song called "The Fake." And it was well received! In fact it ended up being released as a single—though by then we had changed the name of the band to the Vains.

The punk scene in Seattle was all about creating something out of nothing. There was only one bar that booked punk bands, the Gorilla Room. Aside from that, bands had no choice but to do it themselves. Bands rented VFW halls and Oddfellows lodges or played in the basements of communal houses. The houses weren't squats, they were just places a bunch of punks would rent together. They all had names: Boot Boy House, Fag House, Cleveland. You could go hang out at the houses anytime you wanted.

People didn't take themselves too seriously in the scene, either. There was a weird sense of humor. And being musically different was rewarded. It didn't matter whether a band's playing was any good; if they were striving to do something original, people would go check them out. It made for interesting and sometimes cool music. A band couldn't just look good and expect people to go to their show.

In the summer of 1979, I played my first real concert, with the Vains. Because we were all underage, together with two other bands we rented a community center attached to a public park. The week before the show Andy and I stole about twenty plastic milk crates from the back of a grocery store and somehow nailed plywood onto them. Now we had a stage for the gig. That alone was pretty damn exciting for a fifteen-year-old kid. *Our own stage.* Man, now we could play *anywhere*!

I'll never forget the buildup to the gig. I borrowed a pair of pointy black Beatle boots for that very first gig, and wore yellow corduroy pants that someone tapered in for me and a black-and-white, button-front bowling shirt that I'd found at the Salvation Army—this was well before there were "vintage" clothing stores.

There were only 80 or 100 people at the show, but the feeling that I was entering a place that I was destined for was overwhelming. When we finally went on stage—standing on our plywood-covered milk crates—I was *very* aware of everyone staring at me and Chris Crass and Andy . . . then everything stopped . . . and then sped up . . . and stopped again. I was trying to get a handle on what was going on, and that too, just stopped. Everything became a blur . . . a whirl of emotion and confusion and triumph. I don't remember why, but I kicked a guy in the head in the front row. The blur of it all started to feel like warm water washing over me. The noise was all-enveloping and comfortable. I could forget about the fact that I had cystic acne on my face and that I was a confused and unfocused teen. I could forget about my awkward childhood and frac-tured relationship with my dad and all the rest.

Afterward, I didn't remember playing a gig so much as experiencing a feeling. A moment of perfection. Suddenly all I wanted to do was play music. Day and night. But not everyone wanted to rehearse, or at least not as much as I did, so I tried to stay in multiple bands so I always had people to play with. I started practicing multiple instruments, too, so I could fill any position a band had open.

Guitar, drums, bass, whatever, I'll join!

I remember meeting Kim Warnick of the Fastbacks one afternoon in 1979 when I was fifteen. She was about five years older than I was, but she knew a friend of mine and gave the two of us a lift home from school one day.

When she dropped us off we all played some music together. I played bass. She mentioned that her band needed a drummer—their drummer, Kurt Bloch, was a much better guitar player than drummer.

"I play drums, too," I said.

So Kurt switched to his guitar and I joined on drums. From that point on, I was in and out of bands nonstop.

CHAPTER SEVEN

+ + +

For those first few years in Los Angeles I lived beneath the poverty level. I always maintained a working phone line; I had a car, but no car insurance; of course I didn't have health insurance.

When you are making minimum wage, a lot of things can be hard to fit into the budget. My body was forced to realize that it would get only one meal a day. At least while I was working at the Black Angus, that meal was a good one—the daily staff meal.

We couldn't just grab anything we wanted. The owners usually allotted each of us a piece of chicken plus some rice and vegetables. As one of the prep chefs, I did have free rein to prepare the allotted ingredients as I wished. A bunch of my coworkers were from Mexico and Central America, and they taught me how to spice up the simple meal. Under their tutelage, I developed a go-to dish. Sometimes we would eat it every day for weeks on end.

PREP CHEF POLLO

— Skin and rinse chicken breasts, and arrange on broiling pan.
— Depending on thickness of the breasts, grill for approximately five minutes per side under the broiler. During final thirty seconds of broiling on each side, brush on a thick layer of teriyaki sauce.
— In a mixing bowl, toss together diced avocado, julienned jalapeño peppers, and cubed pineapple.

- Cook wild rice together with an ample amount of bread crumbs. This thickens up the rice and adds more gusto and calories to the meal.
- Place chicken breasts on rice and spoon spicy fruit salsa liberally over the top.

To this day, I love to make that dish for family and friends—though now I usually grill the chicken on the barbecue.

For the first three months in L.A. I lived on Prep Chef Pollo. Then suddenly I found myself scrambling to find both food and work: just after Thanksgiving, the Black Angus had to lay me off—I was the last one hired, so the first one to go when things slowed down.

Looking back, of course, I realize I would have qualified for government assistance. I'm not sure why I never applied for unemployment or went to a food bank during the worst periods between various jobs. Part of my reluctance was a legacy of my mom's philosophy, impressed upon us as kids. Much of her thinking on such issues was informed by living through the Great Depression; she emphasized the fact that there were *always* people more needy than we were. I believed that resources were scarce, and that they should go to those with kids to feed or those too old or infirm to fend for themselves. It wasn't that I was too proud, either; I just would have felt somehow dishonest because I knew that if I were really, really bad off, I could have called a brother or sister—I had a last resort. As a matter of fact, my sister Joan did send some money to me once. I didn't ask her, she just knew I needed it.

My reluctance to avail myself of government services had been reinforced a few years prior, while I was still living in Seattle. One of my bands was on tour, and we were stuck in San Francisco without any money. I hadn't eaten in a couple of days, and I was so hungry that I went to get emergency food stamps at a municipal aid office. I felt so down standing in that line at the government office. I had made choices that put me in that predicament, whereas the others in line—mothers with children in tow, for instance—seemed faced with situations largely beyond their control. I realized two things at that moment: my own problems paled in comparison to the level of desperation many of the people depending on assistance faced; and I never wanted to reach that level of desperation. This was definitely a motivating factor in my always keeping a job and usually having an apartment when I lived in Hollywood.

After I lost my job at the Black Angus, food joined the list of things that were hard to fit into the budget. I was left with the task of figuring out a cheap way to cook and subsist with only a hot plate, a single pan, and a small refrigerator. That's when I discovered the wonders of Top Ramen, and after some experimentation I hit upon the perfect modifications to provide a filling meal for about a buck a serving:

HOLLYWOOD (NOODLE) BOWL

— Bring a pot of water to a hard boil.
— Add ramen noodles and a package of frozen mixed vegetables and cook for three minutes.
— Crack a raw egg into the boiling soup and let cook for an additional thirty seconds.
— Turn off hot plate and stir in powdered flavor packet from the ramen noodles.

Another discovery: for an occasional break from ramen, the low-rent hotel on my block offered a happy hour buffet. If you bought a beer, you could gorge yourself on pig-in-the-blankets, fried mozzarella sticks, and french fries.

In front of the hotel was a pay phone. One evening, walking out with my belly filled with its meal of the day, I saw a guy doing business on the phone—a guy dressed like Johnny Thunders. Taking a second glance, I recognized the guy. It was Izzy Stradlin. We had met a few weeks prior, when we both turned up at the same girl's place on the same night. It could have been awkward, but we both shrugged it off and started talking about music. Izzy was into Thunders, Hanoi Rocks, Fear—the rough "street" acts I also preferred to the technical polish of metal. He reminded me of some of the cooler figures I had known back home, and I ended up giving him a ride to some other girl's house later that night. We exchanged phone numbers and that was it. Now here he was on my block.

It turned out Izzy had just moved in across the street. I knew the alley behind Izzy's place was really bad—full of hookers and drug dealers. Shit went down there all the time. What I didn't realize was that Izzy's place was in the back of the building and that he sold heroin out his back window.

Izzy was pretty much strung out the whole time. But he wasn't sloppy, not nodding out. He was a "maintenance guy," meaning he did just enough heroin to stave off withdrawal. As we got to know each other, for some reason I was able to look past his smack habit. In part it was because he handled himself well. In part it was because we bonded over a mutual love of Johnny Thunders—alone in L.A., musical touchstones, it seemed, could trump something that months before in a different setting would likely have snuffed out any budding friendship. In part it had to do with his drive and determination.

Generally, I looked at heroin users as a rung below. I was bitter about dope because of the friendships and relationships it had cost me back in Seattle. I saw what the drug did to people and saw that nobody ever got off it. But for some reason I wasn't bitter toward Izzy. He was different somehow.

During those early months I sometimes had to pawn things to make rent while waiting to get paid. One day I heard a knock at my apartment door. When I opened it, I found two cops.

"Do you own a black B.C. Rich Seagull guitar?" They read out the serial number.

I answered in the affirmative. I had gotten it back in Seattle from Kurt Bloch of the Fastbacks—traded him for it in exchange for another guitar.

"And you pawned it?" They said the name of the shop I regularly used.

Yes, I had.

They then informed me this guitar had been stolen from a music store five years earlier. Pawnshops have to report every item they take in, and my guitar—again, the one I got *in Seattle*—had raised a red flag.

They began to question me as if I had been the initial burglar. It must have been easy to read from my reaction that I was just the guy left holding the bag. They didn't arrest me. But they took the B.C. Rich. Great, I had just recovered a piece of stolen gear and transported it back to Los Angeles for them. I felt pretty down that day.

I already had no money and now I also had no guitar.

CHAPTER EIGHT

+ + +

My childhood experimentation with drugs—speed, coke, LSD, mushrooms—had come to a screeching halt the day in 1981 when I had my first panic attack. I was sixteen.

It came out of nowhere.

Though I had already moved out, I was visiting my mom's house and taking a shower. Suddenly the floor of the bathtub seemed to drop two feet. I fell.

What's happening?

Now I could barely breathe.

I think I just went crazy.

Something had broken inside me and I knew it.

I crawled out of the shower, soaking wet. I didn't want my mom to see me naked, but I needed help. I was terrified.

"Mom! Help!"

My mom came running into the bathroom. She wrapped me in a towel. She managed to get me out of the bathroom and put a pair of sweats on me. She rushed me to the emergency room.

At the ER the doctors determined there was nothing physically wrong with me. They gave me Valium and walked me across the street to see a bearded psychologist. He wanted to talk about what I had gone through. Once the psychologist and I were alone, I revealed to him that I thought the episode was drug-induced—specifically from taking loads of mushrooms and acid. He said he highly doubted it. He drew me a diagram of some sort. He tried to explain.

Despite his dubiousness about my expert medical diagnosis, I cut out the drugs from then on. The timing couldn't have been more fortuitous. In Seattle, heroin was fast becoming a staple in pretty much everyone's diet—not just musicians. With beer in hand, I watched it take over the city. The spread of the drug seemed directly related to the recession that hit the city during Ronald Reagan's first term as president; as jobs disappeared, smack oozed into the vacuum left in people's lives. Up to 1982, I heard about heroin but rarely saw it. Then suddenly I began to see a lot of older kids starting to use heroin openly. As more and more of my contemporaries lost their jobs, smack spread quickly. It would be everywhere by 1983.

At the time of the panic attack I was living with my girlfriend, Stacy. When she and I had originally hooked up, I was a punk-rock outcast and she had been dating the quarterback of the high school football team. I had been playing drums in a band called the Fartz when we started hanging out together. Early on, Stacy rode her moped to a gig the Fartz played with another band called The Fags. That band's singer, Upchuck, was a full-on queen who was one of the first people in Seattle to die of AIDS a few years later. He lived in a building with an eclectic group of gays who liked to call their collective residence the Fag House, and that's where the gig was. There was Stacy, watching me play in the basement of a notoriously debauched punk-rock party house. The cops came to bust up the show. Stacy and I escaped together, running down the street in the rain. We fell in love. For each of us, it was our first real love. I had a loving mom and family, but now I was able to branch off on my own and show another person what I had to offer from my heart.

When Stacy and I got together, guys from her previous boyfriend's circle began to threaten me. The jocks didn't like the punks back then and I had on several occasions been beaten up by groups of drunken high school football players and in one case by a gang of Washington Huskies players. These guys probably looked at such encounters as the culmination of a fun night out. For me, although terrifying, these events some-how confirmed that I was into something new and threatening—and I liked the feeling that the way I looked and the music I made threatened others. Their violence toward people like me also made me understand very clearly that the world wasn't going to be fair—these guys were always much bigger than I was and they ran in packs. Those beatings were also probably a factor in why later I would see red every time I perceived a wrong done to me or someone close to me and would fight at the drop of a dime. Justifiably or not, I saw myself as the protector, and the street-fighting skills I was forced to learn while getting my ass kicked as a teenager meant that I was not reluctant to perform that role with my fists.

I had also stopped going to the same school as Stacy pretty soon after we got together. I switched to an "alternative" high school to make it eas-ier to spend more time playing music. To fulfill the requirements of the alternative school, I had to show up for half an hour every two weeks. It proved too great an obligation, and I got thrown out of that school. That was junior year, and that was it for me and school. Yeah, good riddance, I remember thinking—I was already crafting a new career for myself.

Actually, *career* may be overstating the case. I didn't make a living playing music back then—and never thought I would, to be honest. That just wasn't part of my calculations: I assumed I would always have to maintain a job. The most lucrative jobs I had were in construction—one summer I managed to save enough to buy a Marshall combo amp. My first restaurant job was at a place called Huwiler's. It was popular enough to experience a nightly dinner rush, and even though I was a lowly dish-washer, if the pots and pans weren't clean, the whole kitchen could get thrown out of whack. I really liked the work, liked being part of some-thing with lots of independent moving parts working toward one goal, liked the characters who made up the staff.

After some odd jobs I had landed a full-time slot at Schumacher's Bakery. The place took its name from Billy Schumacher, a local celebrity known as a pioneer in the sport of hydroplane racing. In Seattle, hydro-planes were considered godlike chariots, carrying our heroes at ridiculously high speeds across Lake Washington. This particular hero turned out to be an asshole. I was hired to wash dishes. Scraping out cake pans and muffin tins is hard physical work, which was fine. Except that on top of it Schumacher made me wash his cars, dig a drainage ditch, and clean up his dog's shit. He also treated me—and all the other employees—like garbage. But I couldn't quit. There weren't any other jobs out there. And I had to make rent.

Not long after the panic attack I went away for a week with my family. Stacy was still in school, so when I got home I went to meet her after her classes. She came running up and jumped on me, practically tackling me as she told how much she had missed me. There were tears in her eyes. She did this in front of the entire student body as they spilled out at the end of the school day.

Wow, this is quite a reaction.

I am one lucky guy.

My friends emerged from the building and started whispering to one another just out of earshot. I could tell something was going on. Did they have a surprise for me? Did something happen while I was gone? Then my girlfriend began to cry and told me she had gotten drunk and slept with another guy while I was gone. Right then and there I said we were finished. It wasn't even an issue, not a subject for discussion.

But I couldn't understand the situation.

Is there something wrong with me?

I know she loves me—so how could she do this?

I was destroyed. First my panic attack, now this? I just couldn't understand why Stacy would do this to me. My only understanding of such things was based on what I had witnessed with my dad. I retreated into a weird place.

Stacy was completely distraught, too. And she seemed genuinely contrite. She started calling my mom, my brothers and sisters, and my friends. People said, *Dude you have to give her another chance.* The guy who slept with her apologized, saying it was just a drunken mistake. But I didn't know if I could go back to her after that.

I talked to my mom about the whole thing. She said people just make mistakes sometimes. She said it was obvious Stacy had made a mistake and was devastated because of it.

"I know you love her," my mom said. "You have to find it in your heart to forgive her."

So Stacy and I were back on. It's the only time I've ever gone back to someone after something like that. Things went great for about a year. I even heard about a job opening at Lake Union Café's patisserie that could get me out of Schumacher's Bakery. My hair was dyed different colors all the time, so jobs that put me in the public eye were out of the question. Fortunately the opening was for a dishwasher. And as it turned out, the head pastry chef was an oversized and extremely flamboyant homosexual who didn't look twice when he saw my hair at the interview. He actually liked the fact that I was a musician. I suspect he may have taken me for gay. I got the job.

Then, in 1983, my band Ten Minute Warning got the opening slot on a tour of the Northwest with the big Vancouver punk band D.O.A. When I came back home from a week or so on the road, I walked into our place to find Stacy hanging out with a guy I knew was part of a crew of people dabbling in heroin. I was worried.

We didn't address it directly, but as the signs that she was using began to get more obvious, I would spend more and more time away from our apartment. I didn't want to be proactive, I didn't want to deal. Stacy finally told me she was indeed doing heroin. I moved out. She drowned herself in smack for the next few years. We were done.

I struggled to deal with the loss of that first love—all the more so because of the way it happened. At first I was physically ill—so sick that I couldn't hold down any food. Of course, I also needed a new place to stay right away. One of my best friends, Eddy, had a great idea. His mom bought houses and flipped them; he did renovations on the properties for her. He and I moved into one of the places they were fixing up to resell.

Eddy and I had first met on the basketball court during a third-grade city league practice. I fouled him too hard while trying to block his shot—the kind of thing you do when you have yet to achieve control of your growing body. He punched me right in the nose in retaliation. For

some reason, when boys get into a fight, they will often become insepa-
rable friends. That proved true for me and Ed.

As we came up through junior high together, Eddy and I got into all
of the same trouble and experienced all the same stuff together: sports,
girls, drugs, grand theft auto. At some point in the eighth grade, as Andy
and some other friends and I began playing instruments, Eddy joined
in our new fascination with punk rock. He couldn't play the guitar or
drums, so he started to focus his attention on being a singer. And why
not? He had always been the coolest of us and could certainly stand in
front of a crowd without an instrument to hide behind. It didn't take
long before he was singing for one of the city's most promising punk
bands.

Once ensconced in one of Eddy's mom's renovation projects, we developed a routine. I would get up in the morning and go to work at the
Lake Union Café; Ed would get up and work on the next phase of the
refurbishing—drywall, plumbing, electrical, whatever. Most nights we
would go to gigs, either playing with our bands or going to see friends'
bands. With both of us in bands, we had seemingly unlimited opportunities to meet and sleep with girls. Newly single and working my way out of
an emotional funk, I now took advantage of those opportunities.

I was eighteen, and here we were, two best friends living on our own
in a big house in a nice neighborhood. One night, Billy Idol, who had
just rocketed to mainstream success with his second solo album, *Rebel
Yell*, was to perform on *The Tonight Show* with Johnny Carson. It was the
first time any of our punk heroes had managed to get on a show as big
as this, and we were on a mission to watch it—though not enough of a
mission to stay in for the night. On the way home, drunk, we got pulled
over for speeding just blocks from our house. I was at the wheel of my
"new" car, a 1971 Ford Maverick I had picked up for three hundred dollars. As I rolled down my window, copper penny in my mouth to throw
off the Breathalyzer, I said to the cop, "But officer, we were only speeding
because we can't miss Billy Idol on Carson!" Eddy was snickering in the
passenger seat and I was stifling laughter myself. The rock gods were with
us that night, and the cop let us go.

Soon I could see less and less work getting done at the house. Ed was also coming out of his bedroom less frequently. The good times were coming to an end. In Ed's case, once he started doing heroin, it took away his willpower, stripped it absolutely clean. I watched helplessly as my friend slowly sank deeper and deeper into a pit. It seemed I had lost him and didn't have the means to do anything about it—another casualty to heroin in my innermost circle.

CHAPTER NINE

+ + +

Not too long after I got laid off from the Black Angus I found a steady job again at an office in a back alley near where Hollywood Boulevard crossed the freeway. The company ostensibly sold office supplies, but the specifics of my work made me wonder. A day's work typically consisted of a pistol-packing guy in a tracksuit with a difficult-to-pinpoint East European accent telling me to drive an unmarked truck or panel van between two random, anonymous addresses in the city. Scratch that—to call the hidden alleyways, abandoned lots, and remote underpasses where I found and left trucks "addresses" would be a stretch. I never asked what was being transported. It didn't seem like a safe question, I guess.

With all that driving around town, I began to see how segregated L.A. was. A lot of my colleagues would refuse to make "deliveries" to Watts. That blew me away. In Seattle, there just weren't places people refused to go. Seattle had a "black area"—the Central District—but things weren't delineated nearly as starkly as they were in L.A. I went to school in the Central District. In L.A., people who lived in Hollywood didn't leave Hollywood, people in the Jewish enclave of Fairfax didn't leave Fairfax, people in Watts didn't leave Watts and didn't even seem to know where Hollywood was. Fear swathed the city.

One day in February 1985, as I was coming home from work, I ran into Izzy. He told me he was starting a new band with a couple guys from L.A. Guns, the band Slash had taken me to see back in October. Axl Rose, the vocalist from the version of L.A. Guns I had seen, had grown up with

Izzy in Indiana, and had followed him out to L.A. Axl had just moved into a place on our low-rent high-crime block of Orchid Street, this buzzing hive of prostitution and drug dealing. Izzy's new band also featured Tracii Guns on lead guitar. They were calling the new group Guns N' Roses.

Almost immediately the new group parted ways with their first bass player. Izzy came to me at that point.

"Don't you play bass?" he asked me.

"I *own* a bass," I said. I was getting comfortable playing four strings by then, but I had not come close to developing my own style yet. Fortunately, one of the advantages of being young—I had just turned twenty-one—was fearlessness and unbridled confidence. Not to mention the fact that I no longer had a guitar. At this point it was bass or nothing.

When I showed up at my first GN'R rehearsal in late March, 1985, Axl and I said hi to each other and started joking around about this and that. I liked him right away. Whoever was running the sound then asked Axl to test out the microphone. Axl let out one of his screams, and it was like nothing I had ever heard. There were two voices coming out at once! There's a name for that in musicology, but all I knew in that instant was that this dude was different and powerful and fucking serious. He hadn't yet entirely harnessed his voice—he was more unique than great at that point—but it was clear he hadn't moved out to Hollywood from Indiana for the weather. He was here to stake a claim and show the whole fucking world what he had.

As for Izzy, he wasn't a great guitar player, but I liked that—both in him and in general. I wasn't a great guitar player, either. It was a punk thing. One night when we were talking after a rehearsal, Izzy mentioned a band called Naughty Women. It rang a bell.

"I know that band," I said, trying to place the name. "I think I played a gig on the same bill with them once. Wait, wait, wait. Were they . . . cross-dressers?"

"Yep," Izzy said.

He paused.

"I was the drummer," he said.

Cool, I thought, this guy really was a veteran of the punk-rock club scene. He was the real deal.

Izzy and Axl already had some songs, and the other guys knew them: "Think About You," "Anything Goes," "Move to the City," "Shadow of Your Love," and "Don't Cry." And we did sped-up punk versions of the Stones' "Jumpin' Jack Flash" and Elvis Presley's "Heartbreak Hotel."

Rob Gardner, the drummer, played a double-kick drum set—a metal dude. Tracii was an incredible guitar player, but his sound was also really metal. My initial impression was that he didn't have the feel I had recognized in Slash. Once again I realized with a sinking feeling that this was not the band I was seeking, not one that could move the needle musically.

They had some gigs booked, though, and since Izzy and I had a lot in common and Axl seemed so unique, I decided I would stick it out for a while. After we'd played the Dancing Waters club and another gig so forgettable I can't remember the name of the venue, any excitement I had about the band dwindled. I missed the next rehearsal. Axl called me after that. He could tell I was pulling back and asked me to please come to the next rehearsal. I reluctantly agreed.

Axl met me outside the rehearsal space to talk about my reservations.

"You *have* to be part of this," he said. "Give it another chance."

One thing I soon learned about Axl: if he saw something in a person, he would do everything possible to ensure that person remained part of his vision.

Part of my problem with the band was that I was skeptical about the commitment of Tracii and Rob, who both had comfortable suburban lives in L.A. I had already recognized a difference between people from L.A. and people who had moved there. Axl and Izzy were distinct even from other transplants—they were serious in a whole different way. Axl sometimes slept on the street back then. It was also clear that Izzy would do whatever it took, heroin habit or not. *You can come with us or not,* they seemed to say, *but we're going to make our way and realize our dream.* I liked that. Still, I wasn't sure how best to express this to Axl. I told him

I just didn't think that Rob and Tracii were cut out for going all in and sacrificing everything to work on their craft. Axl didn't argue. We went inside.

During rehearsal I had an idea. I had been through the punk-rock crucible; I was used to sleeping on floors and doing anything else necessary to get my band out there. In my experience, conditions like that also offered a chance to see what your bandmates were really made of. A shake-out cruise could be just what Guns N' Roses needed.

I pulled aside Axl and Izzy.

"Listen, how would you guys like to play some places beside fucking Dancing Waters in San Pedro?"

They nodded.

"If we're going to play for three people," I said, "let's at least go do it other places."

"Fuckin'-A," said Izzy.

I could tell immediately that Izzy understood what I was up to—he had been through this before. He knew this was a way to test the links in a band and find the weak ones.

In the first wave punk bands I played in, we booked our own gigs, functioned as our own tour managers, handled our own dough, made our own concert T-shirts. The do-it-yourself ethic had been strong, and as a result I knew the nuts and bolts of the business. With some songs mastered and these local gigs under our belts, I knew I could use the contacts I'd accumulated over the years to line up some shows for the fledgling Guns N' Roses—a punk-rock tour of the West Coast.

"I think I can book us a tour," I said. "It'll be bare-bones, but we'll be out there playing."

They loved the idea.

"Yeah, let's do it!"

I was excited now, too: we would know by the end of this whether GN'R was the real deal or not. Punk-rock tours in those days ran on pure adventure and adrenaline. You counted yourself lucky if you earned enough to pay for gas and still had something left over to buy ramen noodles. You slept at a crash house if you could find one or on the club floor if the owner liked you. But none of that was important. The main thing was that it offered the chance to prove yourself, to push yourself beyond the confines of your comfort zone, to take music you believed in to other people's towns, to throw all caution to the wind. Come to think of it, there was no caution in those days.

I was able to book us a string of dates, mostly in places I'd played with previous bands or been through while working briefly as a roadie for the Fastbacks. The first show would be a homecoming gig for me—a June 12 slot supporting the Fastbacks at the then new Seattle club called Gorilla Gardens. The rest of the dates were in little punk venues, communal houses, and squats down the coast back toward L.A. We would play 13th Precinct in Portland, the basement of a communal punk house in Eugene, another house in Sacramento, and a club called Mabuhay Gardens in San Francisco. That was the full extent of the plan. We would figure out everything else, including where we would sleep and how we would eat, on the fly.

Rob and Tracii were skeptical about the idea from the start. I guess they weren't sure whether to take the leap of faith necessary to leave home with nothing but your bandmates and wits to depend on. And just a few weeks before we were to leave, they broke the news: they weren't up for a no-budget road trip. Not knowing where we would sleep each night was too much for them. I assured them we'd find places to crash, and anyway, what did it matter—we would be on tour, a concept that to me was pure magic.

It didn't matter. First Rob and then Tracii backed out.

We had ten days before we were scheduled to leave for the tour.

"Don't worry," I told Izzy and Axl, who were fully committed and for whom hitting the road had the same mythic appeal it had for me. "I know a couple guys we can bring in."

CHAPTER TEN

+ + +

By early 1984, my band Ten Minute Warning was becoming the biggest punk act in the Northwest. Back then, to make two hundred bucks for a gig put you on top of the heap. We sometimes made $250 or $300. A weekly alternative newspaper, the *Rocket,* featured us on its cover, and the *Seattle Times,* one of the big dailies, wrote a piece about us. We were headlining concerts in Seattle and playing real shows elsewhere with good bands—we had toured with the Dead Kennedys, D.O.A., and our heroes, Black Flag. We had broken down what had always been an impenetrable wall between punk and metal when we co-headlined a show at a roller-skating rink—where all the suburban metal acts played—with a band called Culprit. Our songs had made it onto some punk compilations. And in early 1984 we signed with Alternative Tentacles, the record label run by Jello Biafra of the Dead Kennedys. They had us recording demos for an album.

The band had evolved from the Fartz. I'd been the drummer at one point and was still close to the Fartz guitarist, a guy named Paul Solger. Paul and I had taken road trips in his '65 Mustang—a gift from his parents—to see Johnny Thunders in Portland and Vancouver. Eventually, Paul and I began to write songs together on the side—both of us on guitars—and we decided to put together a new band. I switched to rhythm guitar and we recruited drummer Greg Gilmore, who went on to play in Mother Love Bone, and bassist David Garrigues, a local skateboard legend. Our choice for singer was a guy named Steve Verwolf, a dude we all knew from the punk scene. Steve was definitely a visionary. His hair was long and he wore black leather hip-hugger pants and little else. Onstage he was a man possessed, mixing Iggy Pop–like antics with the doom and gloom of Bauhaus's Peter Murphy and the shamanic power of Jim Morrison. By that stage I'd formed or played in a lot of bands, but up to then there had always been weak links in the bands. Ten Minute Warning felt different.

We created a new sound, too. By then a lot of us in the punk scene were getting fed up with paint-by-numbers hardcore. Ten Minute Warning's solution was to slow things way down from hard-core speeds and add a sludgy, heavy psychedelic element. Black Flag's singer, Henry Rollins, told us we sounded like a punk-rock version of Hawkwind—the 1970s British band that launched the career of Lemmy Kilmister, who later formed Motörhead. We took this as high praise. Ten Minute Warning had real character and dimension. We had begun to share the stage with other bands also coming out of the hardcore scene and striving to do something new, like the Replacements, a Minneapolis band we played with when they came to Seattle. We were getting better and better.

Paul, who was always dabbling in something, had gone through a few phases of heroin use. But each time he had pulled himself out of it before getting strung out for too long. In fact, I thought he was out of the woods. But I remember vividly the first time he showed up late for a rehearsal downtown at our Bell Street basement space with the telltale nod of an opiate high. I sort of ignored it at first, but the more I saw him high, the more I realized he was swinging back into habit mode. I am not sure whether it was the local notoriety the band was getting that gave him easier access to drugs, but Paul was getting fully strung out, and once an addict finally opens the gates it's a dark and terrifying road from there.

So by the middle of 1984, I had lost my long-term girlfriend, my best friend, and my main band to smack. A lot of my other friends and musical mentors—like Kim from the Fastbacks—were strung out, too. In fact, almost everyone I had so much fun discovering music with seemed to be strung out.

I was still having panic attacks, and I was worried I might have a serious disease: the year before I'd had a tumor removed from my chest, and though it was benign, I was sure there were going to be more. Taken together, the future—with drugs encroaching from all sides—didn't look so bright. I was also starting to drink heavily as a coping mechanism. So much so that my boss at the Union Lake Café had a talk with me about it. It wasn't that I was drinking on the job, but he could tell I was drinking every night. I guess I reeked of booze when I got to work.

I had been at Lake Union Café almost two years. Two things made it a great job: we listened to music in the back, and there were possibilities to advance. My first few months I had worked as a dishwasher, scraping out muffin tins and cake pans like I'd done at Schumacher's. Once I proved a hard and dependable worker, however, one of the chefs had taken me under his wing and taught me some of the simple techniques—making breads, dipping strawberries. The boss took notice of my willingness to learn and started to test me. One day after work he asked me to take the next day off and show up at midnight instead. Midnight? Those were baker's hours! I showed up the following night and they announced that I was now a baker's apprentice. And the boss gave me a raise!

I had mastered Black Forest cakes and various mousses. I could work with marzipan and filo dough. My raspberry tarts with almond-crust lattice tops were becoming works of art. I even had business cards: *Duff McKagan, Pastry Chef.*

One of my buddies at the restaurant was a guy named Bruce Pavitt, who had moved up from Olympia the year before. He had started a music column called "Sub Pop" in the weekly *Rocket.* He told me that summer he had decided to start a record label and put out a single, following through on a dream. He already had a name for his label: he was going to call it Sub Pop, after his column.

An unpleasant thought began to churn in my already agitated mind: Was I at risk of surrendering my dream?

Much as I enjoyed baking, I wasn't approaching my job at Lake Union Café as a potential career. To become a head pastry chef and make real

money, you had to have your own recipes. I wasn't collecting and perfecting my own recipes, I was just executing other people's. But with my
bands foundering and my friends falling like flies to heroin, what exactly
was I doing?

I still had a dream, a dream of finding a team of like-minded musicians who wanted to push the envelope musically, and who were willing
to put in the work it would take to do that. And, of course, ultimately I
would have loved one day to be able to make a living playing music. It
dawned on me that it was time to begin thinking about a way I could start
fresh musically and personally.

I cast about for new avenues—avenues not already dimmed by the
dark shadow of heroin—and started to expand my social circle. One
night, I ended up hanging out with a guy named Donner. I vaguely recognized him from the periphery of the punk scene, but that night we
found we had a lot of stuff in common—most important, a growing dis-
taste for the way heroin was killing our relationships with close friends.
Donner was just then opening a club called the Grey Door in Pioneer
Square. His club quickly became my favorite hangout. The gigs he booked
were always all-ages. Beer was served surreptitiously from a keg in the
basement.

Donner and I even briefly started a band and I went back to playing
drums. It wasn't a serious endeavor, but it was a blast. Like me, he was a
big drinker, and always had a bottle of something nearby. Seattle being
Seattle, we would mix whatever we had with really strong, homemade
coffee—our version of a speedball, I suppose.

The Grey Door is also where I met the singer Andy Wood. His band
Malfunkshun would come over from Bainbridge Island and stay the weekend at the club—it also served as a crash pad. With maybe ten people in
the audience, Andy would point to the rafters and yell out, "I want all of
you on the left side to say 'hell,' and all of you on the right side say 'yeah,'"
just the way his hero Paul Stanley of KISS did in huge arenas. A few years
later, his next band, Mother Love Bone, signed a major-label deal and
recorded a benchmark EP. Then Andy died of a heroin overdose—only a

few days before the band's full-length album was supposed to be released. A couple of the remaining guys soldiered on with a new singer and took the name Pearl Jam.

Andy and I would talk for hours about music in general and Prince in particular. *Purple Rain* came out that summer of 1984 and I bought it the day it came out. I had loved *1999* and listened to Prince's records constantly, either at home on my record player or on cassette on the crappy little boom box I always carried around. A new girlfriend also started making me really cool mixtapes of Parliament, Lakeside, Gap Band, Cameo, and other R&B stuff. Along with Black Flag's *My War,* T-Bone Burnett's *Proof Through the Night,* the Rolling Stones' *It's Only Rock and Roll,* and a new album called *Two Steps from the Move* from the band Hanoi Rocks, this made up the soundtrack of my life during that period of soul-searching.

Prince records had made me realize, too, that being a multi-instrumentalist could open doors. Prince wasn't so much a solo artist as a one-man-band. Maybe one day I could create records all by myself. I had whisky-and-coffee-induced daydreams of moving somewhere like Hollywood, recording cool Prince-like records, making it big, buying a house, and having Donner and all my friends move down there with me to live happily ever after in a pimped-out punk-rock commune.

Those daydreams took on additional heft when another friend, Joe Toutonghi, suggested I leave Seattle. I had always admired Joe. He picked up on new kinds of music—he was among the first to play me Bauhaus, for instance, and British ska, like Madness and the Specials. He was part of the Jaks, a skateboard crew with members up and down the West Coast. Joe would hop freight trains like an old-fashioned hobo—a skateboard under his arm instead of a stick and bundled handkerchief over his shoulder—just to get out and see other places.

Joe was strung out at this point, too, and he pulled me aside one day and spoke conspiratorially.

"You have to get out of here," he said. "I've squandered my chance. You still have a chance—you are *our* chance."

Even though Donner and I were becoming thick as thieves, by the end of the summer of 1984, I began to think that if I didn't get out of Seattle then, I might never get out at all. A lot of my calculations about where to go were based on practical considerations: my old Ford had a slant-six engine that was ultra-dependable, but it already had 200,000 miles on it. Also, my budget was tight and I had punk contacts and crash pads all the way down the West Coast. And my brother Matt was studying down in Los Angeles. Okay, so things were not exactly pointing toward New York City, which had been my initial thought.

Joe's last music tip—during the conversation when he urged me to leave town—had been about a new group called the Red Hot Chili Peppers, a Los Angeles skate-punk band experimenting with funk sounds. *Hmm.* I could make it to L.A. in my old car, leapfrogging from crash pad to crash pad, maybe land at my brother's apartment for a few nights. Beyond that, there was nothing in particular drawing me toward Los Angeles. It was just a place—a bigger place, a place that wasn't Seattle, and with luck, a safer place than the heroin-infested Pacific Northwest.

To some people, moving a thousand miles might be a big deal. For me, in the end, it was just a way to avoid embarrassment. I was out one night, drunk off my ass, and told a bunch of people I was going to move to L.A. So that was it, decision made. I had to do it now.

My move to L.A. presented immediate dilemmas. My drum kit was a piece of shit and falling apart. Drums were hard to lug around and set up and break down all of the time. Hey, I was a multi-instrumentalist—no drums, no problem. Okay, then, settled: I would sell my kit. I got eighty bucks for it.

I decided I would take a guitar—my killer, black, late-1970s B.C. Rich Seagull. But I sold my Marshall combo amp to help pool money for the move. A new amp would be easy to pick up once I got down there, found a job, and settled in. And anyway, I doubted guitar would be the best way to break into the L.A. scene: 1984 was the biggest year yet for Van Halen, and the band's hometown was awash in guitar players inspired by Eddie Van Halen's ornate, light-speed shredding. I doubted people in Los Angeles were going to understand someone coming down and playing guitar like Johnny Thunders or like Steve Jones from the Sex Pistols—raw and fucked up, with the song at the center, not the solo. Of course, I wanted to do that Johnny Thunders stuff, but I thought first I would need to find the right people. And I figured the best way to do that—and to get a gig at all—was to make bass my main instrument. If nothing else, I could get my foot in the door and meet people.

A few years earlier I had played bass briefly in the Vains, but I was not what you would call a great player. I had recently been experimenting on bass again and had bought a black Yamaha and a crazy Peavey head with an Acoustic 2x15 cabinet. To anyone who knows gear, this may seem like an odd combination to play bass through, but it had the beginnings of a unique sound. I was searching for my own signature as a bass player, and this gear was a good start.

There were so many kids and kids of kids in the McKagan clan that there wasn't any drama when I told my family about my plan to bail. The owner of the Lake Union Café understood when I handed in my notice, too. He knew music was what I did. He also respected the work I had done at the café. The head pastry chef wrote a nice reference for me to take along; it would serve me well.

CHAPTER ELEVEN

✦ ✦ ✦

On Friday, May 31, 1985, Slash had a gig at the Country Club with Black Sheep, a band he had recently joined. I had already been thinking that his guitar style would mesh well with Izzy's. So I took Axl to the show and we talked to Slash. The next day I called Slash and tried to convince him to bring Steven Adler and come by to rehearse with us. They both knew Axl, too, having played a few gigs with him as Hollywood Rose in 1984, not long after Axl arrived in L.A. But in the interim there had been some bad blood. Apparently Axl had slept with Slash's girlfriend. Not only that, but when the singer of Black Sheep figured out the reason for our visit to the show the night before, he was so angry he called Slash's mom and told her we were drug addicts—a point on which he was only partly right.

Slash was inclined to try it out because Guns seemed more where he wanted to go musically than Black Sheep. His interest in that job was primarily mercenary: it was a place to be plucked from to fill a gap in an established band—the way Ozzy plucked Randy Rhoads from Quiet Riot. But rather than wait around in Black Sheep hoping to get the call to fill in as touring guitarist for KISS or whatever, Slash liked the idea of joining a band with the intention of making its own mark.

Finally Slash and Steven agreed to come to a rehearsal, just days before a previously scheduled June 6 gig at the Troubadour that was supposed to serve as a warm-up for our tour. We met at a space in Silverlake—we rented it for six dollars an hour, and that included a drum kit. From the moment the five of us leaned into our first song, we could all hear and feel that the fit was right. The chemistry was immediate, thunderous, and soulful. It was amazing and all of us recognized it instantly.

Izzy shared my horror at big, huge, overwrought "heavy metal" drum kits. He and I made sure there was never a second kick drum anywhere in sight, regardless of where we rehearsed. Together we began plotting to hide parts of Steven's own drum kit, too. Every time poor Steven would show up at band practice, the kit got progressively smaller, until he was left with only the bare essentials—the setup that would allow him to hone his signature sound and influence modern rock drummers a few short years later. Without a second bass drum, his frenetic speed-metal beat was cut in half and instead he and I could lock in and create a groove.

During those first rehearsals, the five of us started working up a new song together based on some lyrics I had brought with me in a notebook from Seattle. The song became "Paradise City," and it started to gel in those few days before our Troubadour show and the trip up to Seattle.

On Thursday, June 6, we played our first live show with the *Appetite for Destruction* lineup. The bill at the Troubadour included Fineline, Mistreater, and, at the very bottom, Guns N' Roses. Slash's high school friend Marc Canter—he turned out to be part of the family that ran Canter's Deli—came and shot pictures. He made prints of each of us the next day so we'd have head shots to put up in the places we played on our tour. That was Friday.

On Saturday, June 8, 1985, Izzy, Axl, Slash, Steven, and I got together to set out for Seattle, a happy bunch of malcontents about to hit the road in search of rock-and-roll glory, ready to live by our wits in order to prove ourselves and our musical vision—or not. At the very least we thought we had real musical chemistry. That much was obvious even before the tour started.

A friend of ours named Danny had a huge Buick LeSabre with a powerful 455 big-block V-8 engine and a trailer hitch. Seven of us crammed into the car that Saturday afternoon: the five of us in the band, plus Danny and another friend, Joe-Joe, who had signed up to serve as roadies. These guys would go to the mat for us, really solid friends, and we were glad they, too, had not blinked an eye in the face of the uncertainties of a no-budget road trip. We rented a U-Haul trailer to carry our gear behind the LeSabre. Our plan was to drive straight through to Seattle—it would take something like twenty-one hours—and arrive there at some point on Sunday. My buddy Donner was going to let us crash at his house the first few nights before our show that Wednesday.

As we rose up out of the "Grapevine," a writhing section of Interstate 5 just south of Bakersfield, California, the car started to hiccup and cough and rebel against the weight it had to shoulder in the blazing late-afternoon heat of the San Joaquin Valley. By the time we passed Bakersfield, a mere 105 miles out of L.A., Danny's car up and died. A passing motorist stopped and tried to help, but the best he could do for us was to go to the next gas station and call AAA. The hope of grilling burgers the next evening in Donner's backyard quickly faded with the realization that Danny's car was going nowhere at all until it had some major work.

We were broke, hungry, and sweltering, hunkered down on the side of the highway. Dusk slowly descended but the heat didn't break. When the tow truck showed up, the mechanic was a bit put off to find a whole gang of sweaty, skinny rock guys who wanted to ride in his truck. We ended up walking to the next off-ramp, where there was a truck stop and gas station.

At that point, removed from the whizzing cars, we took stock of the situation. It was the middle of the night. We had thirty-seven dollars between us. If we went back to L.A., we would obviously not be doing this tour. That was not an option, regardless of our current dilemma. We decided that the five of us—along with three guitars—should hitchhike, continuing north while Danny and Joe tried to get the car fixed. They could then catch up, uniting us with our gear either along the way or in Seattle.

I called Kim Warnick of the Fastbacks from the gas station. Our first gig in Seattle was opening for them. I began to explain the situation. Actually I had to go back further and fill her in on the lineup change that had taken place since I set up the show.

"So Izzy, Axl, and I convinced Slash—"

"Izzy, Axl, Slash—and Duff," she said. "What kind of names are those?"

"Well, there is a guy named Steven."

She said it would be no problem for us to use the Fastbacks' gear if Danny wasn't able to get up there in time. Okay, that part was taken care of and now it was time to find a ride, someone willing to transport five guys and their guitars—a tall order for sure.

We knew it was going to be tough to hitchhike in such a big group. To make clear the magnitude of the task at hand, I should add that even though I was in my full-length leather pimp coat, I was not the most menacing-looking among us. Even someone who'd be willing to stop for one bedraggled rocker would never take us all. So we decided to try to catch a ride with a northbound trucker. Truckers had those big empty sleeper cabs and would surely love to have some company, right? Someone to talk to on that long and lonely stretch of I-5 that runs up through California's agricultural outback.

We approached several truck drivers and finally found one willing to give us a lift as far as Medford, Oregon, in exchange for our pooled cash. That was his end destination and for us it was six hundred miles closer to our first out-of-town gig. It was a win for both parties: he would get thirty-seven bucks and we would be heading north at highway speeds.

It was obvious right from the start that this particular trucker was a speed-freak, and that our thirty-seven dollars would be used to supplement his habit. He had probably already been up for a few days, and riding with him in that state in a huge semitruck was a risky endeavor. Fuck it. We were on a mission. Do or die, we were going to make it to Seattle.

I was hoping Kim would spread the word in Seattle that we had broken down and were on the road without a car. Maybe someone would be willing to come down to Portland to pick us up if we made it that far on our own. For now, we piled into the eighteen-wheeler, guitars and all. The other four guys climbed into the sleeper cab. It was tight. I rode shotgun in the passenger seat up front.

The guy couldn't believe our story.

"Let me get this straight," he said. "You guys are fucking *hitchhiking* to a gig—*a thousand miles away*?"

"Yep," I said.

"And you don't have any equipment—or even any food?"

"Well, yeah, but our equipment . . ."

"I don't mean to sound like a prick, but, I mean, can't you play anywhere in Los Angeles?"

I tried to explain the swashbuckling magic of playing to strangers, in strange places, us-against-them, us-against-the-world . . . winning over listeners a few at a time.

He shrugged.

The drug-induced sleep deprivation started to take its toll on our driver about two hundred miles into the drive. By the time we hit Sacramento in the morning, he said he needed to rest his eyes and clear his head of the speed demons. It was okay with me. I had been talking with the dude for this first part of the ride and noticed that he kept looking into his sideview mirrors and sort of jumping around in his seat. This kind of stuff happens when you don't sleep for several days. I had a little bit of experience with speed from my teenage years, enough to know what was happening to the driver.

Sacramento sits at the top of the arid central California valley—the area became a center of agriculture only with the aid of intense irrigation. When it's hot in the valley, Sacramento always has the highest temperatures. Our venture into the valley coincided with an absolutely scorching heat wave. Now, for some reason, the driver stopped in front of the state capitol building.

"All right, boys, I'm going to need you to hop out here."

We didn't know what to say, and were in no position to argue anyway.

"I've got to take care of something," said the driver. "But I'll be back for you, don't worry."

Yeah, right. I was convinced our driver had just tricked us and left us behind. I'm sure the rest of the guys shared the same suspicion.

We were left sitting on the curb.

No one said a word. No one even made a face, sighed, or raised an eyebrow.

As we sat there in front of the capitol, wilting in the heat, exposed to the intense sun, it became clear: as of this moment, Guns N' Roses was no longer *a* band, but *the* band—*our* band. *These are my fucking boys— they're willing to fight through anything.* I already knew this trip had set a new benchmark for what we were capable of, what we could and would put ourselves through to achieve our goals as a band. This band became a brotherhood under that oppressive Sacramento sun. *Fuck yeah!*

Then, as I sat there silently rhapsodizing about my friends and our collective determination, the eighteen-wheeler suddenly pulled up and the driver nodded.

"Let's roll, boys," he said.

He had actually come back to pick us up. Unbelievable.

"You have a fucking show to get to!" he said.

I hopped back in the passenger seat. He was cranked out of his mind. He must have dropped us off to go score some more speed, and to this day I have no idea how, in that state, he remembered to come back for us.

That afternoon, just after Redding, I cautiously suggested we pull over at the next rest stop and take a break. I could see it was getting even more dangerous being in a huge moving vehicle with him. He had huge black circles under his eyes and he was sweating profusely. By some miracle, he agreed—and he actually slept there for a few hours while we just hung out nearby, trying to be as quiet as possible. We had no money for booze or food. I'm not sure what Izzy had with him, but he wasn't showing any signs of withdrawal yet. After the driver came to, he took us the final hundred and fifty miles up to Medford.

"I'm actually sorry I can't take you any farther," he said. "Shit, I might even try to make it up there myself on Wednesday for your show."

It was now Sunday evening. We found a pay phone to check in with our contact person in L.A., who Danny was supposed to call with an update on the broken-down car. Danny hadn't been able to get the car fixed yet. The replacement part would have to be shipped down to Bakersfield from San Francisco on a business day.

With no money left, our only hope now was to straight-up hitch-hike on the side of the freeway. From a less determined perspective, it would have seemed a hopeless long shot that anyone would pick up five fucked-up-looking guys with their guitars—if anyone even had enough space. But we didn't see it that way at all then. We just had no alternative.

After only about forty-five minutes, a Mexican farmworker in a Dat-sun compact pickup pulled over to give us a ride. In broken English, he made us understand that he was going only as far as Eugene, Oregon, but that we were welcome to pile into the back. After only a few miles, it became painfully obvious to us that this ride would not last. The little pickup couldn't bear the weight; the wheel wells kept pressing down on the back tires and began to take rubber right off of them. Our victorious feeling from just moments earlier sank as the man pulled over to drop us off. I will never forget how apologetic he was. I hope to this day he real-ized how grateful we were to him for at least trying to help us.

Back on the side of the road, we started to walk while we thumbed. I knew how far it was to the next town because I had driven back and forth from Seattle to San Francisco more than a few times on tours; it was too far to walk, that's for sure. But as driven as we were at that point, we thought at least we would be making headway. So we walked.

Eventually we found ourselves in the middle of an onion field. When you're hungry and don't know where and when your next meal is coming, you can eat almost anything. Those were the best damn onions I've ever eaten. At that moment they tasted as sweet as apples.

After a few more hours of walking, I was only slightly aware of the passing cars. No one was going to pick us up, I thought to myself. My hope was that maybe we would come to a farmhouse with a phone and I could call Donner or Kim up in Seattle. Maybe someone would be able to come get us.

By morning, I was so fucking hungry and thirsty. We all were. Just then, a full-size pickup swerved to the side of the road and stopped in front of us. Two women in their mid-thirties told us to get in the back. They were sorry, they said, and explained they had passed us without picking us up when they first saw us. They were scared. But then they had talked about the way they, too, had been passed so many times on the roadside as hippies back in the early 1970s; they scolded each other, turned around at the next exit, and came back for us.

They asked us if we were hungry. We were. They asked us if we were thirsty. We were. They asked us if we were broke. We were. They pulled over at the next gas station, bought us sandwiches and beer, and told us they could take us all the way up to Portland. Almost three hundred miles! These women were like angels sent from heaven. Food and drink never tasted so fucking good. Friendship from strangers couldn't have come at a better time.

I tried Donner's number from a pay phone at the gas station and he actually answered.

"Dude, here's the deal. We broke down in Bakersfield and we've been hitchhiking for a day and a half. We're in Medford now and some girls are going to drive us as far as Portland. We'll be there early this afternoon."

Donner grew pot. He had grow operations going in a couple of unused buildings. He always had dough. And he had already met some of the other members of the band—Donner had visited me in L.A.

I asked him, "Can you help us out somehow?"

So we started talking: Could he arrange bus tickets maybe? Then he blurted out, "Fuck that, I'll pick you up. We're going to have a party at my house tonight, we'll have a feast, there'll be girls, it's going to be a Seattle welcome."

We made it to Portland on Monday afternoon, and Donner was there. By the time we arrived in Seattle, it seemed everyone I knew had apparently heard of our trials. They welcomed us with open arms, open liquor bottles, and open drug stashes. People in Seattle knew me as a drinker—they knew that as a result of my panic attacks I was not into drugs back then. For this reason, I guess, nobody offered anything hard. I think Izzy was a bit disappointed by this, and by then perhaps a tad sick from withdrawal.

Donner had, however, baked a batch of pot brownies. I think they were intended for people who would be coming over to the party later that night—people familiar with the potency of local weed.

Izzy just needed to catch a buzz off something, and I guess he thought pot brownies would be a lightweight short-term fix. Axl followed suit so Izzy wouldn't be alone.

"This shit is strong," Donner warned them. They ignored him.

In the 1980s, Seattle led the nation in the fine art of hydroponic pot growing. I'm not sure why the city excelled at it so, but the weed up there was getting potent. Really potent. Around 1982, a new strain of weed was developed for the basement water growers—the luckiest and most deep-pocketed started to cultivate what would be known as "a-strain" and later as "chronic." Up in the Northwest, we knew the strength of this shit, and also knew it was nothing to trifle with. It was like a mix between a strong muscle relaxer and LSD. Until you knew what was right for you, the best thing to do was to take just the tiniest puff and see where that got you; you had to build up a sort of tolerance.

Next thing I knew, Axl and Izzy went and curled up on Donner's couch with wide, scared eyes. I went over to make sure they were all right.

"What the fuck did they put in these brownies?" Izzy asked me.

Nothing, I assured them, it was just very strong weed.

"No way, man," he said. "I think there's acid in here."

They were completely paranoid. I told them not to worry. I felt horrible. I was hyper-sensitive to what my new bandmates were experiencing that first day in Seattle. They were a curiosity to my friends, that's for sure. But we were all dead tired and hungry and I wanted to make sure that Axl, Izzy, Slash, and Steven were well taken care of. I was proud of my city and my friends and wanted to cast them in the best light. It took Izzy and Axl hours and hours and a lot of beers to come down off of their first a-strain high. Fortunately, by the time the party started to get into full swing, they were returning to earth. But to this day, I am sure, they still think they were dosed with something.

Donner threw a barn burner that night: barbecue, beer, girls. Life was suddenly, really, really good.

Danny, Joe-Joe, and our gear still hadn't arrived when we played the show on Wednesday night at Gorilla Garden. We were sloppy on borrowed gear, though on the plus side only about a dozen people were subjected to our set. Kurt Bloch of the Fastbacks is always nice, and made a point of telling all the guys we had played great. We knew we were better than the actual gig—or at least we now knew we would be. The important thing for us was that we had made it there at all. Together.

After the Fastbacks set, we helped pack up their gear then hung out for a while with the crowd at the club—which was pretty much just old friends of mine at that point. Hanging out, of course, meant drinking, and drinking heavily.

One of the people I was most glad to see was Big Jim Norris. He was a tough guy from the wrong side of the tracks who had finally found a comfort zone in our little Seattle punk-rock scene. Jim had always had his struggles with drugs and drink, but he was one of those guys who had the spirit of life in his eyes. Jim was a leader. And when I left for Los Angeles, he made it a point to keep in touch. Once I got my apartment, he sent me letters, and we talked on the phone when we could afford to. Our friendship had actually deepened since I left.

Finally, as the place cleared out, the members of Guns went back to the club owner's office to pick up our gig money, no doubt looking like a pack of hungry wolves. When I had booked the show, I somehow managed to finagle a $200 guarantee out of the venue. Of course, I hadn't gotten a contract—not for this show or for any of the others. But then again, I'd never gotten a contract. Back in the day, punk shows were always handshake deals—and often the handshake part was just implicit because you had to come to terms over the phone. Our plan now was to wire this first $200 to Danny and Joe-Joe the next day and continue the tour.

English was not the owner's first language, but he quickly made it clear that he wasn't going to pay us.

We were stunned. I tried to reason with the guy. Then I played the sympathy card, telling him of our plight and our long journey, of the sunburn and hunger, of the onion fields and tweaking truckers. But the club owner didn't give a shit.

"You not bring any people to show," he said. "How I pay when I no have money from ticket?"

We made vague—and then probably more explicit—threats of violence. He held the office phone in his hand ready to speed-dial the police, and made sure we understood this.

Eventually we left his office and went back into what was now a deserted club.

"Fuck that asshole," said Axl. "We went through HELL to get here and play this show. And he treats us like scum?"

Suddenly there was just one thought in my head. It was the only solution I could see. The only way to get justice.

"Let's burn this fucking place down!"

The members of the band looked around the empty club and at one another. There were no objections.

"Let's burn it the fuck down," I said again.

Axl and I threw matches into a garbage can full of paper toweling and we all hauled ass outside.

Nothing happened.

We had failed as arsonists, but the mere attempt was enough to exorcise our ill will for the night. And it may have saved us a stint in the slammer.

After running out of the Gorilla Garden, we went out to see a local band called Soundgarden. The initial rumblings of what would become the Seattle sound were just starting to happen then. Buzzing on our newly solidified camaraderie—and plenty of booze—we stormed the stage when they were done and asked to play a few songs on their gear. They looked at us blankly and explained in the nerdy kind of way a kid on a playground might respond to a request to share his toys, "Um, no, that's *our* gear."

It didn't matter. Nothing could bring us down that night: we had played an out-of-town show.

The next day we found out we had also played our last out-of-town show for a while. Danny and Joe-Joe weren't going to make it. That didn't matter either. The shake-out tour had already accomplished everything I had hoped and more.

One of Donner's friends drove us all the way back to L.A. a few days later, and we arrived home a genuine band—a gang with the shared experience of a road trip gone wrong, an out-of-town gig, and the knowledge that we were all fully committed to Guns N' Roses.

PART TWO

JUST AN URCHIN LIVING UNDER THE STREET

CHAPTER TWELVE

✦ ✦ ✦

When we returned from Seattle, our first stop back in L.A. was Canter's Deli. We were starving after being on the road and getting only a few solid meals. But equally urgent was the determination to conquer the hometown club circuit—and for that, we needed photos to use to try to book gigs and make flyers. Marc Canter did a photo session—and by "photo session" I mean he took a black-and-white snapshot—in a booth at the deli while people ate at the adjoining tables. That picture became the flyer for our second-ever L.A. gig with this final lineup. Then we went out into the alley behind Canter's and Marc took the shot we'd eventually use on the back of the *Live! Like a Suicide* EP.

We began to look for gigs the second we got back. And we started rehearsing with a burning sense of purpose fueled by the knowledge that each of us was all-in. Initially we met at a rehearsal space owned by Nicky Beat, a well-known figure in the early L.A. punk scene. His facility was in an industrial wasteland out by Dodger Stadium. It was also Nicky's house—or rather, he also lived there. And apparently Nicky had become obsessed with exercise. Every day when we walked in, Nicky was lying on his back on a weight bench, stark naked, doing sit-ups. He would stop and say, "I'm doing a thousand a day!" We'd give him a thumbs-up and walk through to the practice room.

The timing for me and Steven to meld as a rhythm section was perfect. Steven had tons of drive, and we kept at it hour upon hour, day after day—just mercilessly. At that point, I was probably a better drummer than bass player. Not that I was so talented, but at least I had played drums in working bands. By contrast, I was still working on my bass style—Guns was the first band in which I played bass in earnest. I was heavily influenced by R&B and soul music at that stage, and for Steven and me, listening and playing along with Prince, Parliament, Cameo, and Sly and the Family Stone became our gauge and music school.

Of course, I definitely fashioned myself after punk bassists, too, especially those whose work had really propelled their bands' songs, like Barry Adamson of Magazine and Paul Simonon of the Clash. In 1979, I had seen the Clash at the Paramount Theater in Seattle and Simonon struck me as the embodiment of what was good in rock and roll. A year later, when *London Calling* came out, the cover art showed him smashing a bass on a stage. Greased-back hair, rolled-up sleeves, black engineer boots—cool incarnate. Some of the great bass players from the post-punk and noise era introduced more of a mood—almost a sense of color: Raven from Killing Joke is a good example. The actual playing is not the thing that grabs you—it's the attitude behind the playing that makes you want to break shit. Then there was Lemmy Kilmister of Motörhead, whose bass tone is still second to none. Mötley Crüe's first EP, 1982's *Too Fast for Love,* got a lot of play at punk-rock parties, and Nikki Sixx—the bass player—was the musical leader of the Crüe. So while many people felt guitar players like Eddie Van Halen forged the sound of the early 1980s, it was easy to see an alternative history where bass players led the way.

Another new band called Jane's Addiction was using Nicky Beat's space, too. They had an interesting rhythm duo made up of Eric Avery on bass and Stephen Perkins on drums. I suppose competition makes for a better "product," and Steven Adler and I would go watch Jane's Addiction play gigs whenever possible once we got to know them. It made us better—and I think we made them better, too.

As Steven and I crafted our sound as a rhythm section, I got to know him a lot better as a person, too, and quickly realized I couldn't have asked for a better musical partner or a better friend. I also realized that, as with all the members of the band, what you saw with Steven was not necessarily what you got. Despite his metal-dude hair and the fact that he'd go off and see Leatherwolf shows, he liked nothing more than to listen to Frankie Valli and the Four Seasons.

One night when we were out together, Steven said to me, "You know, all I want in life is to make enough money one day so I can have a bag of good weed and a big ball of crack around—all the time."

I laughed.

"We'll never make that kind of money," I said.

And besides, I thought to myself, *if we ever do, you'll look back at that dream as nothing more than a teenage joke.*

The Seattle road trip marked the start of a period of almost round-the-clock interaction between us five Guns members. We would go see bands together, play acoustic guitars together, learn to play as a unit, work on songs together, and post flyers together for the increasing number of gigs we started to book. Of course, we got into a ton of mischief together, too, and drew and redrew new lines in the sand as we pushed toward the outer edge of survivable behavior. Sex was blissfully plentiful and carefree; booze and drugs remained inextricably tied to partying, not coping; and rock and roll became the redemptive raison d'être of the next two years of our lives in a way it never had been in any of my other bands and, unfortunately, in a way it would cease to be in Guns a few years later.

Our social circle soon included a group of recently transplanted New Yorkers who moved out west to—I always suspected—escape legal problems. "Red" Ed, Petey, and Del melded nicely into our lifestyle, which included twenty-four-hour alcohol consumption, scoring any available drugs (I was starting to warm up to various kinds of pills at this point), sundry debaucheries, and plenty of Motörhead, Rolling Stones, and Sly and the Family Stone.

In addition to Big Jim, I had been corresponding with Eddy since I'd left Seattle, too. It seemed he took my departure as something of a wake-up call. He'd been trying to clean up. He got himself on a methadone plan with the help of his mom. When he got out of a stint in rehab, Eddy's mom called and asked if he could come down and spend some time with me. She thought it might be a good idea for him to come join me in Hollywood to get away from all of the dealers and junkies up in Seattle.

Eddy flew down and I picked him up at the airport. Over the next few days I guess I was too busy rehearsing to notice much beyond the work right in front of me. I didn't pick up on the fact that Ed had gone off methadone and slipped back into a nice heroin run right there in my tiny apartment. It took about four days. Junkies can always find other junkies. And in this case it happened to be our rhythm guitar player that Ed found. I just didn't think Eddie would put it together so fast. I couldn't deal with him or his drug use at this point, and I told him that he would have to leave. Over the next few years, horror stories trickled down from Seattle about how strung out Eddy was. I heard that someone Ed knew well was murdered. I heard Ed was on the run. Hearing things like that made me put on my blinders even tighter and forge forward.

I had been seeing a girl named Kat for a while at that stage, and we decided to move in together. I moved out of Orchid Street to another ground-floor place (they were always the cheapest) on El Cerrito, which I shared with her. The apartment was definitely a move up because of the cross streets: instead of being between Hollywood and Franklin, this building was half a block up the hill from Franklin. Lots of strippers lived on the block, but there were no longer hookers plying their trade outside my window. And I could leave my gear at home without constantly worrying it would get stolen.

When Kat and I moved in there, I didn't have much more than a mattress. This little troll of a guy came out as I was moving in and helped me carry the few things I had. His name was West Arkeen, and he lived in the apartment next to ours. Turned out he was one of those guys studying at the Musicians Institute around the corner from my previous apartment. West was one tough motherfucker. He was one funny motherfucker. And he quickly became valuable not only for his friendship but for his songwriting.

He wasn't the type of guy who wanted to play in a band, but he was an incredible guitar player. He ended up writing songs with several of us.

He had a hand in an unreleased song called "Sentimental Movie," and in "Yesterdays" and "The Garden," which eventually turned up on *Use Your Illusion*. All of those songs were written there on El Cerrito together with various members of our band. West also showed me open-E tuning, an alternative way of tuning a guitar so it plays an E-major chord when strummed with no fingers on the frets. That's why he got a songwriting credit on "It's So Easy"—without open-E tuning, that song wouldn't have happened. I didn't know alternate tunings existed.

Kat and I had heard that an eccentric old musician lived above us, but we didn't care. We weren't the best neighbors, either, what with Axl, Izzy, Slash, and Steven dropping by, cranking up music all the time, drinking, singing, and strumming with West. But the guy upstairs turned out to be none other than Sly Stone, whose music Steven and I jammed to almost every day, working on our groove. He started to give me cassettes of cracked-out demos he made on a four-track in his apartment. Then he began to use my place as a sort of psychic bomb shelter. It didn't go over too well with Kat.

I'd be next door at West's place, working on some lyrics, and I'd hear her cursing and then she'd scream down the hall.

"Duff, that motherfucker is smoking crack in our bathroom again!"

That was one of those pellucid moments in life. I watched the illusions I had about one of my idols evaporate before my eyes. Was the great Sly Stone living the good life, jamming in a home studio tucked away somewhere in his sprawling mansion? Nope, he was sneaking past my girlfriend to smoke crack in my bathroom.

Our first gig back in L.A. was on June 28, 1985, at the Stardust Ballroom, out east of Highway 101. They had a club night called Scream. It had started as a Goth night; Bauhaus and Christian Death were the most popular acts the DJ played. We were at the bottom of a four-band bill and had to go on stage at 8 p.m. The next show was on the Fourth of July at Madame Wong's East, a restaurant in Chinatown that hosted a lot of punk-rock shows at night. Guns played second on a four-band bill that night. Only three people showed up for our set, including Kat and West.

The gig at Madame Wong's was like many of our first shows in that we were booked alongside punk bands. Early in our career we played shows with Social Distortion, the Dickies, and Fear. I guess at first we must have been perceived as that—punk. But the cool thing about our band, and what set us apart from the beginning, was that we couldn't be pigeonholed. Sometimes this could work against a band. If you weren't punk enough for the punk-rock set, or metal enough for the heavy-metal crowd, you risked ending up without gigs. But with the addition of Slash and Steven, we somehow seemed to capture the best of both worlds. In the right setting now, Axl appeared both more punk and more metal than the whole L.A. scene put together.

The glam scene across town seemed like a private club with some mysterious secret handshake. We got a few gigs with rising glam bands, but it was clearly a mismatch. Rather than treat it as an opportunity to mix things up, insiders in the glam scene made sure to rub our outsider status in our faces. The Sunset Strip scene was all coke and champagne, and we were definitely from a different place. The people who came to those shows were a bit scared by us, too. We meant what we were doing; it wasn't safe or choreographed or pretend badass in any way. We also went through a period where we played a shit-ton of gigs with Tex & the Horseheads and other cow-punk bands, but we weren't an easy fit in that scene, either.

All the while we eyed the Troubadour in West Hollywood. Most bands started there in an opening slot on a Monday or Tuesday night. If and when you began to draw an audience, you could earn a chance to move up the bill, maybe even to a headlining slot, and you could shift to more desirable days of the week, and finally to weekend gigs. The Trou-badour was always packed on weekends. If you could manage to headline there on a Friday or Saturday night, well, that was an indicator of real potential: some weekend headliners got signed to major-label deals out of the all-important "Troub." For now we were a little too dirty to get even an opening slot on those coveted Friday and Saturday night bills. We would have to start at the bottom and get there on our own.

One of the staples in our early sets was a tune called "Move to the City," which was eventually recorded for our *Live! Like a Suicide* EP. We always heard that song the way it was recorded—with a horn section. And sometimes, even at the smallest venues, where we could barely all fit in the backstage area, we put together a few brass instruments to come onstage for that song. I recruited my brother Matt, who played trombone, to be part of the horn section. The first time he played with us, he looked out from the backstage area and said, "Where is everybody?"

He was right. Our early gigs were practically empty. Often the few people who were there had come to see the band playing after us. People would throw cigarettes at us and spit on us. Not that it was meant as an I-hate-you thing; people were just rowdy and having fun—that was the way some of the L.A. punk venues were back then. We got used to being treated poorly by everyone—audiences, promoters, clubs, and fellow musicians.

As soon as Guns began to play regularly in L.A., we started up a phone and mailing list. We obsessively made sure people who came to shows signed up—well, actually, what we did was send stripper friends out into the audience and have *them* convince people to sign up. Obviously we had to write good songs and play well live to get a bigger audience. On that front I already knew we had the components we needed. But the mailing list really worked for us—within six months we had a thousand names with contact info for each. Other bands had mailing lists, but one of the secrets to GN'R's success was how much time and effort we spent building and maintaining ours. We knew we had to make it on our own, and after our Seattle road trip, failure was not an option with this crew.

The established rock clubs in Hollywood at that time had devised a brutal system to ensure themselves against low attendance. By instituting "pay to play," they shifted the financial risks of the nightclub business downstream to the musicians. A club would require an act to pre-buy, say, thirty tickets at ten dollars a pop. At that point the club didn't care anymore—their money was already in the can. The band would have to sell those tickets on their own to recoup their money.

The problem for us was getting together the initial balloon payment. Rich Hollywood parents could loan their kids' bands money, but we didn't have that cushion. That's where Slash's best friend Marc Canter came in—Marc was the unsung hero of GN'R. Without him, I don't know how we would have done half the shit we did at the beginning.

Marc believed in our band from day one. His faith was such that, in addition to photographing us, he was willing to front us the money to buy the tickets that allowed us to get shows in the pay-to-play clubs. We paid him back once we sold the tickets. We were relentless about calling the names on our list. At first we had to hustle really hard just to pay Marc back, but we grew our fan base faster as a result; as our mailing list expanded, it was easier and easier to sell tickets to our shows. Of course, we also had to borrow money from Marc to buy stamps.

We made cool flyers and, in addition to sending them to people on our list, we posted them all over the city. We always posted flyers as a band, at night. The first time I discovered Night Train wine was on one of these epic nocturnal flyering campaigns—which were best accomplished while drinking from a brown paper bag. Afterward I was happy to find that the liquor store around the corner from our storage space also stocked it. At $1.29 a bottle, Night Train instantly became a band staple; we started piecing together the song "Nightrain" a week later while rehearsing before another flyer-posting outing.

Soon we decided to rent a makeshift rehearsal space. Even though we would have to come up with a monthly nut of a few hundred bucks, we would save money versus paying by the hour at other rehearsal spaces. (We rehearsed *a lot* of hours.) We felt we were now on a roll, and scraping the money together at the beginning of each month would allow us a lot more freedom, too: we could leave our gear set up all of the time instead of having to tear it down for the next band the way we had to at the per-hour rehearsal places. Still, given our limited resources, we had to improvise.

Half a block north of Sunset on Gardner was the mouth of a dead-end alleyway that ran east behind what was then the Guitar Center. Halfway down the alley, the slender lane opened into a tarmac lot behind a public elementary school. Along this lot, there were half a dozen doors to self-storage spaces used for various types of commerce. We found one for rent for four hundred dollars a month and knew it was our spot, though we'd have to fudge a little bit about what we planned to do in there. Once we finally jumped through all of the various hoops presented to us by the apprehensive landlord, we got the keys to our new rehearsal studio.

If Orchid Street was ground zero of Guns N' Roses when Axl, Izzy, and I all lived there, the alleyway behind Gardner was where the whole thing came together once we had discovered we were a real band. We set up the garagelike, ten-by-fourteen structure as our gang headquarters—a place to rehearse, party, and, much of the time, to spend the night.

The storage space itself had a door and unadorned cinder-block walls. There was no bathroom, but for four hundred bucks a month, who expected a bathroom? And anyway, there was a latrine in the parking lot. There was also no a/c or heat, but there was electricity and we could make noise twenty-four hours a day.

We raided a nearby construction site for some two-by-fours and plywood that we used to install a ramshackle loft in our tiny new home. The loft added some dimension and much-needed sleeping space to the room. If you were to walk in the door, everything in the room would be to your left. First there was my bass amp, then Izzy's Marshall half stack, then Steven's drums, and then Slash's guitar rig. This is also how we would set up onstage for each and every gig until Izzy left in 1991.

Our gear was all very old and beat-up, with the vinyl covers shredding off the cabinets and all. But in this room our shitty gear sounded magical, clear, and *huge*. We did not have a PA for Axl, so we basically improvised and made do. There is a photo out there somewhere that shows Axl screaming into my ear at the Gardner space. This was the only way that he could get his ideas across in that setting. Among the benefits of playing shows as frequently as possible was that it offered us our only chance to hear what Axl was singing.

It was funny having crappy gear and no PA and constantly looking at the back wall and dumpsters of the Hollywood Guitar Center all day. That place was a veritable toy store to those who could pay for the things in there—or had credit with the powers that be. It was like a sick joke to us. By the time we did finally get our record deal and the advance dough that came with it, I knew exactly what new gear I wanted to buy.

To the right of our space was another one being used by a band called Johnny and the Jaguars. The members had come out together from Denver. The unspoken truth in Hollywood back then was that if a band moved to town from another city as a unit, it never lasted. I suppose all the influences and amusements L.A. offered were just too divisive. You had to wade through a lot of new shit in Hollywood, and your life was going to take some turns. For five guys to experience all those turns at the same time and react in the same way was almost impossible. Sure enough, before long Johnny and the Jaguars broke up. The other thing about bands from out of town? They were usually awful. True to form, Johnny and the Jaguars were not a great band. But they were a nice bunch of guys, and we later tapped their keyboardist, Dizzy Reed, to join our touring band for the *Use Your Illusions* tour.

Just across Sunset, in a nondescript row of one-story buildings, stood a cheap Mexican restaurant that served strong margaritas. The interior was kept so dark you couldn't see a thing when you stepped inside. You had to wait for your eyes to adjust before a dark bar appeared on the left and even darker vinyl banquettes and booths slowly swam into view on the right. No matter how long you let your eyes adjust, sufficient murkiness remained to allow for discreet blow jobs and drug use right at the booths. The Seventh Veil strip club was a few blocks down Sunset from here. The important thing about the Seventh Veil was the girls. That might sound obvious. But to us it was the girls, not the show and the venue. We spent a lot of time with off-work strippers, and a few began to dance onstage at our concerts.

Between us and the other bands, the alley began to attract a lot of drugs, booze, girls, and other musicians. Strippers from the neighborhood constantly came by the space, often bringing quaaludes, Valium, coke, or booze to share. I still avoided blow because of the effect I assumed it would have on my panic attacks, but to pills I didn't always say no. As we started to play more gigs and met more people, word spread about our alleyway and it became a go-to after-hours party spot. This translated into more people hanging around the fringes of our scene. Among them was a guy named Phillipe, who drove a bus for the city as his regular job but sold crack on the side. He was older than we were. Phillipe was not a rocker per se, but he liked the fact that there were hot young girls around. He got them high and tried to take advantage of them—creepy stuff. He was emblematic of a certain element that orbited our band.

As more and more people showed up to party in our alley after the clubs closed on Friday and Saturday nights, we also started to sell beer by the can. We could buy cases of rotgut beer for $5.99—which was only twenty-five cents a can. We sold them for a buck a pop. That translated into major income, at least by our standards. Shit, we could make the rent on our space with income like that.

Not surprisingly, we started to run into trouble with the police— though oddly, it wasn't the LAPD so much as the West Hollywood sheriffs, who would leave their jurisdiction to mess with us. Raids were difficult to escape because we were in a dead-end alley, after all, and there was no place to run. I remember the cops coming there and asking who was who, let's see IDs, blah, blah, blah. In retrospect, it probably wasn't much of a big deal. Izzy was smart about his dealing, and even the sup- posed complaints from girls were probably just ruses that were held over our heads to scare us—a response by the West Hollywood cops to getting an earful from parents of kids who showed up late and wasted after a night in our backyard. Of course at the time it all felt much more serious and sinister, and some of us would hide out for periods of time after the police turned up asking questions.

I had another run-in with the police on my way to work at six o'clock one morning. The brakes went out on the Maverick. I drifted into the intersection of Hollywood and Highland and caused a six-car pileup. The name tag on the cop who pulled up read *O'Malley*; I happened to be wearing a green sweatshirt one of my brothers had sent me—it read IRE-LAND across the chest. The drivers of the other cars—all Mexicans—were irate. Officer O'Malley looked at my sweatshirt, then at the other drivers.

"Ah, your brakes went out, what are you going to do? It's not your fault."

He let me walk.

After I totaled my car, I had to walk everywhere. Hollywood's system of alleyways offered places to seal shady business deals, to hide out, or to pass out—and a lot of places for skeezy motherfuckers to come out of. Of course, now that we had our back-alley headquarters, we felt as though we *were* those motherfuckers. What could be skeezier than living in a storage space behind the Guitar Center? Well, I guess the food chain in Hollywood at the time was more limited than I realized, because I got jumped by four dudes while walking from work to the space one day. They had knives and wallet chains—before wallet chains were a cool accessory.

CHAPTER THIRTEEN

+ + +

In 1985, AIDS was definitely starting to enter the national dialogue, but it didn't yet occupy a prominent place in the heterosexual psyche. I never used a condom, not once. I was lucky. The scene in Hollywood was an orgy of shared needles, and shared girlfriends and boyfriends. Perhaps there has been no other time in recent history when the doors were so wide open. Everyone seemed to be living in and for the moment, and it seemed as if nothing was off-limits. Our Gardner storage space was at the epicenter of all that, the place where the members of Guns N' Roses lived our reckless lives.

Three of my bandmates were using heroin at least occasionally by this point and Izzy was continuing to deal, but everybody put in the work. Even then, though, the singer's personal issues were beginning to affect the band in a way that drug habits were not (at least not yet). Axl had intense emotional swings marked by periods of incredible energy followed by days on end when he would be overtaken by black moods and disappear—and miss rehearsals. Since I had suffered from panic attacks since I was seventeen, I knew all too well how crippling things like that could be. Axl and I talked together about it once in a while, and I told him about my panic attacks. I quickly realized that while each of us in the band had his own things to deal with, Axl's was closest to mine—a sort of chemical imbalance that he had no more control over than I did over my panic attacks. After that, we had an understanding. Which made me much more comfortable with the situation: between growing up in a big family and playing team sports as a kid, I had found it important to come to understandings with the people around me.

Axl's unpredictable mood swings also electrified him—a sense of impending danger hung in the air around him. I loved that trait in him. Artists are always trying to create a spark, but Axl was totally punk rock in my eyes because his fire could not be controlled. One minute the audience might be comfortably watching him light up the stage; the next instant he became a terrifying wildfire threatening to burn down not just the venue but the entire city. He was brazen and unapologetic and his edge helped sharpen the band's identity and separate us from the pack.

We rehearsed at the space twice a day regardless of anything else going on in any of our lives. Many of the songs that made up *Appetite* and *Lies*—as well as more than a few from *Use Your Illusion*—came together in this back-alley lair. When any two or three of us were together, there were always song ideas percolating. Our disparate musical voices somehow managed to mesh. Axl was into Nazareth, Queen, and the Ramones. Slash was the Aerosmith guy. Izzy brought a no-pretense rock vibe—Stones, Faces, New York Dolls, Hanoi Rocks. Steven was a San Fernando Valley metal guy with a soft spot for the soaring harmonies of 1960s vocal music. I brought in more of the funkier, groove stuff and the punk-rock ferocity.

Another key was the way we could be completely open with one another while working on songs. Writing songs is a highly emotional thing. Working on them in a group exposes you to others. Either you hold back or you risk feeling vulnerable. But the closeness in our band fostered intimacy; we weren't afraid to expose our ideas and to have the rest of the band tweak them, kick them around, repurpose them—or not. That comfort level helped us all work together to create great songs. And nobody was holding on to stuff for another day or another band, either. This was the band, this was the moment.

We were also learning how to write lyrics, especially Izzy, Axl, and me. And as we developed songs, we put a lot of emphasis on anything that veered away from the main melody—we all felt that diverging from a good tune was only justifiable if the other part was just as good. That meant we rejected cookie-cutter songwriting that demanded bridges for bridges' sake and strictly delineated between verses and choruses. Instead we only went places we really felt strongly about. There's a reason the codas in songs like "Rocket Queen," "Paradise City," or "Patience" sound so distinctive—we didn't feel compelled to add them; we were just so excited about certain ideas that, working together, day after day, we found ways to incorporate them. (We wrote "Sweet Child o' Mine" later, and the "where do we go now" coda of that song actually was just sort of tacked on, which is one of the reasons we didn't anticipate it being a hit—or even a single, for that matter.)

When we started to write the songs that would become *Appetite*, it was clear that Slash saw this as a chance to finally perfect his sense of melody on leads and his crunch when it came to riffage. Slash wrote and perfected those classic parts from some dark and beautiful place within himself. The shy introvert I'd first met had at last found the true medium to express himself.

I remember "My Michelle" coming together. Slash had a great riff, a typical Slash riff. It was a slinky, spidery thing, but he was playing it really fast at first. (His initial riff shows up, slowed down, in the intro of the recorded version—that brooding, eerie horror movie bit at the beginning.) While working on it together with the whole band—collaboration was the magic ingredient for almost all the songs—we hit on that *bomp, bad-a-dam, bad-a-dam* that kick-starts the song in its final version.

One of our signature songs from that period had an even longer gestation—part of it went back to the very first song I ever wrote. Now in L.A. seven years later, the main riff from that first song came back to me as we were putting together another tune about the hardscrabble lives we lived. As with "My Michelle," one of Slash's amazing chiming staccato riffs became the intro, and the main section of the song hurtled along atop the riff from my Vains song "The Fake," now played on bass. Axl had some lyrical fragments he'd been working on since the Seattle trip, and we created an extended bridge around those—a dreamlike section echoing the words *when you're high* devolved into a churning, nightmarish wash of sound out of which Axl howled, "Do you know where you are?"

We called the result "Welcome to the Jungle."

We played the song live for the first time when we opened a show at the Troubadour on a Thursday night in late June 1985. Also on the bill was a band originally from San Francisco called Jetboy.

"Jungle" went over great, and from then on crowds would get agitated as soon as they heard Slash's intro riff—it became one of our first calling cards. We also hit it off with Jetboy. I had an immediate connection with Jetboy bass player Todd Crew. He was so damn smart that I truly believe he had to drink to slow down the inflow of information to his brain. I also understood without asking that he was self-medicating some deep pain. But Todd was also fucking funny. He was always the life and light in a room. We quickly became best friends.

I hadn't been in L.A. for even a year yet, and I was still very conscious of being away from home, away from my family and from my boyhood friends. It is difficult to describe how much this early friendship with Todd—which almost immediately became a hang-out-all-of-the-time kind of friendship—meant to me. Todd, together with the guys within Guns, formed part of a new foundation for me, like a family. And fuck, we had fun. Todd was a *heavy* drinker, often passing out at the most inopportune times. Clubs, apartments hallways, sidewalks . . . whatever.

It's also difficult to express the level of excitement I felt as I saw the number of people who were into our music explode. Within a few months we went from playing to a handful of people to packing some of the coolest venues in town. When things are working and you're seeing progress, it kicks major fucking ass. Especially since that progress was largely based on new songs we continued to write together.

The next time my brother Matt played with us—a few months after the time he looked out and saw an empty club—people knew the songs and were singing along. I could see the relief in Matt's face.

Not that it was a completely steady upward trajectory. We still played a lot of random gigs. Shit, the night after we unveiled "Jungle" at the Troubadour, we played a UCLA frat house. We got $35 and free beer for that show. It was one of those spontaneous gigs—it was set up the same day we played. The students at the frat party weren't sure what to make of us and hung back a little. Axl's assless chaps may have had something to do with our tepid reception, too. Still, free beer.

Obviously we still had to work other jobs. Steven was the only one of us who was not working. He had been kicked out of his house when he was twelve and learned early how to make his way on the streets. But he was completely unselfish. If he scrounged up the money for a hamburger or a bag of Cheetos, he would share it with me or any of the other guys— no matter how hungry he was.

Slash worked at a newsstand at the corner of Melrose and Fairfax called Centerfold News. Lucky for us, the stand had a phone. Slash routinely left Centerfold's phone number with bookers and club promoters. He would sometimes be on the phone his entire shift trying to get us gigs, calling people on the mailing list to sell tickets, spreading the word about shows. Slash was a natural-born salesman when it came to getting people to buy tickets to our shows. Eventually he got fired from the newsstand because he was on the phone so much.

I was still working for the mobsters of indeterminate East European origin transporting "office supplies." At first, I found the guys who ran the company pretty intimidating. They were right out of central casting: heavy-looking features, unidentifiable accents and a clipped way of talking, tracksuits with pistols in the waists of their pants. The whole situation made me wary. But they were really cool to me, it was steady work, and after I'd been there for half a year I felt like part of the team.

Maybe that's why I tried to get Izzy a job at the same company. He ended up in the one room where they really did sell office supplies over the phone. He came in late his third day, and one of the bosses took me aside.

"Mikey"—even my mom had called me Duff, but these guys used the name on my driver's license, Michael—"Mikey, your friend . . . he no good. Your friend—he on drugs."

Another guy who worked there with me was a white guy named

Black Randy, who was in the L.A. punk band Black Randy and the Metro Squad. He was insane—shot speedballs all day at work. But somehow the bosses liked him enough to keep him around.

Black Randy loved our band. He always told us, "I'm going to manage your band and you'll have the swagger of the New York Dolls and you're going to shit on this town."

He took the bus down to our rehearsal space and brought children's Halloween costumes he wanted us to wear. He videotaped us, and video-taped himself shooting speedballs. I guess it goes without saying that he became our first manager. Obviously.

But Black Randy also had AIDS, and he died soon afterward.

After that, I called my brother Bruce, who was booking bands and DJs for a restaurant chain.

"Dude, do you know any managers?" I asked him.

"Yeah, I can call a buddy of mine," he said.

He called me back. The guy wasn't interested.

I had broken up with Kat and moved out of the El Cerrito apartment by then. Some nights I crashed at a girl's place near our rehearsal space; some nights I spent at the space itself. The same was true for the other guys. We bounced around, hooked up with stripper friends—those girls always had apartments and money—or crashed in the alley off Gard-ner, where, as Izzy told a local paper a few months later, we lived "like rats in a box." Each member of the band now existed solely to write and play, and almost all other concerns had melted away. In my case, this was one of the few periods of my life when I didn't have a fixed address. It was an amazing rite of passage. The camaraderie within Guns N' Roses deepened to a level so unquestioning and intense that it could only be compared to blood relationships; it was primordial. And as when the first creatures began to slither out of the primordial ooze, it could get messy.

The clap was absolutely rampant back then, and venereal diseases swept through the band members' crotches while we were all living and fucking in such close proximity. Fortunately, since my last experience I'd gotten a tip from one of my brothers-in-law, who was a doctor. You could get dirt-cheap antibiotics—intended for use in aquariums—at pet stores. Turned out tetracycline wasn't just good for tail rot and gill disease. It also did great with syphilis—and with no doctor visit, no expensive prescription, and no need to feign shame for the nuns at a free clinic, like I had to that time in Seattle.* Who needed health insurance when there were pet stores?

---

* Note: The American Medical Association would not approve.

CHAPTER FOURTEEN

✚ ✚ ✚

We continued to expand our song list and started looking for headline gigs. By October 1985, we added "Paradise City" and "Rocket Queen" to our set list and headlined a show out in Reseda at a place called the Country Club. In November we headlined a show at the Troubadour with a national touring band we had always liked—Kix, from Maryland—opening for us. By the end of the year we had added "My Michelle" and "Nightrain" to our regular live repertoire.

An independent record label named Restless called us near the end of the year and asked us to come down to their office in Long Beach. There were some cool bands on Restless, and the label people were into our band. They were ahead of the curve—no other labels had contacted us at that point. Izzy bought a book about the music industry in preparation for the meeting. I remember looking through it. I could understand the sections I read, but there was a lot of shit to master. When we went to their office, they offered us something called a pressing and distribution deal, plus something like $30,000 toward recording costs. It was a simple two-page deal, and they explained the whole thing to us. Still, we thought, if they're going to offer that, someone else will, too.

We left their office without signing. But we were nervous—had we just fucked ourselves? I thought of Sly Stone. I knew you could blow it.

Kim Fowley, the fabled manager, bullshit artist, and generally shady figure behind the success—or lack thereof, depending on how you want to look at it—of the Runaways, came knocking at the end of 1985, too. By the time I moved to Hollywood, the Runaways had come and gone, and Joan Jett, the Runaways' guitarist and main songwriter, was a successful solo artist. But Kim Fowley was still trolling the gutters for the next rising stars. Once GN'R was up and running and writing songs and we were attracting a regular and growing audience, Kim set his sights on us. He wanted to manage our band.

One thing that we knew about ourselves by that point was that Guns was the best and most committed band that any of us had ever been in, and we had become very protective of it. Kim had a storied but checkered past; I had opened for Joan Jett when I was with the Fastbacks shortly before she became a household name with "I Love Rock 'n' Roll" and I knew the stories. We were dubious.

When Kim sensed that we were not going to let him manage us, he came at us from a different angle. He invited us to breakfast at Denny's on Sunset. Slash, Axl, and I went. Kim said that he wanted to buy the publishing rights to our song "Welcome to the Jungle." He had a contract with him and a traveler's check for $10,000. To us, this was big money. But if Kim Fowley was offering this money to us now—if this one song was worth so much money to him—wouldn't that mean we had something valuable? Shouldn't we play this out a bit? I think in a weird way, we owed it to Kim that we eventually ended up keeping the publishing rights to our songs when we later signed our record deal. If Kim Fowley thought our music rights were worth something, then by God, they probably were. He could spot this stuff, and we knew it.

Kim intensified his efforts, coming to see us again a few weeks later to offer $50,000. But it didn't matter. By that time we knew to hold on to anything that was ours. It was all we had and all we believed in.

Like Joan Jett and the Runaways, we were chasing a dream and the world was exciting and wild and fast. We avoided getting involved with people like Kim Fowley not because he wasn't fascinating and smart, but because by 1985 we had heard lots of stories about bands that had been ripped off. Between what happened to the Runaways—they never really got the shot they deserved and lost control of their name and songs—and the financial straits the members of Aerosmith faced in the early 1980s despite their enormous success in the 1970s, we were familiar with the full spectrum of rock-and-roll pitfalls.

We could see the sharks beginning to circle us, and we were wary.

On January 18, 1986, before our show at the Roxy, a friend ducked his head into the backstage area.

"This fucking gig is sold out!"

When we looked out at the crowd, we still saw the same faces. We knew most of the people in the audience, even after we started selling out venues like this. Del, West Arkeen, Marc Canter, and assorted girlfriends assembled backstage as usual. The big difference? One of my nephews stood in front of the backstage area as "security."

There were no high fives. And yet I was proud of how far we had come. I had played some big gigs with Ten Minute Warning, and GN'R's shows in early 1986 had that feeling. Except this was L.A., one of the biggest cities in the world. Still, the members of Guns never looked at one another and said, "Fuck yeah, we rocked it!" We celebrated that kind of stuff onstage—we would be better onstage than in rehearsal. We recognized that there were transcendent moments, but we didn't need to talk about them. You have this silent relationship as players in a band; it takes all these parts and you have moments—whether it's between a guitar player and singer, a bassist and drummer, or everyone together. And when you saw that look in the audience—people just blown away—that feedback from the crowd was enough. Especially since we were playing to a lot of the same people, we could see the looks on their faces and feel the electricity when we hit a new high.

Around this time a friend of Izzy's named Robert John became our "official" band photographer. Robert had shot pictures of another L.A. band, W.A.S.P. His girlfriend, a dominatrix at some club in Hollywood, was the bondage girl in W.A.S.P's horror-movie-style stage show. Nice girl. I liked her. Robert had come to one of our shows to hang out with Izzy and took a few shots of the band. They looked great, so we started having him shoot more and more for us.

He also believed in the band from day one.

"You guys are going to be huge," he always said.

"Yeah, yeah, just take the pictures."

We gave him a lot of shit when we did photo shoots.

Not only did we begin to sell out everywhere we played in early 1986, but the club owners suddenly *loved* us. The crowd we brought included punkers, rockers, and, best of all, lots of women. And they all drank. A lot. We broke the liquor-sales records at the Troubadour. Once you start doing that kind of business, people notice. And also, once you start head-lining, you don't have to sell tickets on your own anymore. There was no more paying to play.

A&R staff from major labels started to pop up at gigs, too. On Friday, February 28, we had the coveted headline slot at the Troubadour again, and at least a dozen record execs were rumored to be in the audience. Creepy manager types were oozing around, trying to get backstage to charm us. Having my nephew there came in handy that night.

Los Angeles was also a beacon for national and international tour-ing acts, and now that we could fill clubs, we started to get offers to open shows for big artists. When my boyhood rock idol Johnny Thunders came to town in late March 1986, the promoters asked us to open both his shows. For me, this was a huge deal. Probably for Izzy, too. I had seen Johnny play a bunch of shows on the West Coast in the early 1980s, and had even gotten a chance to jam with him after a show in Portland. Of course, by 1986, I didn't hold Thunders in quite as high regard as I once had—the romantic notion of a junked-up vagabond like Johnny had faded a bit for me with direct experience of heroin. I could even admit in hindsight that the chance to jam with him probably happened only because he had shot up a post-show speedball and was looking for any-thing to do, even if that meant jamming with some teenage straggler. But still. Sharing a bill with fucking Johnny Thunders! I was really looking forward to that first show at Fender's Ballroom.

Unfortunately, one of the first things that happened when we got down to Fender's for the show was that Johnny started to chat up Axl's girlfriend Erin while we were onstage doing our sound check. Johnny also wanted to know where he could score some dope. Axl flipped out when he got wind that Johnny had hit on Erin, and began a tirade backstage. Axl could be intimidating when he started yelling and carrying on. Johnny spent the rest of the night hiding in his dressing room, jonesing for a fix. Whatever remnants of a romantic and swashbuckling image I had of Johnny Thunders disappeared that night.

During the weeks between that Troubadour show and the Thunders gig, the record-label frenzy to sign us peaked. We were having fun doing what we were doing, playing live all the time, courted by all the clubs, near hysteria at our shows, blowing the doors off places. We were in no rush to shift gears for the sake of a record deal. We knew we were good. And we had songs we liked. I was convinced we were too hard and too dirty ever to be huge. Yet everybody was in the hunt, or at least pretending to be, as industry people started falling over one another to talk to us.

Robert John had been haranguing us to approve some photos he had taken so that he could start to submit them to magazines as coverage began to spike. Slash and I finally agreed. One afternoon the two of us went with Robert to some girl's apartment right on Hollywood Boulevard to look at his proofs. Robert explained we'd have to look at the contact sheets through a little magnifying glass shaped like a shot glass called a loupe.

When we arrived at the girl's apartment, we were relieved that she had air-conditioning, as it was in the high nineties that day and we had walked there from the Gardner alley. Phillipe, the bus-driving drug dealer we knew from Gardner, came out of the back bedroom as we arrived. It was obvious that both he and the girl whose apartment this was were flying on crack. No big deal, we were used to this shit.

Slash and I were not exactly looking forward to going through this stack of proofs for Robert. It wasn't a very rock-and-roll thing to do, but we grudgingly acknowledged that it was part of the deal for a working band. Now we saw there were hundreds of individual shots that we had to approve or deny. Right at that moment Phillipe offered me some crack.

Crack cocaine was one of those drugs I had always passed on when it was around. Between Seattle and then Hollywood, I saw a lot of people get addicted to the stuff and crack addiction wasn't a pretty sight. But on this day, I decided to try it. I'm not sure why. I had been drinking; maybe

I needed something to get me over the edge so I could look at this heap of photos. My first experiences with most drugs were the result of something as dumb as that. In the sixth grade I dropped acid for the first time because an older kid, one I looked up to, offered it to me on the way home from school. I didn't want to embarrass myself, so I did it.

The crackling sound from the torched rock in its receptacle and the sight of the glass tube filling up with smoke that smelled both sweet and acidic was mesmerizing. I inhaled. The high I experienced from that first hit of crack was one of the most euphoric sixty seconds I had ever felt. My senses sharpened and I felt stronger than fucking Atlas. I found myself horny. I was filled with a powerful feeling that I could accomplish anything.

The resultant crash was just as extreme. It seized my whole body in an acute and all-encompassing craving.

"Hey, Phillipe! Set me up again, okay?"

He gave me a sizable rock and I dove headfirst into another hit. *Ahhhhh,* I thought, *this shit is good!*

Crack accentuated everything in a good way. The features of the girl's drab, cookie-cutter apartment suddenly became beautiful. The Formica-topped island that separated the kitchen from the living room suddenly took on architectural perfection, a use of space so logical and brilliant its beauty blew me away. What had at first glance looked like an ugly orange shag carpet was now as magnificent as a priceless Persian masterpiece in the window of an expensive Beverly Hills rug shop. The traffic I could hear outside on Hollywood Boulevard transformed from a noisy nuisance to a source of enchantment: I wondered where these people might be headed. Maybe some of them were on crack, too, and as happy and elated as I was!

I started to come down again but had another rock at the ready. No worries.

Slash was doing the same thing as me, and now we fought over the loupe to start the process of approving individual shots among the reams of photo sheets. We raced through the images, somehow doing it in tandem so that neither of us would have to wait around with nothing to do.

God forbid. But alas, our rocks started to dwindle and finally disappear. Phillipe now wanted money if we chose to continue. Oh fuck, I didn't have any money!

I bolted from the apartment. The impossibly hot sun singed my whole being as a ridiculous crash almost doubled me over with despair. All my muscles seemed to contract at once. I felt dark and used and stupid. The ten-block walk back to our Gardner storage space was one of the hardest physical challenges I had ever endured. Sluggish. Jonesing. Lonely. Depressed. Ugh.

For some reason, I stopped at a pay phone and did something really stupid—I called my mom. I tried to act cool and just see how she was doing, see what was going on with the family in Seattle. The truth was I wanted to hear the voice that always made me feel better as a small boy when I was sick with the flu or when jocks beat me up for being a "punk-rock faggot." I knew she could tell something was wrong with me. The stench from the ghetto phone booth was making me dry-heave and it was impossible to see out of it because of graffiti that blackened the glass. Claustrophobia washed over me. I couldn't breathe. I tried to keep my cool on the phone.

"No, Mom, I'm okay, just a little tired," I said. "I might be coming down with something." Yeah, I was coming down from fucking crack.

After I hung up the phone, I trudged the last few blocks to the rehearsal place. Normally I would be happy to see any of my bandmates or the few friends we had. This time I was hoping to find something—anything—that could help me take the edge off of the plummeting feeling I was going through. Pills, Night Train, maybe even some coke. Or all of those things together.

When I rounded the corner into our alleyway, the sun hit me dead straight in my eyes. I let out an audible groan of shock and pain. The door to our space was open a little bit and luckily Joe-Joe and Del were there with some Night Train. After gulping down an entire bottle by myself, I told those guys what I had been up to.

"Shit, dude," said Joe-Joe when I had finished. "I have a little bit of money on me. I'll go get some more booze."

He took off down to the corner liquor store. That was the thing about our inner circle. We would do anything we could for one another. We did not judge one another. We just had one another's backs.

I settled down a little bit after that first bottle. Being in our little rehearsal space helped, too—it was a safe haven. The dingy floor with the old brown carpet was filthy, but it was *our* filth. The amps that lined the wall were worn, but they were the only sure bet we had to be heard musically. These amps were *our* sound. The loft was only six feet high, so anything up there—whether it was a guitar case or a naked girl—was easily accessible. This was *our* refuge. And our friends were there for me.

Joe-Joe came back with a big paper grocery bag of alcoholic fortifications and my crack-cocaine crash faded into the past, just another experience to tally up. I would end up doing crack many more times, but I was never as ill-prepared as I was the first time with Phillipe.

CHAPTER FIFTEEN

+ + +

Just as the record label frenzy around us was heating up, some fallout from our Gardner space partying hit us. The cops busted down our door one night looking for Axl. They wanted him to answer what turned out to be a bogus rape charge. Our days became numbered there at Gardner. Axl didn't do the crime (or time), but the incident inspired a great song, "Out to Get Me," which we quickly added to our sets in early 1986. You can hear the depth of our collective anguish in that song, shitting ourselves that the record labels might get wind of the situation and break off their courtship: "You can't catch me, I'm fuckin' innocent!"

Axl avoided the storage space for weeks—eluding capture until the charges were dropped—and the news didn't get out that our singer was looking at jail time. Everybody took us out for meals—different management companies, all the labels. The swank restaurants where people had business lunches weren't just a side of L.A. I hadn't seen; they were a side of life I hadn't ever experienced—well, except in the bowels of the establishments where I worked as a dishwasher and later a baker.

I called Kim from the Fastbacks after a few of these outings, trying to adjust to the idea of being pursued for a record contract.

"It's weird," I told her. "These guys, men in business suits, take us out for lunch. You can order anything you want."

They didn't take us to Spago. We weren't worth that much, and we were also pretty filthy. I remember going to meet David Geffen at his office. As we were hanging out in the lobby, employees coming and going didn't realize we were a band—they thought we were street people.

After a while we asked to go to the same place as often as possible, a place up on Sunset at the edge of Beverly Hills called Hamburger Hamlet. I never had a hamburger there, but they had a full bar.

Despite all these meetings, I was nervous when it came time to finalize a deal. I deemed myself more experienced than the other guys, having been through this once before, albeit with a tiny indie label. But I was out of my league. I didn't fully understand the business. In fact, I didn't really understand it at all. I wasn't even going to pretend that I could handle a deal like this.

We still didn't have a proper manager. Fortunately we hired a lawyer. He explained things to us. Preparing to enter into a contract brought changes in our intra-band relationships: we had to create a legal framework for what had been just a one-for-all-and-all-for-one gang. I didn't even know we needed a partnership agreement. Why would we? Hey, we're bros. But our lawyer got us protected within the band, and I will always be thankful for that. He did a great job lassoing in a bunch of guys and making sure we understood the implications of various aspects of the contracts among the band members and between the band and the label.

Splitting future publishing royalties caused a real clash. In the old days, with Rodgers and Hammerstein and other writing teams of the American songbook tradition, one person did music and one did lyrics. But songwriting didn't work that way for most bands by the 1980s—and certainly not for our band. Guns wasn't one of those bands where one person wrote all the songs. Or even a band where two people collaborated on the songs, like the Stones. We had done everything together—and in so many different ways. We found ourselves arguing about things we'd never had to deal with before: No, *I* wrote that part; no, *I* wrote that part. Everyone had his own version of how things had gone down. It got heated for about a week as we tried to hash it all out. Since it was so difficult to say who had done what with our songs, we finally agreed to split everything equally across the board. Our lawyer enshrined it in writing—and thank God for that.

After all the liquid lunches, Chrysalis offered the biggest advance, something like $400,000. We weren't going to go with Chrysalis—like most of the record companies, they wanted to soften us up, both musically and imagewise. Geffen's offer was much smaller, $250,000. But Tom Zutaut, the A&R guy pursuing us on Geffen's behalf, was saying all the right things about how we should be produced. He got it.

Tom said we would have absolute artistic freedom at Geffen, and that was the clincher for us—but only after it was in writing. Our lawyer took care of that, too. Our songs were by far the most important thing to us—worth far more than the extra money offered by labels not willing to give us free rein. No one was going to tell us how to make our record.

Every step of the way I was thinking, *Nobody can ever take this away from us—we will have been signed by a major label.* Getting a major-label deal was considered massive, life changing.

There was no big fanfare when we finally signed a six-record deal on March 26, 1986. We never even looked at one another and said anything like, "Holy fuck!" We took $75,000 of the advance up front, divided it by five ($15,000 for each of us), and took half of each of our shares ($7,500) immediately. We had our new accountants sock the other half away to pay for personal expenses as we recorded our debut album. The balance of the advance, $175,000, would be administered by the accountants to cover legitimate band costs and the making of the album.

While the ink was still wet on the contract with Geffen, we rented a cheap rehearsal space out in Glendale, near the Burbank line. We had to get out of Gardner for various reasons, but we were careful not to go to SIR in Hollywood or some similarly expensive place. Our new space was in an old run-down shopping center—now long gone—called the Golden Mall. There was a stage. We had to move our gear out every day. It wasn't ours twenty-four hours a day with a lock or anything—we didn't have that kind of money. Our room at the Golden Mall is where the checks were delivered to us. Slash and I took our checks to a bank out in Glendale. We didn't open accounts; we went in and asked to cash the checks. That raised alarms, I guess. They had to call a bunch of people, including the accountants at Geffen. It didn't help that Slash's check was made out to "Stash."

Axl didn't get a bank account, either. Like Slash, he had yet to change his name officially and refused to take out an account in any name other than Axl. So all of us ended up keeping our money in our boots or stashed under our mattresses. Not that the money lasted long. I had gone into Guitar Center by our Gardner space so many times to scope out the perfect setup for myself that I'm sure the sales guys there were totally shocked when I suddenly walked in one day and bought all of the stuff I had just looked at so many times before—with cash! I'm sure they had long since put me in the never-going-to-buy-a-damn-thing category. I bought the Fender Jazz Special and Gallien-Krueger 800RB that have helped mold my bass sound to this day. I also got my first tattoos: two guns and a rose on my left shoulder, a dagger that says GUNS N' ROSES, and a dragon—all three of them within a few weeks. I bought some cowboy boots and a couple pairs of pants. We all bought new clothes, which had been a rare luxury up to then.

I also bought a steel chain and a chunky little padlock and started to wear that around my neck. It was just like the one worn by Sid Vicious, the bass player in the Sex Pistols. I was determined to carry that torch—the punk-rock torch—regardless of where this major-label deal took us. Call it punk-rock guilt.

At the time we received our advance, I was crashing on and off with a girl in Hollywood. We all had a few girls with whom we could stay if we needed a break from the loft at the rehearsal space on Gardner—some were friends with benefits, some were just friends. Now, however, I put myself on a small stipend that could pay my rent—or half-rent, I should say—for about six months. Another friend of mine was looking to move to Hollywood from her parents' house somewhere down in Orange County. She and I decided we could share a one-bedroom apartment we found on Crescent Heights just below Sunset. She would get the bedroom, and I would get the floor of the dining room, which I cordoned off with a sheet to create my little den of darkness. The finishing touch on my lush new lifestyle was to fill the refrigerator. I could afford to eat. This was major-label success!

Suddenly I didn't need to keep my job anymore, either. I had $7,500 in an envelope in my boot. We were going to be entering a recording studio to make an album. We were going to tour. As at every job, the guys at this place knew I was a musician, and knew that was my thing. They had even come to a few shows—tracksuits and all—to see what it was all about. The problem was, I knew a lot of things about a business that wasn't exactly run by the books. How do you quit a job like that? Was there a debriefing process for leaving a mob job? This eventuality had never crossed my mind in the year I worked there.

I went into the office of one of the bosses after we signed.

"We just signed our deal this morning and I don't have to work anymore."

His expression didn't change for a second. He just sat there, looking blankly at me. I began to sweat. Was I going to have to give him a cut of the money in my boot?

Then his face slowly lightened, he took an unhurried breath, and he said, "You do good, Mikey, you do good."

He wanted to know that the label wasn't ripping us off. I let out a silent sigh of relief.

We played a celebratory gig at the Roxy, or rather two—an early show and a late show—on March 28, 1986. To be honest, the shows had been booked prior to our signing with Geffen. They were supposed to be label showcases. Events overtook our plan, however, so we took out full-page ads in the local music papers to announce the gigs: *Geffen recording artists Guns N' Roses, live at the Roxy.* Everyone in Hollywood already knew, of course—we were throwing money around, buying rounds of drinks for friends.

We all had fresh tattoos at the Roxy shows, and people wanted to touch them. We felt like we ran the city that night. My old bosses even came. They stood out like sore thumbs in a room packed with Hollywood street trash like us, helping us celebrate our collective takeover. They sent a bottle of champagne to us backstage. I was touched by the gesture, and we thanked them during our first set.

The icing on the cake came a week later, when Guns rechristened the Whisky a Go Go on April 5; the legendary Sunset Strip venue was being converted back into a club after serving as a bank for a few years. The poster asked, WHEN WAS THE LAST TIME YOU SAW A REAL ROCK N' ROLL BAND AT THE WHISKY A GO GO? And, since it was assumed we'd be making a record soon and then be off to tour the world—or, as eventually was the case, one-horse towns in the Canadian rust belt—below that was written: THIS COULD BE YOUR LAST CHANCE.

Reopening the Whisky was sweet. It meant that somehow, despite the fact that nobody gave us the time of day on the Strip during the year it took us to find an audience for our idiosyncratic sound and style, we now embodied L.A. rock and roll to the extent that this legendary venue wanted to associate itself with us to restake its claim on the city's musical landscape.

We had moved the dial at the club level. Now, could we do the same on record, on radio, on MTV? Fat chance.

CHAPTER SIXTEEN

✦ ✦ ✦

With a legal framework overlaying our brotherhood, a sudden expansion of free time, and wallets (or rather, boots) flush with cash, it was clear things were changing. One change I didn't see coming: heroin use in the band started to expand. Certain guys you just don't peg as the type to fall for the romantic image of the rock-and-roll junkie. Slash and I were really big drinkers—alcohol addicts, if you will. Of course, if you are easily addicted to one thing, then chances are pretty good you'll be easily addicted to others. Bingo. Though he'd dabbled a bit in the past, after we signed our deal and were all relatively flush with dough, Slash got himself strung out. And then so did Steven Adler. He was smoking crack, too. I think Stevie was willing to try anything that might dull the memories of his nightmarish childhood. Poor fucker.

I knew I was an alcoholic and assumed I would address that problem at some unspecified point in the future. These were only shadowy thoughts, though, and I really had no plan as to how I would one day tackle it. Still, I was the most responsible guy in the band during this period. I drank every day, but I still drank mostly beer. I had also found this killer belt—a boxing championship belt decorated with Budweiser bottle caps. Like I was the heavyweight champion of fucking beer. Since it was Bud, Axl started introducing me at shows as Duff "King of Beers" McKagan.

Axl continued to drop out of sight for days on end as a result of his erratic moods. Sometimes it was as if he was on speed, bouncing off the walls; then he would sleep for three days. When he was around, he was a bundle of energy: we're going to do this and that, and, oh, yeah, let's write some lyrics. And we were like, yeah, we're going to do those things but we can't do them all at the same time, Axl. I was always aware of what a fundamentally different type of person he was from me—*what a spectacle,* I thought, *what a figure*—but we continued to get along great, and I loved his sense of conviction about the band.

As 1986 wore on, Slash, Steven, and Izzy were in a constant cycle of cleaning up and going back out on the dope. It was hard to watch sometimes, but we were young and they held it together for the most part for the sake of the band—nothing was more important to any of us.

Getting signed didn't earn us entry into some special fraternity of Hollywood elite or anything like that, though we did meet Nikki Sixx one night. Tom Zutaut, the guy who signed us to Geffen, had signed Mötley Crüe while at his previous job at Elektra. We went to Nikki's house and drank. At first we were like, *Whoa, it must be amazing to make enough money from music to have a house!* Then we got really fucked up.

For us to start making *any* money, much less enough to buy a house, we needed to make an album. To make an album, we needed a producer. We wanted somebody who would capture us in the studio in a way that was true to our live ferocity. We made a mixtape for Tom to try to express how we wanted the recordings to sound: Motörhead, the Saints, Fear, Bon Scott–era AC/DC, Led Zeppelin, the Sex Pistols. Copies of the tape ended up circulating through Geffen's offices, but our search for the right person to produce us went nowhere.

Part of the problem was that people didn't really know where to put us—we didn't fit comfortably into the sort of categories industry people dealt in. The knee jerk inclination was to shoehorn us in with Whitesnake, W.A.S.P., Autograph, Poison: heshers and poodles. We didn't like the sound of those kinds of records. Most bands being signed at the time—Warrant, White Lion, BulletBoys, all that shit—fit the bill. We were different. Poison wasn't playing alongside punk bands, that's for sure. And we didn't hang out with the types of people who formed bands like BulletBoys. (Like us, Jane's Addiction didn't fit in, but *Nothing's*

Shocking wouldn't be released until almost two years later.) The guy who signed us really believed in us and tried to help us find the right producer, but we kept running up against the same attitude. Everyone wanted to take the edge off our music or to transform it into something they already understood.

The first candidate came in and said Steven needed more rack toms and china cymbals. We had worked so hard to get Steven down to a small drum kit and get that groove going. Next up was Paul Stanley of KISS, who wanted to produce our record, too. He came out to see us play at Raji's, which was a grubby little place where a lot of underground bands played. We were surprised he showed up at such a dive, and we agreed to meet with him as a result. When he arrived at our rehearsal space to talk about his vision, he said he wanted to add double kick drums. Steven loved KISS, absolutely *loved* them, and for a member of KISS to suggest he revert to his teenage drum setup was something beyond his wildest dreams. "Yeah, yeah, great idea!" Izzy and I looked at each other, though, and we both had the same thought: *This isn't going to work.* We didn't tell Paul to his face that we didn't want him to produce us, but it was over from the word *go* (or rather, the word *double*).

For a time we thought we could get Mutt Lange, the producer behind AC/DC's *Back in Black*. But Mutt wanted $400,000 to walk into the room, plus a cut of the future earnings of the record. We had to pay for the studio and the producer out of our $250,000 advance, and we had already taken out $75,000. We weren't going to borrow money to pay for a producer.

With these pressures mounting and the band still recovering from the feuds over various aspects of the signing process, Geffen asked us to stop playing live. By then we were doing gigs nearly every week, and sometimes more often than that. Those regular appearances were a chance to—depending on your mental state—channel everything into your performance or block everything out. Just as important, the transcendent experience of playing our songs for an audience was a way to regularly refresh the brotherly bonds of rock and roll that held us together. Now, just when we needed that most, Geffen pulled the rug out from under us.

The rationale? We had to build *mystique* by dropping out of sight, putting a premium on our performances.

To say we didn't see eye to eye with this decision is an understatement. We acquiesced at first, though we had some gigs already booked that we honored. Soon, though, we had to figure out ways to play—we just functioned best when we could get onstage regularly. And we got bored. So we began to play a bunch of shows as the Fargin Bastydges to get around the label's injunction. We took the name from a scene in the movie *Johnny Dangerously*. It was an alias, not an alter ego: the set list and everything else was exactly the same as our normal Guns shows; it just allowed us to avoid fighting with Geffen. One of the shows we played was at Gazzarri's, a venerable Hollywood dive we had always sort of wanted to play—just to say we had—but not the sort of place a band signed to a major label was supposed to play. But that was us. The industry had one set of priorities. We had our own.

We picked up another Fender's gig at the end of July, playing—as Guns N' Roses, that is—with Lords of the New Church, a punk supergroup featuring Stiv Bators of the Dead Boys and Brian James of the Damned. In hindsight, we might have seen the seeds of later trouble being sown at this show: Axl turned up so late we had to start without him.

We played at the Whisky again on August 23, a month after a "Farewell to Hollywood" show at the Troubadour. Still, it's hard to imagine the label people were too upset, because we debuted two new songs in concert that night, "Sweet Child o' Mine" and "Mr. Brownstone."

We continued to take high-profile opening slots for national tours—I suppose Geffen saw those gigs as different from shows in a club milieu, as we were getting in front of new audiences. We played with Cheap Trick, Ted Nugent, and Alice Cooper. The night of the Alice Cooper gig, Axl showed up late again and then was unable to get into the venue. Izzy and I sang. At the time it was almost funny—though we were definitely pissed, too, and we absolutely trashed the dressing room. We traded some words with Axl when we found him in the parking lot afterward, but at the end of the day the situation lacked much in the way of consequences. We did the show, we got paid, and the crowd was there to see Alice anyway. That was that. For now.

Probably the most memorable show of this sort took place on Halloween, 1986. The Red Hot Chili Peppers, who were just starting their rise as a national act, and the Dickies were headlining a show at Ackerman Hall at UCLA, and we opened. We still had yet to enter the studio. We were feuding with Geffen about whether we had enough songs to warrant recording, and we still hadn't found a producer we liked. We reached a compromise with the label to put out a limited edition "bootleg" EP, *Live! Like a Suicide,* and we had finished it just before this show. That night we felt like we were finally making some forward motion.

The Dickies were still a big draw then and, aside from Social Distortion, pretty much the last band standing from the original wave of L.A. punk rock. For me, the cool thing about this show was that Black Flag's Henry Rollins watched our entire set from the wings of the stage and came up to us afterward and told us how much he liked our band. I considered him the most credible guy in rock, and he had a reputation as a guy who didn't mince words. He definitely wouldn't fawn over a band just for the sake of doing so. And we got the thumbs-up. *Kick ass!*

It turned out he had seen us once before. The year before, someone in Black Flag's crew had dragged him to some Hollywood club to see a couple glam bands. Apparently we had opened the show. Rollins described the night in his journal, published years later as *Art to Choke Hearts:* "The opening band was called Guns and Roses and they blew the headliners off so hard it was pathetic."

And then we met Mike Clink. He had produced a couple of Triumph records. I hated Triumph. But Clink loved GN'R and had seen us live a few times. He said he would come down and record us for nothing and convince us with his recording. When we got together, he said a cool thing about how the microphone picks up the sound and it goes through a cord and onto a tape—it was his way of saying he didn't want to change us, couched in producer-philosophy speak. He did a playback and said, "This is how I think your record should sound." And it was basically us live. And I immediately thought, *That's exactly right.*

CHAPTER SEVENTEEN

+ + +

With my favorite punk bands, the bass was the loudest thing and led the way. And now as Mike Clink started to produce the songs that would make up *Appetite,* the bass was the loudest, roundest thing on the recordings. It had a lot of space. And it wasn't on the outside or underneath the way it was on a lot of records back then—Clink had it right in the middle.

We were pretty disciplined about the sessions, but outside the recording studio it was business as usual in our world—partying, fighting, getting into scraps with the police. Half the band slept at the studio sporadically because they still didn't have beds anywhere else, though I was actually moving in the opposite direction on the personal front. After a period without an exclusive relationship, I started to see a girl named Mandy. She was in a band called the Lame Flames. By spring 1987, as Guns was finishing the record, Mandy and I moved in together. Our apartment became an oasis of stability not just for me and Mandy, but for people around me—like Todd Crew. His band, Jetboy, had just signed a major-label deal. Whenever people needed to find Todd—his band, their management, his family—they called my number. Now that I had an actual phone instead of having to use a pay phone, I was also able to call home a lot more. I talked to my mom frequently, excited to tell her about Mandy and the foundation I seemed to be building with her. *For the first time since Stacy, I feel as if I am in a relationship with long-term potential, Mom.* I talked to Big Jim a lot more, too. He had continued to write me, always managing to track down my latest address as I lived like a nomad during those two years since the trip up to Seattle for GN'R's ill-fated shake-out tour. Jim confided in me during some of those long conversations that he was thinking of moving down to L.A. I was psyched at the prospect of having another solid friend around.

Once the *Appetite* sessions were over, we needed another outlet as we waited for all the peripheral stuff to get done—the record wouldn't be released until July. Axl, Izzy, and Slash went to New York to sit in on the mixing process. I started playing rhythm guitar in a side band called Drunk Fux, just screwing around with various friends.

One afternoon Todd was sitting in my apartment when my phone rang. Jetboy's manager was on the line. I handed the phone to Todd. The conversation didn't last long. Todd looked devastated as he hung up.

"What's wrong?" I asked.

"They just kicked me out."

"What the fuck are you talking about?"

"I'm no longer the bass player in Jetboy. They fired me."

"What? That's all he said?"

"He said they decided I drink too much and hang out with the Guns N' Roses guys too much."

Todd was absolutely crestfallen. The payoff for several years of hard work had suddenly been jerked away from him at the last minute.

At the time I was royally pissed off at Jetboy. In essence, they fired Todd for being too fucked up. It ruined the camaraderie we had with that band. Unfortunately we would face a similarly heartbreaking situation within our own band in a few short years.

For the short term, Todd joined Drunk Fux, which now consisted of him on bass, me on rhythm guitar, Steven Adler on drums, Del singing, and West Arkeen on lead guitar.

Then I realized I hadn't heard from Jim in quite a few days. I couldn't seem to reach him, so I started calling a few other Seattle people to see what the story was. But then my phone rang. It was Jim's girlfriend. She was crying. Jim had died of a heroin overdose. At first I didn't understand. He wrote me letters. He sent me pictures. He was coming down to L.A. Now he was dead. Oh, god. My heart sank. It felt as if something inside me had been ripped out.

Why didn't you move to L.A. before this happened, Jim?

I flew home for Jim's funeral in Seattle. All my old feelings about heroin came flooding back: Joe Toutonghi, who had urged me to get out of town three years prior, spoke at Jim's funeral—and as he eulogized yet another overdose victim, Joe himself was clearly nodding out. Seeing my old friend and roommate Eddy again at the funeral, I was really scared he might be next. It was clear he was what people called a "to die" junkie. The kind who just couldn't stop no matter what—only death would break the habit of a "to die" junkie.

But there was no time to hunker down and reflect on the macabre events. Guns N' Roses was on our way to London. The gig came about because of our *Live! Like a Suicide* EP, released six months before, in December 1986. The EP was a fast and furious collection of songs, two originals and two covers. At the time we were relieved to have something—anything—out on vinyl. (By the way, the crowd noise on that EP is from recordings of a 1970s rock festival called the Texxas Jam—we thought it would be funny to put a *huge* stadium crowd in the background at a time when we were lucky to be playing to a few hundred.) But the EP didn't make a stir anywhere in the world. Except, we soon found out, in Britain. Unbeknownst to us, a cult following was building over there and was champing at the bit for any news about the band. When *Kerrang!* magazine sent a photographer over to Los Angeles to shoot us for a cover article in early 1987, we had been completely baffled. *Kerrang!* was the biggest rock magazine in the UK. We had received some local press coverage in L.A. at this point, but *Kerrang!*? We were half convinced somebody was playing a prank on us, but the photographer showed up and the article ran. Then a London concert promoter had contacted us and asked us to play the famous Marquee club in June, before the release of *Appetite*. Up to then, the only place I had been outside of the United States was Vancouver, Canada, to play punk-rock shows with my various Seattle bands when I was a teenager. So this was big news to me. Huge. Magnificent.

Kids in the UK would sort of latch onto one band and make a big deal out of it. In the mid-1980s, that band was Hanoi Rocks, an amazing group of Finns who had relocated to England and were writing some of the best and dirtiest rock on the planet. When Hanoi came to tour America in 1984, their drummer died in a car crash while making a booze run with Vince Neil of Mötley Crüe during a few days off in L.A. that December. I had just moved to Hollywood that fall, and Slash and I had tickets to the Hanoi Rocks gig that never happened because of the car accident. It was an incredibly sad moment in rock and roll, and Hanoi Rocks never recovered—they broke up soon after.

Flash-forward to our gig in the UK in June 1987. After the first Marquee gig sold out in record time, they added a second date. That sold out just as fast, so they added a third night. By the time we arrived in London, we were minor celebrities. We discovered we had become the "it" band the youth of England had been looking for to fill the void left by Hanoi Rocks. We stayed in a rent-by-the-week apartment because it was much cheaper than a hotel, and at times people would stop us on the street. They actually knew who we were! It was a weird sensation, even on such a small scale.

I learned to ride London's subway system, the Tube, because there were great gigs every night we were there. Slash and I went out one night to see the Replacements and got so drunk that when we caught the Tube after the show, we ended up on a train heading the wrong way. When we arrived at the end of the line, there were no more trains running and we didn't have anywhere near enough money to take a cab back. And anyway, we didn't know the address where we were staying. We only knew how to get there from our local Tube stop. We ended up sloppily swinging at each other out of frustration before passing out in the train station.

The real reason we were there, of course, was to fucking rock. In that period of the band's career—and with pent-up energy from half a year of virtually no gigs—nobody fucking rocked with as much purpose and sneer, or with the same level of recklessness and bad intentions. This is not me bragging; we were just firing on all cylinders. At sound check before the first show on June 19, 1987, we ran through a cover song. We played it just once, but somehow our feelings found a perfect vessel in this Bob Dylan song and our emotions just came pouring out. Todd Crew showed up unexpectedly that day—he was bumming around Europe on a Eurail pass he'd gotten for graduation but never used—and he told us he was blown away by the way we played the song.

When we walked to the Marquee that first night for the show itself, we were met by a crowd filling up the entire block in front of the club. We were absolutely amazed that all of these people had come to see us. Trusting Todd's judgment, we ended up closing the show with the cover song we had tried during sound check that afternoon, "Knockin' on Heaven's Door."

We all hung out in the street in front of the Marquee after that show and before and after the next two gigs. We felt awed by our reception.

When we arrived back in the States in early July, nothing was happening for us. We took an opening slot on a tour with the Cult, a British band with Goth roots. They'd had success with "She Sells Sanctuary" off their second album, *Love,* and beginning in mid-August, they were touring across Canada and the western United States for their third album, *Electric.* With our record coming out, we would have a small budget for a crew, so Todd Crew and I hatched a plan: he would come out on the Cult tour and be my bass tech. He could make some money working the tour and then return to L.A. and start a new band.

There was still a month or so to kill. Slash went off to meet with merchandising companies in New York City just prior to the U.S. release of *Appetite.* Todd got a wild and drunken hair up his ass and flew out to New York to join him. Todd thought it'd be a fun last hurrah before he had to sober up a bit to work the tour, I guess. Todd always called me about eight times a day, and this didn't change when he went to New York. But then the calls stopped. I thought that maybe he'd found some girl and was holed up in her apartment without a phone.

But that wasn't it.

At three o'clock on a Sunday morning, my phone rang. The sound woke me from a deep sleep. I picked up the phone and heard Todd's mother's voice.

"Duff! Please tell me Todd is at your apartment with you. Please tell me he is there."

"What?"

I had no idea what she was talking about, and I was still rubbing my half-closed eyes.

"Todd is not dead. He *can't* be!" she shrieked.

Now I was completely dumbstruck. The New York Police Department's coroner had called her to tell her that they had her son's body. He had died of a heroin overdose, the coroner had told her.

It can't be true. He'll come bursting through the door any minute now.

I made some frantic calls. It was true: Todd was gone. Gone.

To this day, it is hard to talk or even think about it. At the time all I knew was that two of my best friends had suddenly been washed from this earth in quick succession. First Jim and then Todd. I felt as if I had been left to swim upstream in a world that was getting darker and darker all of the time.

I didn't know where to turn. Eddy was unavailable. Andy was a thousand miles away. My mom was always on the other end of the phone, but I still felt suddenly lost.

I feel so alone.

I had moved in with my girlfriend Mandy a few months before. Now I asked her to marry me. Premature, for sure. But I needed to try to create something solid, to shore up the foundations of my existence. She said yes.

Guns N' Roses started the Cult tour in Halifax on August 14, with shows almost every night for a little over a month. Halifax is in Nova Scotia, in the easternmost corner of Canada. Despite everything else, it was an exciting prospect. Nobody in my family had ever been out to Nova Scotia—nobody I knew had ever been out there. I was going to be the first. Every time there was a first like that, I used to think to myself that I should savor the moment. It would also be the first time ever that I was part of a highly organized "campaign" behind the release of a record. We had a tour bus! We had a couple of real hotel rooms! And catering! *Fuck, yes!*

Backstage the first night of the tour, I saw Billy Duffy—the Cult's guitar player—sitting down to dinner at one of the tables in the catering
room. I gave him a sort of half-assed "dude nod" in the hopes that maybe
he knew my name—you know, he's Duffy, I'm Duff—and that we would
have a conversation starter. Nope. Didn't happen. He just saw some tall
geezer with a strange tic. He ignored me and went on about the business
of eating his fucking dinner. I felt like a complete goof.

Hitting the stage that night was extra special. It did not matter in the
slightest that there were maybe fifty people in the audience when we took
the stage. One thing I hadn't reckoned on were the barricades between
the stage and the audience, leaving a ton of space where the building's
security personnel could gather and show their force. Because of that gap,
the stage lights did not illuminate the few people in attendance. And all of
those lights were blinding. The overall effect was to make us feel like we
were playing to this big yawning void.

We had decided to add "Knockin' on Heaven's Door" to our set as a
tribute to Todd, who had loved it so much the first time we played it back
in England. When we played it onstage the first night of the tour, the
song's sentiments were further magnified by our decision to use it as a
way of publicly acknowledging the death of our friend.

We had filmed a video for "Welcome to the Jungle" just before we
left on the Cult tour, but MTV refused to air it. So nobody knew who we
were. In fact, the Canadian release date for *Appetite* was six weeks later
than the U.S. release date for some reason—so our record wasn't even
available until halfway through the tour. We continued to play to empty
rooms because nobody turned up for the opening act. After our set each
night, I would go out into the audience and bum Canadian quarters to
call home on the venue's pay phone. Mandy, my mom, my friends back in
Seattle—they all got to hear about the strange mix of elation and tragedy
that accompanied me across Canada.

From Canada we swung down the West Coast of the United States.
When we played the Paramount Theatre in Seattle, I got a bunch of my
friends in for free. Seeing Kurt and Kim and Donner and Andy and Brian
again put me somewhat at ease, though Eddy was still strung out. Andy

Wood came and brought Stone Gossard and Jeff Ament—they were in the process of putting together Mother Love Bone. Jerry Cantrell and Sean Kinney from Alice in Chains came, too. And I got a chance to stop by my mom's the day after the show. The next tour stop where any people came early enough to see Guns play our set was at the Long Beach Arena; it was a homecoming show for us after not playing there much that year. But the rest of the tour—which then went east to New Orleans via Arizona and Texas—nobody knew us and nobody cared.

A few days after the Cult tour wrapped in mid-September, we went as a headlining act to Germany and Holland and then back to the UK. I was sick as a dog in Amsterdam with the flu. I was sharing a room with Izzy and Slash and they got hold of some heroin and smoked it. For some reason, despite Jim and Todd's deaths just months before, when they offered me the tinfoil contraption they were using to smoke it, I accepted. When I inhaled, it felt as if I floated away on a silk pillow. It was the perfect antidote to the flu, but I was still a drinker, not a junkie, and I wouldn't touch heroin again for quite a few years.

In Britain we played in Newcastle, Nottingham, Manchester, Bristol. Returning to London on October 8, three months after our first visit, we had a date at the Hammersmith Odeon. This was a huge step up. It was a legendary theater—both the Clash and Motörhead had written songs about the place. When I found out we would be playing the Hammersmith Odeon, I thought to myself, *Whoa, that's it, we've made it.*

When we came back to the States we played our first ever East Coast gigs, headlining a small-scale tour in places like Allentown and Albany. It was a bare-bones operation: one bus and a Ryder truck for our gear. In clubs, the lights and sound were already installed and you got what you got. Good or bad, you couldn't do anything about it. We just hoped the places had a shower we could use. We played the Ritz in New York City for the first time. The buzz about us seemed finally to be building in New York—we played another show at the famous Brooklyn hardcore club L'Amour billed only as "mystery guests." Rumors that it would be us were enough to fill the place. And we did an acoustic set at CBGB on October 30, 1987, where we debuted "Patience."

Next we nabbed a slot on Mötley Crüe's "Girls, Girls, Girls" tour starting in Alabama in November. The Crüe had a big production show. Tommy Lee was in a spinning drum riser on a crane arm that could rotate him 360 degrees. Our back line was tiny—just a few amps and my bass rig. After we dumped our gear at each stop, we just waited around while they set up. We ate the free backstage food and started cocktail hour. We could only get onstage a little while before the doors opened and do a quick sound check. Our setup was barely visible in front of the Crüe's KISS-scale stage set, and at one point our manager wanted to bring out dummy Marshall stacks and make it look huge. We said no way—it wasn't about the back line, it wasn't about video, lighting, or dry-ice smoke. It was about us. We had forty-five minutes as an opening band and we just tried to kill it every night.

Back in the halcyon days of GN'R, when everyone in L.A. thought we were the most badass hard-drinking and hard-drugging motherfuckers around (and maybe we thought so, too), we quickly found out we were in the minor league compared to Mötley Crüe. After their shows, we often ended up partying together, learning their code names for different drugs, even flying on their private jet a few times. Our peek into their world was a look into an abyss. They'd found a way of skating around the edge of that abyss while perfecting the dark art of drinking and drugging for a while there back in the 1980s.

My brother Bruce, the one who first got me started playing bass, now worked for a music management company. He tracked the pop charts as part of his job. And he tracked Guns because of me. He kept all the weekly *Billboard* magazines. He watched *Appetite for Destruction* creep from the high hundreds up to 110. He called me when we cracked the top 100.

"Brother, you're ninety-five!"

After a quick interview on MTV's weekly late-night metal show, *Headbangers Ball,* the video for "Welcome to the Jungle" was finally getting some plays on MTV, and audiences on the Crüe tour were receptive to our sound. In December, we joined Alice Cooper's tour as the opening band for the opening band: the bill went us, Megadeth, then Alice. That meant going through the Midwest in a bus playing in front of two bands' gear. We finished the year with four homecoming shows at Perkins Palace in Pasadena.

Whew, what a year. Our first album, our first taste of national and international touring, CBGB's, and the fucking Hammersmith Odeon. It had all been very exciting—in my case, the fulfillment of dreams I'd had since I started playing in bands at fifteen. But I had also found that flying triggered panic attacks. Sometimes the attacks were so bad that I couldn't see, couldn't breathe. I would sweat profusely. I wanted to take off my clothes because everything felt like it was binding me, but at the same time I was freezing because my breathing was so shallow. It felt like I was going to suffocate. People around me—the guys in the band, friends— could see the frantic look on my face, but there was nothing they could do to help me. I began to drink heavily prior to our increasingly frequent flights. The trick was to be able to walk straight during boarding but pass out as soon as they sealed the aircraft doors.

Yeah, what a year. I'd lost dear friends; in fact practically every triumph had been tempered by a deep sense of loss.

CHAPTER EIGHTEEN

✦ ✦ ✦

We spent most of the first few months of 1988 back home, right up until we shot the video for "Sweet Child o' Mine" in early April. We also did an acoustic recording session to lay down tracks we figured would be good for B-sides or whatever.

Among those tracks were "Patience," and a song Axl brought in lyrics for called "One in a Million." When he first showed them to us, I cringed at some of the words—especially *niggers*. It wasn't that I thought Axl held racist views—there was never any question on that front. I realized Axl's lyrics represented a third-person observation about what Reagan-era America had become: a nation of name-callers, a land of fear. It was just a word my mouth would not form. Among my earliest memories as a child was my mom pulling me out of kindergarten to march in a peace rally after Martin Luther King was shot and killed. But Axl was bold. And nobody at the label seemed concerned.

A few months prior, Axl had also come up with a great idea for "Patience," seemingly out of nowhere, that had immediately become the story and melody of that song. The whistle part at the beginning was another ballsy and unusual move by Axl; the song just wouldn't be the same without it. "Patience" quickly became one of my favorite GN'R songs to play live.

When we went out in L.A., which was every night, people at the rock clubs recognized us, but life was still quite similar to the way it had been for the last few years. We had our bars, our clubs, our friends, we were always together, and we were not public figures except when we wanted to be—buying rounds of drinks or hopping up onstage with friends in other bands. We had no idea it would be the last time we would ever be able to walk around L.A. without feeling like we were in a fishbowl, isolated and on display.

One night Slash and I went out to the Rainbow, a restaurant next to the Roxy on Sunset that was famous as a rock-and-roll hangout. They gave us a booth. This was a new level of deference. A booth! At the Rainbow! As we proceeded to get blasted, a really big, drunk guy wandered over to our table. Though he looked like an overgrown hick, he was in fact the guitar player from a band considered quite big just then—much bigger than Guns. He addressed himself to Slash:

"Niggers shouldn't wear tattoos," he said.

What? Was this his idea of a joke or something?

He wasn't laughing.

I stood up.

"What the fuck did you say to my friend?"

"You heard me. Niggers shouldn't wear tattoos."

I slugged the guy. Then I slugged him again. And again. He reminded me of the bullies back in Seattle, the meatheads who beat up punks in packs, who called everyone faggots. I'm not sure how many times I hit him—I just completely lost it—but he went down. I found out later that three of his ribs had broken.

We did make a trip east in late January to play at the Ritz again—the show MTV taped for broadcast. Two nights before that show, we decided to play a semi-acoustic surprise show at a venue in Manhattan called the Limelight, a former church. By the time we headed into the sanctuary, everyone in the band was so fucked up that we lost members one by one as the set progressed. Eventually everyone except me and Axl went down. It was a comical gig, but I took something serious away from it. I told myself I would *never* get so deep into my cups that I wouldn't be able to play.

Back in L.A., Mandy and I began to plan a big wedding at the Hollywood Roosevelt Hotel. My brother Matt, the trombone player, volunteered to put together a big-band jazz combo for the event. Mandy and

I had been living together for ten months at that point, though I'd been away much of the time. Still, we seemed a perfect match; it felt like she was going to be the girl forever.

My brother Bruce called me again in the spring, after MTV aired the Ritz concert.

"This is getting fun," he said. "Your record is up to number fifty-five."

Appetite was doing okay at this point. A record company is just a bank: they loan you money to make a record and then they take a cut if you start selling records. We started to pay back our loan and were starting to see a little bit of money—but not much.

We did a swing through the Midwest on our own that spring, then signed on to the Iron Maiden tour, making the same swing across Canada and the West Coast we'd made with the Cult. When our manager broke the news to us, he apologized.

"Yeah, yeah, I know," he said.

In the 1980s, for a band the size of Maiden, touring Canada was like spring training: you got your show together so everything was ready for the American tour. Places like Toronto and Vancouver were big markets, but most nights you were in Moncton, Moose Jaw, or Red Deer. Not only that, Maiden was straight-up metal. Metal crowds could be pretty narrow-minded back then. If you were a little weird and you were opening for Maiden, they called you "faggots" and "punks"—and "punk" was meant as an insult. It meant you couldn't play your instruments.

To be fair to the audiences, what they were picking up was correct: much as I respect metal, we didn't fit the bill musically. We *wanted* to be different. After all, Steven had only one bass drum. And while Axl sang in a high voice much of the time, he wasn't operatic. His howl was pure, unadulterated rage and anguish, not a vocal exercise; clearly, the first time that sound came out of him, it had come from the pit of his stomach. Oh, and also we didn't write songs about elves and demons and shit—unless, of course, you considered Mr. Brownstone a demon.

All five of us were still sleeping in one tour bus, and we salaried ourselves $125 a week. Most of that went back to L.A. to pay rent; I probably had $20 a week for walking-around money. It felt like a step backward in some ways. Our reward for succeeding—for building an audience, creating excitement in L.A.—was to go out and play to a sprinkling of people who didn't give a shit about us. Well, that was on the good nights. Some nights the silent treatment gave way to name-calling. But despite that, and the occasional beer bottles that came flying our way, we didn't care. Shit, a couple years prior we were hitchhiking to a gig with no gear. Now we were on a fucking tour bus. We could eat for free at a catered backstage buffet. Life was good.

And anyway, we knew it was all part of the process. We'd been to England and gotten a good reaction there on our own. We had won over New York. Our music was starting to catch fire in some corners of the world. Certain areas just took more work. We would work. We *loved* to work. For us, work was quite literally play. What the people hurling glass and invective at us didn't realize was that for Guns N' Roses, this was fun. *Bring it on.*

In May 1988, I flew home from Canada for my wedding. The prospect of a long flight was not welcome, never was, but a short respite from all the boozing wasn't the worst thing ever—especially when it allowed me to wrap my arms around the girl who would be my foundation from then on. I would like to have had my band at the wedding, but I understood better than anyone that the band came first, and that if anyone was missing, it was me from the band and not the band from my wedding. A guy named Haggis filled in on bass for the show I had to miss—he had been with the Cult when we opened for them. It wouldn't be the last time we found a replacement player from among the frequently changing personnel of that band.

I returned after a couple of days, but the Maiden tour was soon cut short when Axl had some throat problems. We went back to L.A. for a month just as the video for "Sweet Child o' Mine" was released. As the video picked up steam, people began to recognize us on the street for the first time.

Kim from the Fastbacks called me from New Orleans one day: "I just heard you on the radio!"

We assembled an accomplished crew in preparation for our next engagement, joining Aerosmith for their national summer tour. These crew guys were the first outsiders to join our gang—not friends or even friends of friends, but bona fide professionals. Slash's guitar tech, Adam Day, had been working with George Lynch of Dokken; he ended up staying with us for years. McBob handled my bass and Izzy's guitar; he stayed with me for twenty years. His brother Tom Mayhue came aboard as the drum tech and also remained for years. We became a close-knit bunch almost immediately.

At one time singer Steven Tyler and guitarist Joe Perry from Aerosmith had been such big users that they had the nickname the Toxic Twins. But all the guys in Aerosmith had recently gotten sober. And though that was the last thing we were interested in for ourselves, we didn't want to see these guys—legends whose music we all loved—falter. All through the tour we made a real effort to keep our drugs and alcohol hidden from them as much as possible.

The video for "Sweet Child o' Mine" was on MTV when we set off in July, but on the first few dates we still got a tepid reaction from the crowd—polite applause. Soon, however, the song became a phenomenon, much to all of our surprise, to be honest. We had not even seen it as a potential single when we put it together.

We found ourselves in a novel position: we idolized the band we were on tour with, but crowds were coming to see *us* now. The amphitheaters we played were packed by the time we went on for our abbreviated opening-band set. The less-than-ideal elements of being an opening band—cramped positioning of our gear onstage, second-class-citizen status at the venues, and so forth—remained, but the feeling that we had been banished from our fans when we left L.A. to play those other opening slots quickly evaporated. Suddenly we had fans in force all over the country.

In early August 1988, we were sitting backstage one day when some people from our record label came in with a sheet cake from the local grocery store.

"Congratulations," they said, "you're number one!"

I remember thinking, *Uh, wow, cool . . . a cake.*

And then, *What does this mean?*

Shit was crazy.

Shit was great.

I was hammered.

But after a little while I remember going back out to the bus and thinking about the whole thing.

Really?

I knew *somebody* was making real money as a result of our record reaching the top of the charts. It certainly didn't seem to be us. There was a party back at the record label in L.A., I was pretty sure. Limos out front of the Geffen office to take people to celebratory dinners. Champagne all around. But was anybody from the label there when our friends died? Did anyone from the record label send flowers to their parents? Hang on a minute now, was it anybody at Geffen's responsibility to do that? This was a business, after all. Maybe I shouldn't have expected anything different.

· I didn't know what to think. I was a dumb motherfucker.

Our album had reached the top of the chart almost exactly one year after its release. My brother later told me this was a very unusual feat— albums typically reached their peak chart position within the first few weeks after they came out. Still, I never really celebrated *Appetite* reaching number one. Maybe I still haven't.

Lots of people think it was an upward trajectory from there. But for me, it was the opposite. About a week after the sheet-cake ceremony, we flew to England again to play the outdoor Monsters of Rock festival at Castle Donington. This was the kind of thing you heard about other bands playing—big bands, household names, not grubby kids a year or two removed from living in a back-alley storage space and treating their venereal diseases with fucking fish food.

Looking out at the sea of faces on August 20, 1988, I realized I'd never even *seen* a crowd that size, much less stood in front of one. The festival had been going for a few years, but this was the biggest one so far—107,000 in attendance. It was stormy, and the lawn—the infield of a racetrack—was thick with mud. Wind swirled. The PA had problems and a giant video screen blew over.

We were near the bottom of the bill and played early in the day. When we started playing, tens of thousands of people surged forward.

Shit almighty, people really want to see us. This is fucking crazy.

As fans swarmed toward the stage, I could see people getting pushed around, losing their footing.

"Back up!" Axl screamed at the crowd.

Security stopped the show during the third song to fish a few people out of the scrum. But they were also occupied dealing with the video screen that had collapsed in the wind. People refused to get out from under it—it was still showing the video feed.

We continued playing after getting the okay from security.

When we played "Paradise City" the crowd surged forward again, a writhing mass of bodies, singing, screaming, nodding.

Suddenly I could see kids piled on top of other kids, horizontal in the mud. It looked like some kids might be getting hurt.

Should I jump in and try to do something?

I was too scared.

We stopped playing again.

"Don't fucking kill each other," Axl said to the crowd.

This pause lasted about twenty minutes. Dozens of people were pulled out of the mud by security. Then once again we were told we could resume playing and finish our set. Only later did we hear the news: two fans had died, suffocated beneath other fans in the mud.

Oh, fuck, no, no, no.

Those two fans, Alan Dick and Landon Siggers, had just come to see a rock concert. They had tried see *us,* to sing along with *us.* And now they were dead. All I could think about were their final moments of an-guish, the horror they must have faced as they struggled to breathe in the knee-deep mud and other fans fell on top of them. *Oh, God, no. I wish we'd never played this fucking show.* I wanted to apologize to their families.

The tragedy woke me to the sheer power of a crowd and the way things could turn on a dime—those casualties happened in an instant.

Adulation comes with a dark side. Never forget that. Never.

This is supposed to be fun for everyone—and ESPECIALLY for the people who come out to support us.

No more casualties. No more blood on your hands.

The next day we returned to the States with heavy hearts to finish the Aerosmith tour.

Geffen had officially released "Sweet Child" as a single in the United States the day we'd flown to England for Donington. By the time the Aerosmith tour wrapped up about three weeks later, in mid-September, the song had hit number one on the singles chart.

The last show was near L.A., at the Pacific Amphitheatre in Orange County. The place had lawn seating back then and could hold almost 20,000 people. It was sold out. It seemed as if much of the crowd that night was there to welcome us home after a momentous year during which we had become conquering local heroes but barely played the L.A. area at all.

Prior to the last gig, Aerosmith presented each of us with a set of Halliburton luggage as a thank-you gift. I think they felt sorry for us: despite the chart success of *Appetite* and "Sweet Child," we were living out of duffel bags held together with duct tape—still just urchins living under the street.

The byproduct of us keeping drugs and alcohol on the down-low during the tour was that we were also a little less extreme even when behind closed doors. But at this last show, everyone we knew came down to congratulate us on our success and to revel in a victory for street-level rock. Half of L.A. suddenly wanted to be our friends, and a lot of them brought drugs in order to ingratiate themselves. After we played our set and came offstage to party, I was handed an eighth of an ounce of cocaine. I was still not a cocaine guy, and with my panic disorder, anything with an "up" scared me. But hell, I had some Valium and plenty of vodka to counter any effects. We were number one. We were home.

Okay, I thought to myself after a few more drinks, *I'll do some cocaine.*

A little while later I was invited up onstage with Aerosmith to play along with the final song of the tour. I froze. They wanted me to play "Mama Kin," a song Guns had covered on *Live! Like a Suicide,* a song I had loved my whole life.

Fuck, I am so fucking high on coke!

Okay, quick: drink a huge cup of vodka and take a pill.

When I hit the stage with Aerosmith, I was experiencing that toxic mix of uppers and downers for one of the first of what would become countless times in the future. Little did I know it would become my secret potion and cure-all for the next six years. I did it when I was happy. I did it when I was sad. I would do it until I was almost brain-dead, hopeless, and left for dead.

In hindsight, I can see that night as the moment I started the transformation from a guy who had spirit and soul and who looked at the cup as half full into a blackened shadow of my former self.

PART THREE

LOADED

CHAPTER NINETEEN

+ + +

"Sweet Child" was bumped from number one by "Don't Worry, Be Happy," but *Appetite* climbed back to the top of the album charts and stayed there for a few weeks that fall. Our lives began to change irrevocably.

All the guys in Guns came out of humble, working-class families. Money was never a thing any of us understood—at all—because we didn't have any. We had long been comfortable with subsistence living. Now we had a hit record. I remember the first check I received from that: we each got $80,000. It was an incomprehensible amount of money. It might as well have been a billion dollars.

The check made me think once again about all the stories we now knew about Aerosmith getting fleeced and about guys from the Alice Cooper band having to hock their guitars. I thought about seeing guys in Hollywood—like Sly Stone—and thinking, *Wow, you'd think they had some money, but they're living in some shitty apartment.*

I was always fearful of somebody ripping me off. With no knowledge of how to act or what to do to avoid that happening, I reverted to street smarts, something we all had in spades. I went to each of our accountants, including the head CPA, and demanded their home addresses: "I want to know where you live."

Right or wrong, that's what I did.

When we got that $80,000, the accountants said there was a lot more money coming down the pike. They said we should start thinking about what to do with it. They suggested we should each buy a house. I didn't know what interest rates were, what a mortgage meant. I was kind of freaking out. But we got another check about three weeks later and I thought, *Okay, I guess I can get a house.*

I started working with a real-estate agent and we looked all over the area. We looked in Hollywood at first, but I decided I wanted to get out of there. When we got back to L.A. after *Appetite* had gotten so big, everybody there was suddenly dressed like us, in bandannas, and trying to sound like us. It was suffocating. So I wanted to be away from that. I ended up buying a nice little place in Studio City, two bedrooms with a little pool. It was as close as you could be to Hollywood without being in it—just over the other side of the hills. I bought it at the height of the real-estate market, but I didn't know what that meant. We all bought houses at the height of the market right after we finished the Aerosmith tour. The five of us all ended up buying in the same area, dotting Laurel Canyon. We all bought right on the main road or just off it. Obviously, in thinking accessibility would be a plus, we failed to recognize the way our lives were about to change. We'd soon want to be out of this fishbowl.

I bought a brand-new car for the first time in my life—a Corvette. Soon afterward, my brother Jon came down to L.A. to visit.

"Oh, you bought a Corvette," he said, eyebrow raised. "You sure? Don't get used to this or your money's going to be gone."

We McKagans had grown up with the idea that you didn't live beyond your means. None of my brothers or sisters went out and bought cars or houses they couldn't afford. I was the first one of us—the last kid, ironically—who started making real money, big money, money none of us had ever thought about. And my brother checked me.

By this point, I thought my life had already gotten strange. But I wasn't prepared for what happened one day in November 1988, when I went to a Ralph's grocery store on Laurel Canyon to buy a pack of smokes. People started staring, and audibly whispering, "Holy shit!" People were freaking out.

Then a couple people came running up from the magazine aisle, clutching stacks of magazines, saying, "Hang on, please, hang on, please wait for us to buy these so you can autograph them!"

They put the magazines down in front of me at the cashier. Guns N' Roses was on the cover of *Rolling Stone*. I vaguely remembered being interviewed for a *Rolling Stone* article during the Aerosmith tour, and someone probably told me the magazine had changed its mind and decided to put us on the cover instead of Aerosmith, which had been the original plan. But somewhere along the line, I must have forgotten.

Being out in public meant hysteria from then on.

Once *Appetite* topped the charts, the label packaged the acoustic tracks we had recorded along with our old *Live! Like a Suicide* EP for what became *Lies*—which came out at the end of 1988 and joined *Appetite* in the top five just a few weeks after we were on the cover of *Rolling Stone*.

Axl's lyrics in "One in a Million" immediately caught attention. The press labeled us things like David Duke's house band; I heard that the KKK—or some faction of the Klan, at least—started using the song as a war cry. I stood by my original interpretation of the song and of Axl's intentions. Art gets misunderstood all the time. Still, I found myself uncomfortable as a result of this particular misunderstanding. I had always looked up to my oldest brother-in-law, Dexter, who was married to my sister Carol. Dexter was a black man with a Black Panther tattoo on his left forearm, and having him in the family meant I never distinguished between black skin and white skin as a child. Carol and Dexter's kids— two nephews and a niece of mine—were half-black. Or was it half-white? And they were very close in age to me; we had all grown up together. Now I worried what they might think of me and my band with all the controversy swirling around the song.

Prior to the release of *Lies*, David Geffen, the head of our label, had arranged for us to play a charity gig to benefit AIDS research in New York. Axl had used another slur in his lyrics for "One in a Million," too: "faggots." Again I felt he had used this word as an indictment of the attitude behind such statements, not an endorsement of them. Even so, the plug was pulled on our charity appearance as protest mounted.

We were happy to get away from the controversy and finish 1988 by headlining our first-ever shows in Japan, Australia, and New Zealand.

When we left Japan, the promoter gave each of us a nice camera as a thank-you gift. I had never before flown home with something I hadn't taken with me. The first two times we came back from England, we didn't have enough money to buy anything. So obviously I didn't have to declare anything and fill out any customs forms. This time I had the camera, but I didn't know to declare it—it was a gift, after all. When we returned home the third week of December, our port of entry to the United States was the airport in Honolulu, Hawaii. It will come as no surprise that a young, scruffy (and in my case, of course, plastered) bunch of rock-and-rollers didn't get waved through the express lane at customs. As a customs official went through my bag, he pulled out the new camera. He asked where I got it.

Still in the vodka-induced haze that was mandatory for me to be able to fly, I just assumed the best thing to do was to pretend it was mine all along. "Got it in L.A.," I told the officer.

Then he opened it up and started examining the writing on the camera body. "Hang on," he said. "This is Japanese."

When it became clear that U.S. Customs was going to confiscate my camera, I hoisted it up and viciously smashed it on the ground as hard as I could. Twenty-five years later I'm still trying to get that incident cleared from my passport file.

Mandy and I went back to Seattle for Christmas that year. I had fucked up my thumb at the end of our Asian tour. Freak accident. My bass tech, McBob, had been diagnosed with cancer and had to go home for treatment. I took the replacement tech, Scott, to a dinner in Sydney, where we were awarded an Australian gold record. I had a couple of gold records already, so I gave this one to Scott. We went to high-five and my thumb caught on his hand awkwardly. It started swelling up as the night went on, and I had to duct-tape the pick to my hand for the last two gigs of the Asian tour because I couldn't hold it. In Seattle, my brother-in-law, a doctor, reconnected the ligaments. I had a cast on when I flew back to L.A.

There's no way to prepare for how strange and claustrophobic it makes you feel to be constantly recognized. There's no training for it. One day you can pop into the grocery store to pick up a pack of smokes; the next there is hysteria as soon as you walk through the door. In theory, my world and future were opening up, and the money and fame represented seemingly limitless opportunities. In practice, my world felt as though it was shrinking, as there were fewer and fewer places I could go without attracting attention and having to function in front of an audience. I began to feel like a zoo animal: king of the jungle, stuck in a cage.

At first I didn't know how to deal with that—I simply lived a public life. It never occurred to me to try to distinguish between a private life and a public one. I didn't know how to do both. I was all public all the time. Still, the sense of being in a fishbowl was unnerving. If I'd had any wits about me, I would have bought a house back in Seattle and just maintained an apartment in L.A. That would have been common sense, but no. It was about our band, it was about our gang; we had to go out and conquer and kill it every night. Even in our town. We had houses in the hills now but lived like we were still crashing in the alleyway off Gardner, still fighting to keep our fingernails dug into the bottom rung of society's ladder. If that meant scrapes and bar fights, so be it. If that meant using my cast as a weapon, so be it. That's just the way we were.

In my wife, I thought I had a tether to a more normal life. I looked to my older brothers and sisters' stable marriages as examples. I had always held a very romantic and idealized vision of what love and marriage should look and feel like, right down to smiling children and a white picket fence. Mandy and I set up the new house for the perfect domestic life we anticipated. We bought a dog named Chloe, a gentle yellow Lab. We even put in a picture-perfect brick walkway in front of the house to give it a more idyllic look. I laid it myself.

But what should have been a source of stability didn't work out that way. In fact, it was almost as though the moment we got married our relationship completely changed. Once I was home, it quickly spiraled downward. I suppose if I'd been more coldly analytical about it, I could have seen the marriage wasn't going to last. But I couldn't believe it could turn so sour so quickly. For now I clung to her, to us—or rather to what we had been for the year prior to our wedding.

Anyway, not to worry, I always had my band to fall back on. Guns N' Roses was still the most important thing in the lives of us five members. At least in my mind I chose to see it that way. Somehow, though, while we were off the road in 1989, we began splitting at the seams.

Our new houses provided sanctuaries away from the other members of the band—something we had never known in the four years since we had started rocking, writing, and reveling together. We had a bit of money now and ample and easy access to any and all types of vice. With Izzy and Slash, smack returned with a vengeance. And it turned out Steven hadn't been joking about wanting nothing more in life than a bag of good weed and a big ball of crack—except now, with more than enough money to realize his dream, he added heroin to the mix. At the same time word was getting back to me that people were whispering in Axl's ear, saying all the ass-kissing clichés: *You're the guy, you're the basis of the band's success.* That's a cancer for any band.

Still, I never doubted our bonds would hold. Sure, Slash started jamming with Dave Mustaine from Megadeth and there were rumors that they were talking about starting a new and separate band. I, for one, recognized this as an expression of his frustration with the directionless path that GN'R was on. Nothing more. Slash just wanted Guns to get back to being a gang of dudes who hung out together all the time. As equals. With no bullshit. But there was no communication.

I went up to Axl's condo on a few occasions and the two of us discussed how worried we were about our comrades.

"What are we going to do?" he asked.

I had no answer. We talked, but all we could do was hope they would find it in themselves to pull back and get into the swing of things as far as the band was concerned. We never thought of rehab or interventions back then.

We wanted to begin writing for our next full-length release. Everyone in the band had seen *Lies* as just a stopgap move. Then it, too, had gone to number one and "Patience" became a hit in the spring of 1989 just as we were trying to figure out our next move. Guns already had ideas for some new songs—in toying with riffs and ideas at sound checks in late

1988, we had created a skeletal version of "Civil War" and now Axl and I were writing lyrics for it. Memories of marching with my mother as a child provided the inspiration for one section: "Did you wear the black armband / When they shot the man / Who said peace could last forever?"

In the summer of 1989, it was decided the band would relocate to Chicago to start writing our follow-up record. Part of the idea was to recapture the hothouse effect the Gardner space had provided as the songs for *Appetite* had come together. There, we were always together in close proximity, for hours, even days, at a time. Now that we all had houses and cars and separate lives, that aspect of the process was impossible to re-create in L.A. Moving in together in Chicago was an attempt to re-create it, though I didn't like the idea of going away. I had already pulled up roots once with my move from Seattle a few years earlier, and I had just bought my first house and even had a dog and something that resembled a home life in L.A. But I didn't voice any opposition. Chicago was Axl's idea. He wanted to be closer to his roots in Lafayette, Indiana. It was the last vestige of a romantic notion he had of going back to Indiana and leading a normal life. In the spirit of band unity, we bowed to Axl's wishes.

I knew absolutely no one in Chicago.

This would be interesting.

CHAPTER TWENTY

+ + +

Slash, Steven, and I arrived in Chicago first. Our work ethic always pushed us to get things rolling. We wanted to be sure everything was up and running. I assumed Axl would follow after us shortly—after all, we were here at his insistence. The likelihood of Izzy's participation in our heartland experiment was less clear. He had recently been arrested for, um, disrupting a flight. By pissing in the galley. So he was taking a stab at getting sober. And, yeah, well, there were also the urine tests he had to take as a result of the arrest. It was understandable at the time that he might not want to be around the rest of us too much.

The first thing we had to do was find a place for the whole band and a couple of our techs to live. We also had a security guy—in our management's eyes, it was probably to protect the public from our antics and not the other way around. Then we had to find a place where we could rehearse and write.

We found two apartments above an Italian restaurant across the street from a church off Clark Street. For our rehearsal spot, we rented an empty old theater—Top Note Theater—above the rock club Metro. Unbeknownst to me then, some regulars at the Metro were also tightly linked into the city's drug chain.

After two weeks in Chicago, Axl was still a no-show. Slash, Steven, and I started to get a little resentful. I mean, what the fuck? Here we were in a city in which we had no interest, no friends—and no singer. We were fucking pissed off. I started to drink harder.

One night I was so fucked up that somebody pulled me aside and said, "Here, do a little coke and you'll sober right up." And there you go, that was the secret potion. I had been looking at coke the wrong way. I never wanted to be *that guy*—the asshole coke guy. But now I realized coke wasn't an end in itself, or didn't have to be; it was a means to an end, a tool. I didn't have to become a coke guy to make use of it. Coke just allowed me to pursue my favored mind-altering regimen—vodka—harder and for longer periods of time. That guy I could be. I started to drink more and more, and now I, too, tapped into the drug connection available to us via the club downstairs.

On top of that, a Chicago newspaper did a piece about the band living there in town, writing songs for a record, and even revealed the street where we were living and the location where we were rehearsing. Perhaps the lone advantage Chicago could have offered was anonymity, and now kids came to seek us out from all over the place with the hope of getting a glimpse of us or even partying with the band now tagged as the most dangerous in the world. This was not good.

We did get some work done. We finished "Civil War" and wrote "Get in the Ring" and "Pretty Tied Up," to name a few. We were still prolific songwriters in our creative prime at that point, and even with just three of us there, we were a locomotive.

Unfortunately this was also the point at which Steven really started to go overboard with his cocaine and heroin intake. I was nothing close to sober then, but I maintained a line I would not cross—which meant, first and foremost, that I would not let my work suffer. Also over the line: putting my life in jeopardy, putting someone else's life in jeopardy, getting arrested. Slash maintained a similar line—especially when it came to rehearsing and playing live shows. And Slash and I had an unwritten pact to keep an eye out for each other and to make sure these lines were never crossed. In Chicago, Steven started to become frightening even to us, a couple of guys not accustomed to getting spooked when it came to intoxicants.

Ever since the band had started, there had been some vague animosity between Axl and Steven. This happens in bands. All bands. I could never quite figure out what these two guys had against each other, but the longer Axl continued not to show, the more Steven began to vent to me and Slash about him. I understood where Steven was coming from, but I was always more of a solution-based type of person. Getting pissed off and throwing food across a room or whatever never made much sense to me. Between Steven's cocaine intake and his ever-more-vitriolic rhetoric, the situation in Chicago was becoming worrisome. *Another drink, please.*

In the daytime, I would try to do somewhat healthy and normal things to offset the nightly pollutants I was pouring down my gullet. I joined a gym, but really remember going only once. Health clubs were definitely not in my comfort zone back then. No, I would just go out for a run from time to time, or even go across the street to the church lawn and throw a football around with whatever kids were hanging out there. I grew up in a huge family with scores of nephews and nieces, and tossing a ball with some kids offered a comforting, familiar respite from the drugs, drink, and drama.

One day, while I was tossing a ball around with a couple of kids and their parents, four unmarked police cars came careening down the street and screeched to a halt on the sidewalk in front of us. The detectives jumped out of their cars, screaming and yelling for me to get on the ground facedown. I complied. Now, I did have an open container of beer, but still, I thought this show of force was slightly excessive for drinking in public—even if it was technically on church grounds. *Whoa, they take this stuff seriously in Chicago,* I thought to myself.

It was muggy and I wasn't wearing a shirt. The cops kept looking at my back. I have a ton of old acne scars on my back and I assumed these guys had never seen acne scars like mine. Kind of rude to stare, though, right?

Big Earl, our new security guy, came bursting out of our apartment and started to quarrel with the cops about the exact reason they had me in cuffs and were now throwing me in the back of one of their cars.

"Get the fuck back, sir," came the answer.

Earl yelled to me that he would get right down to the station and bail me out. I resigned myself to an afternoon in the pokey. That's when it got a little interesting.

As we were driving, the cops continued to look at my back. They were also looking at me with a stare that expressed some serious disdain. The threat of violence hung in the air. *Wow! Drinking in public is really frowned upon here,* I thought. Then suddenly they pulled the car over and a cop told me to get out. I looked up and down the street for someone who might witness the beating they were about to put on me. But the cop walked around behind me and uncuffed me.

They said that they were sorry. They'd picked up the wrong guy.

"Wrong guy for what?" I barked.

Apparently, there was a child molester in the area who fit my description—except he had an identifying tattoo on his back. My scars had looked like tattoos to these guys from afar, and they thought they'd found their man.

I started to scream at the assembled officers: the kids on the church lawn were probably scared shitless and now thought I was some kind of bad guy. I was indignant. The cops went from being apologetic to bristling at me again in an instant. They told me that they could still take me to jail for an open container and would be more than happy to do so. I suppressed my anger and shut my mouth. They let me go and I walked all the way back home.

Axl did finally show up in Chicago. It was too little too late. He got there, got into a fight with a girl we had befriended, and trashed the place where we were living. That happened the day Izzy showed up. Already nervous because of his court-mandated sobriety, Izzy came upstairs, took one look at all of the damage Axl had just wrought (not to mention the various powders all over the place), and hightailed it the fuck out of there. He would still send in riffs and ideas for *Use Your Illusion* and didn't officially quit until 1991, but his day-to-day involvement with the band pretty much died that day.

When the dust settled, Slash, Steven, and I sat down. The three of us agreed that enough was enough. We were out of there.

I felt used and foolish about going out to Chicago for so long and in the end getting dusted by Axl. Up to then I had not wavered in how I perceived us—as a band and a family and a gang. But this trip solidified some of the flimsy walls that had begun to go up between various parties in our unit. Sure, we were young, wild, and somewhat dumb, but this ill-conceived trip cast a dark cloud over the band—and additional clouds on the horizon were soon to render things darker still.

After the doomed stint in Chicago, I had to reexamine my steadfast belief in the band. The harsh reality was that the old us-against-the-world mentality had waned this year for sure. Steven was fully strung out and babbling incoherently much of the time. Slash had one foot out of the band as a result of feeling betrayed. Izzy had all but checked out. The techs, I soon found out, were secretly looking for other gigs. And to top it all off, we had an expensive bill to pay for the rehearsal space and apartments, the plane trips back and forth, and all the destruction Axl had inflicted on the apartments. We did have the songs that would make up the more meaty, up-tempo sections of the *Illusion* records. But the damage was done and all forward progress stopped for quite some time.

I did, however, have one epiphany in Chicago: cocaine was a nice supplement to my drinking. On cocaine, I could now drink twice as much as I had before. Fucking brilliant.

CHAPTER TWENTY-ONE

✦   ✦   ✦

Back in L.A. we retreated to our houses. They provided privacy for each of us to pursue his own brand of debauchery. Though things with Mandy continued to get uglier and uglier after I returned home, I pulled back a bit from the extremes of Chicago. I rode a mountain bike here and there in a token effort to be healthy. I would take our dog Chloe for walks. I tried not to drink so much and rarely did coke or took pills.

I would hang out with Slash from time to time, but things were getting dark up there at his house in Laurel Canyon. One day he pulled out a stack of Polaroid pictures he had taken around his house.

"Duff, look at these," he said. "It's some of those Martian bugs I was telling you about. They're infiltrating my house and watching me all the time."

There was, of course, nothing on these Polaroids. But he kept flipping through the stack and pointing.

"See, there's another one—right there, in the corner!"

Steven was careening off the deep end, too. He had bought a house just three blocks from mine and as a result I was able to check on him more often; what that amounted to in practical terms was watching helplessly as his crack and heroin use escalated. It got so bad, and he seemed so incapable of reining it in, that at one point I found out where his drug dealer lived and took a shotgun to the guy's house. Fueled by booze, obviously. I waited for him, intending to threaten the fuck out of this dude to get him to stop supplying Stevie with the things that were going to kill him. It's lucky this guy never showed up—lucky for him, of course, but also for me.

Then we got an offer to play four shows in October 1989 as the opening act for the Rolling Stones at the L.A. Coliseum. It was a huge shot in the arm for us at the time—though that's probably a poor choice of idioms given the situation in the run-up to the shows.

Mick Jagger negotiated the terms of our gig himself and took care of all the details. We didn't deal with a Stones lawyer or agent or somebody like that. We expected to, of course. Nope. It was Mick. We would say, We want this much per gig. And Mick would say, No, you're going to get this much.

Despite the work we now needed to do to prepare for the Stones shows, Slash and Steven showed no sign of pulling out of their drug habits, and Izzy slipped back into heroin use, too. Sometimes those guys put their drug use in front of band practice. One or the other often showed up late or left early from rehearsal—if they showed up at all. But we never talked about the problem. We were never any good at communication, especially when that meant confrontation. If we could have developed those skills then, the story of GN'R might have been very different.

With the shows looming, the *Los Angeles Times* ran a big piece about us supposedly staking our claim in rock and dethroning the old guard. There is one thing no band can ever do, and that is dethrone the fucking Rolling Stones. That would have been true regardless of the state of our band. And I was very nervous about the state of our band going in to the shows. The *Times* article seemed a bad omen to me. Later in life, I would be more apt to listen to that first instinct when committing to various things, but come on, this was a chance to open for the world's best.

By the time of the actual shows, everything melted into the background because I was so excited. My brother Matt put together the horn section again to play along with a few tunes. He was student-teaching. In the evenings before the shows, he came to the hotel where we were staying, got dressed, hung out in the hospitality room, and drove out to the Coliseum in one of the band's vans to get ready to play to tens of thousands of people; he told us that during the day he saw kids with GN'R cut into their arms at his school. By this point, the magnitude of our success was weird not only for us, but for people around us as well.

The Stones were great hosts—they hooked all our guests up, and the whole scene was charged. I flew my mom down for the shows. While she was in town, she picked up on the problems between me and Mandy. It was dispiriting to have a relationship I had taken seriously, and had such high hopes for, unraveling—and particularly for that disappointment to take concrete form in front of my mom. But for the moment, Guns was playing with the Stones, a fact that could buoy me in the face of almost any personal setback. Guns was fucking playing with the Stones.

Prior to the first show, Mick Jagger came up to me during sound check. I had on my cowboy boots, as usual, and it was misty and drizzling.

He motioned to my boots and said, "You going to wear those tonight, mate?"

I shrugged and smiled. I wasn't sure if he was making fun of me or what.

"You're going to slip on our stage."

This was the *Steel Wheels* tour, with an all-metal stage set.

"I've got some trainers," he said. "What size do you wear?"

"Eleven," I said.

"Me, too," he said. "We must have the same size willy."

Wow, I thought, *Mick Jagger says we have same size willy, and he's going to let me wear his sneakers.* Despite his kind offer, though, I didn't wear them in the end: Mick was cool, but his spare sneakers, I'm afraid, were not.

As showtime approached, Axl wasn't there and everyone—us, the Stones' people—was sweating and frantic. But he made it at the last minute, the first concert went off without a hitch, and I didn't slip on the metal stage. Sure, the guys were smacked out of their minds, but I had family and good friends around me, and I did not really pay much attention to what was going on with those guys backstage. I knew that we should have had a band sit-down before the gigs to get everything out on the table, but things had been moving too fast in the run-up to the shows.

Then came the second night.

Before we played our first note, Axl suddenly announced to the 80,000 people in attendance that "if certain people in Guns N' Roses didn't stop dancing with Mr. Brownstone," this would be our last show.

The crowd became absolutely quiet. People in the audience looked at one another; they seemed as confused as we were. They really had no idea what Axl was talking about.

I shrank. I was so fucking embarrassed. And I was so fucking mad that Axl felt he could do this to me. I would have been supportive if he was sufficiently pissed off at certain guys to want to confront them for what was going on—I was with him, the situation was bad. But he needed to talk about that shit in private! Not out here. Never out here.

Once Axl took his concerns public, the times of being a gang—us against the world—were over. We played the rest of the show, but it was a halfhearted effort at best. Afterward, and really for the remainder of our career, we just went our separate ways. That night officially rang the bell for the end of an era in GN'R.

CHAPTER TWENTY-TWO

+ + +

We should have had a band meeting to talk things out after the Rolling Stones gigs. But we didn't. I never even told Axl how upset I was. Other things came up, and when not putting out those fires we all just retreated back into our separate lives.

By the end of 1989, there was no longer any way around the fact that my marriage to Mandy was falling apart. Somehow, making our relationship legal had added a level of seriousness that neither of us foresaw. Before we'd gotten married, we never had arguments; we also never saw any reason to look deeper into long-term expectations. Neither of us cheated or lied to the other as things unraveled, but we were both sort of crestfallen that our passion for each other was somehow waning. She had started to take some things out on me, and I was in turn taking things out on her. I think we both hated ourselves for doing it, but it continued to happen. Mandy and I were both extremely young—I was twenty-five at this point—and naive and vodka-filled. It was a match made for friendship but in no way for marriage and children.

The problems in our relationship also seemed more real now that my mom had seen the full magnitude of them. With no more shows on the horizon and both of us constantly together in the house on Laurel Terrace, things came to a head.

Living down the street, Steven had the best vantage point on our relationship. He knew Mandy and I had sought marriage counseling, and he could see I was in a lot of pain even afterward. He was the one who finally confronted me about things—on Christmas Eve.

"Dude, if you don't have her stuff out by tomorrow, I'm going to do it," he told me. "That'll be ugly. You don't want me coming in there, because I will."

He was right. It was over. I had to admit it. And I had to act. On Christmas Day, 1989, I gave Mandy the Halliburton luggage Aerosmith had given me and asked her to get out. I was adamant. And I was keeping the dog. Merry fucking Christmas.

I felt completely lost and heartbroken. I thought I had let my mom and family down. I thought I had been caught living a lie. Or rather, *lies*, those little lies you tell yourself to help make your life fit a more idealized image. Now they had all suddenly been laid bare. For me it all boiled down to one simple thing: *Just like my dad*, I thought—in whose footsteps I had tried so hard not to follow.

I was so depressed that McBob, my bass tech, quietly slipped into my house one day and removed my shotgun. He later told me he just didn't want to leave it sitting around given the way I was acting. He stashed it inside one of my bass cases and left it in a band storage space.

A lot of people around me hoped that once the day-to-day pain of the marriage and its immediate aftermath faded, I would be able to pull back a little from my everyday vodka habit. But instead of straightening out, I kind of fell apart. My drinking had taken off as the marriage went sour. When Mandy left the house, I started to add more drugs to the mix.

My first drink of the day slipped forward, from about four in the afternoon to more like one. I also started to score larger amounts of cocaine so that I could drink more for longer periods of time. It proved a diabolical cocktail for me. Now I could drink until I finally had to sleep—and if you're doing coke, you don't have to sleep for up to four days in my case. Only then would I start to see trails. The only other time I slowed down was if someone I respected—like my brother Matt—would say, "Slow the fuck down." I also found that Valium or codeine could help to bring me down when I finally needed to sleep after a multiday binge. In my mind I was simply using modern scientific methods to get me through a tough time, and I figured I would cut back on the drugs and booze at some stage when the heartbreak subsided.

One day early in 1990 the phone rang at my place.

"Yeah, uh, is Duff there?" said the voice on the line.

"This is Duff."

"Uh, hi, it's Iggy."

I knew instantly it wasn't some knucklehead friend of mine playing a prank. It was Iggy Pop, and he was in L.A. to make a new album. He asked whether I'd be interested in playing on the record.

"Of course!" I said.

Then, trying to sound somewhat cooler than I was, I added, "I mean, yeah sure."

I had actually met him a little more than a year before. Two days after the end of the Aerosmith tour in September 1988, Guns played a strange festival-type gig at the home of the Dallas Cowboys in Texas. INXS headlined and the opening bands included the Smithereens, Ziggy Marley, and Iggy. I was excited to meet him. After the show, Iggy and I both ended up at a party in the hotel suite of Michael Hutchence, the vocalist for INXS. I was nervous as hell to be in a room with Iggy, a guy who had inspired a dream that stuck with me for the rest of my life—a dream that cemented the direction of my life in many ways. So I commenced to get really fucked up. Michael Hutchence was already as famous for dating models and appearing in paparazzi photos as for singing "Need You Tonight," and I think Iggy felt as out of place as I did—so he joined me. We got fucked up together.

Now he was asking me to play with him. Slash was also enlisted, and we went into the studio along with the kick-ass Kenny Aronoff on drums. I showed up expecting the sessions to be one big drugging and drinking fest—the absolute perfect way to spend a few weeks, I thought. Folklore would surely be passed down about how we rewrote the book on debauchery. But when we got down to Ocean Way recording studio in Hollywood the first day, producer Don Was informed me that Iggy had recently cleaned up his act. I could almost smell the brake pads burning as my runaway ideas about the sessions came to a screeching halt. Oops. I had a full-on drug and drink habit, and now, out of respect, I would have to keep it somewhat on the down-low while recording.

Iggy was no rookie to such games and soon caught on to the fact that Slash and I kept disappearing to the bathroom for lines of cocaine and gulps of our hidden bottles. Iggy was more than cool about our little indiscretions and never sweated us about it. And in the end, one of my all-time favorite gigs was the record release party we played together later that year for the album, called *Brick by Brick*. Sobriety had not changed one thing: whether in a studio or on a stage, Iggy flipped a switch when he performed and on came an incandescent, uncontainable rock-and-roll force, whirling, yelping, raw and fucked up. Raw and fucked up.

Slash and I began to hang out a bunch again. I still eyed an imaginary line and I tried to anticipate potential pitfalls—I would ride a bicycle everywhere so I didn't have to drive home once things got sloppy, for instance. I'd be in shorts and Converse sneakers with a bottle of booze taped to my bike frame. I discovered bike trails in Wilacre Park just above my house and started to detour through there. It was a wild park and pedaling through its arid but tree-covered glens created a sensory effect like sitting at the bottom of a swimming pool: the city suddenly receded, its noise and activity dampened.

Slash's guitar tech, Adam Day, was living down the road with Steven at the time. I liked biking through Wilacre Park so much that I convinced Adam to ride with me sometimes. I'd call him up and we'd go out for a little exercise, riding on Betty Dearing Trail.

For the most part, though, idle time gave me trouble. Work kept me engaged. Sure, I might start drinking toward the end of rehearsal, but I always showed up and always remained coherent. Steven, on the other hand, was beginning to get erratic. His participation in rehearsals and writing and recording sessions became less frequent, and his ability to perform suffered big-time.

Izzy had gotten sober for good by this stage, and he kept his distance from us. During the songwriting process, he would send us homemade cassette tapes of his songs and ideas. There was no animosity about his reluctance to come to rehearsals, and his songs—like "Pretty Tied Up" and "Double Talkin' Jive"—were great.

We decided to contribute our first finished song to a charity album, *Nobody's Child,* being put together by the wives of the members of the Beatles to benefit Romanian orphans. Early in 1990, we went into the studio to record it. Up to now we had always recorded basic tracks together. Slash, Izzy, Steven, and I played in the studio to get the rhythm tracks on tape. The first thing we wanted was a full fluid drum take. Bass and drums always got done quickly in the early days. I hardly ever had to do bass fixes because Steven and I were so solid as a rhythm section. But when we had tried to lay down the basic tracks for "Civil War," producer Mike Clink and I had to patch together the drum track from dozens of inadequate takes—by hand, as this was before digital editing made that sort of thing much easier.

This all coincided perfectly with the implosion of what was left of the band morale. Axl had figured out that if he said he wouldn't do this or he wanted that, ten people would jump. People from the management company, the label, would-be concert promoters, it didn't seem to matter as long as somebody jumped.

Axl also started to see a psychologist, who seemed to consciously feed his megalomania. As far as I was concerned, she took advantage of him and milked the situation.

Sometimes he talked to me about the things she told him.

"Come on, man, this is me you're talking to," I would say. "She's blowing smoke up your ass."

"I know, I know," he would say. "But listen to this . . ."

Of course, I was in no position to throw stones. I dealt with my shit with booze; Axl had now found his way to deal with things.

My marriage was shot, and now the other thing I most loved and cherished seemed to be slipping into a dysfunctional state as well. The band was so huge that like any big bureaucratic or corporate entity it had acquired a momentum of its own. There was no stopping some things. Once again, I didn't know how to deal with it, how to fix it.

Instead I fixated on my belief that my time on earth would be fleeting. *Better go out swinging,* I thought.

And I don't remember a day of peace from 1990 until 1994.

CHAPTER TWENTY-THREE

+ + +

I decided I needed to start fresh in a new house. I found I could rent out the place on Laurel Terrace and cover the mortgage that way, and I started looking for a new place, one without the ghosts of a marriage past. Or maybe just one strategically positioned to make it easier to drink and drive without getting caught.

I bought a new place in 1990. It was also in Laurel Canyon, but this time right at the top, on Edwin Drive, perched on a cliff overlooking Dead Man's Curve on Mulholland Drive. The place was up the hill from the old mansion built by Houdini. Here on the Hollywood side of the hills, Laurel Canyon was still quite countercultural—it was certainly no Beverly Hills. The name originally came from a studio owned by Stan Laurel, as in Laurel and Hardy, and the road up and over the Hollywood Hills through Laurel Canyon had originally been built to connect to that studio. The first places put up in there were hunting lodges. Later Houdini and Marilyn Monroe moved in, development mushroomed, and it became a countercultural enclave. By the 1980s, the Houdini mansion had been split up and a bunch of unreformed hippies lived there in a sort of wizened dorm-party milieu.

There were secret entrances to the area and I could avoid main roads and cops. This seemed important because it was getting harder and harder for me now to wait until 1 p.m. to start my daily doses of pain management.

Early in the afternoon on the day I moved in, Billy Nasty—one of my partners in crime—and I were hitting golf balls off a tee we'd stuck in an artificial fire log. Neither of us knew how to play golf; both of us were wasted. My dog, Chloe, looked on with an expression of placid amusement on her face. She never seemed to hold my shortcomings against me. One ball hit the fence, ricocheted off, and—*crash, shatter*—went right back through the massive picture window of my brand-new place. Chloe flinched. I couldn't stop laughing. The movers looked at me like I was an asshole. I just didn't care.

The house itself had a cool loft space with a spiral staircase. It was fun, light, airy. It provided the inspiration for another new hobby: shooting shotguns off the balcony. Another perk: my go-to coke dealer, Mike, lived right around the corner, and I could whip down to his place and get in and out via little local roads. Or he would deliver the stuff to me.

There grew such trust between us that I had a key to his place and he had a duplicate of my ATM card. I knew he wouldn't steal from me—I was too good a customer. Shit, he even helped me paint things in my new house. We had an ingenious system whereby he would write me fake receipts for stereo components or music equipment, or for servicing or installing the phantom electronics. With these receipts, I had some explanation for my accountants for my constant drug expenditures. Only later did I realize the expenses were always the same amount, three hundred dollars. I didn't really care whether the accountants caught on or not. I was living a constant lie at this point and only halfheartedly trying to hide it.

I needed multiple dealers in case one of them ran short. A guy named Josh was my other main dealer. He brought supplies to my house himself or sent his wife, Yvette. I became social friends with Mike, Josh, and Yvette. I knew that they were not really the type of people I should be hanging out with, but I also convinced myself that they had my best interests at heart. It was just another one of the lies I was telling myself.

I bought a potbellied pig. Again, Chloe took it all in stride. But with me in a haze of drug-fueled partying, the house became quite literally a pigsty. It barely registered with me that there was pig and dog shit everywhere. In fact, it didn't register at all until one of our accountants came by; soon after, he recommended a housekeeping company to me. And I thought, *Oh, is that what you do—house cleaners?*

Pig shit notwithstanding, my house quickly became a regular stop for hard-core partiers. The pool behind the house clung to the very top of the ridgeline and offered a spectacular view out over the valley side of the Hollywood Hills. Now that I was finished with the divorce and was partying for nights on end at various L.A. club nights, that basin of sapphire-blue water often ended up a naked free-for-all. Somehow I still lived the life of a Gardner alleyway urchin: sex, drugs, and, um, excrement. Nice.

One of the girls I started to hang out with was a newscaster. She had pictures in her office of herself with Ronald Reagan and Jesse Jackson. She repeated a catchphrase to close all her on-air reports. Years later she landed a job at a national news network, and every time I heard her finish up with that catchphrase, the image on TV would fade and I would see her paddling around nude in my pool.

A circuit of clubs dominated Hollywood—Bordello, Scream, Cathouse, Vodka, Lingerie, Spice. There was a club to go to each night of the week except Wednesday. I have no idea why Wednesday was an off night. I didn't care. Wednesdays—and after-hours the rest of the week—the party came to my place. I plucked the stand-up bass to accompany Tony Bennett onstage one night in the VIP section of Spice. I got up and played drums with Pearl Jam the first time they came to L.A. for a show at the Cathouse; there was a lot of alcohol consumed that night, but I think we played a song by the Dead Boys together.

I swelled with pride at what was happening up in Seattle—even if I was a little jealous it had taken off without me. Although I loved and lived for GN'R, with things going off the rails I began to do the obvious—to torture myself with what-if scenarios. What if I had stayed in Seattle? Would I have been in Soundgarden or Mother Love Bone? Would I be making records for Sub Pop, the hip and suddenly successful label set up by Bruce Pavitt, my old coworker from the Lake Union Café? I could have stayed close to my family and childhood friends, people I missed more and more as the fabric of Guns—my surrogate family unit—began to fray.

When Alice in Chains came to L.A. for their first gig—at the Palladium right as "Man in the Box" was blowing up as a single—they asked me to come down to the show and play that song with them. Awesome. After their gig that night, I invited the whole band and various hangers-on back up to my house for an after-show party. The party went on for three days straight.

Other news reached me from Seattle—unexpected news about Eddy. He had cleaned up for real. Life was funny: from now on, I was hiding from him, and not the other way around.

My brother Matt moved in with me on Edwin Drive while he fulfilled his student-teaching requirements. He lived in the back bedroom; off his bedroom was one of only two bathrooms in the house—one of the few shortcomings of the place. He taught every day, so he'd come home and sleep while I headed off to wherever the party was that night—and eventually showed up late at night with a gang of people looking to continue the party. I had installed a billiard table and a drum kit in a room abutting Matt's. One night Lars Ulrich from Metallica came over and went up to the bathroom off my brother's room without realizing Matt was there. Lars came out and sheepishly discovered Matt sitting up in bed, wincing. All he said was, "Uh, sorry, man, I just took a big shit."

Sometimes my student-teacher brother had some fun when the parties raged at my house. Mostly, however, he just dealt with the fallout of my dissolute lifestyle. Sometimes I'd head off in the morning to keep partying someplace else and leave any half-dressed, passed-out girls in the house for Matt to drive home. At the time I didn't even realize somebody was driving these girls home. I just knew they were gone when I came home. Yeah, I wasn't exactly the world's most thoughtful roommate at this stage.

There was always a core group of friends around, but the people on the periphery changed all the time. There were hangers-on, interested only because of the notoriety of the band. Those people always changed. People started to ask for money now, too. Not family members; I'd give them anything. All these other people started asking for loans to start businesses. Friends, or friends once removed. "I'm going to start a record store in Manhattan—be my backer on this." At first I would just give money away, feeling my punk-rock guilt.

One solid group of people I hung out with were the guys in some of the gangsta-rap groups of L.A. I became friends with Dr. Dre, Eazy-E, and Ice Cube from N.W.A. as well as people in Ice T's posse. I had seen the sensationalized reaction Guns got by presenting an unedited look at *our* lives on *Appetite*. And white boys in Hollywood weren't exactly a marginalized group. The glimpse of street life presented by N.W.A. and some of the other new hip-hop acts from black Los Angeles was a true shock to the system. These guys lived hard, too, and we had some great parties up at my house.

I did still have some level of self-awareness. I must have harbored an inkling that I was in the process of jumping the rails. That summer I bought a small vacation place in Lake Arrowhead, California, to get out of Los Angeles. I hoped periodically to escape my bad drink and drug habits, and to retreat from the fishbowl effect of living a highly public life in the city.

Lake Arrowhead turned out not to be the ascetic wilderness retreat I had envisioned. Little did I know that Tommy Lee of Mötley Crüe also had a place up there. Bikers and meth ruled the whole area—the sleazy juke joint used for the Patrick Swayze movie *Roadhouse* was the local bar. Instead of drying out on my trips to the lake, I used its remoteness as an excuse to act more extreme. I invited my coke dealers—Mike, Josh, and Yvette—to come up with me for weekends. I bought a boat for waterskiing; parts and service for it provided a new source of fake receipts. Musician friends made road trips up to Lake Arrowhead, too, people like Lenny Kravitz and Ernie C, the guitar player from Body Count—the band that got threatened by the FBI for their song "Cop Killer." The house quickly became an even more debauched party scene than my place above Dead Man's Curve. Back in L.A. one day, Ernie C told me he was scared for me after seeing my intake up at the lake.

Sure, I could scare the shit out of most people who partied with me. But for the second time in my life I realized that nobody—not even me at the time—could hang with the dudes in Mötley Crüe: within two months of buying the house at Lake Arrowhead, I was throwing up blood at Tommy Lee's cabin.

Back in L.A., Chloe broke through the fence around my yard and got pregnant. I had never had her spayed—just couldn't bring myself to have a vet do anything to her that would cause her pain. She had a huge litter of fourteen puppies. Lucky for me, my brother Matt was doing his student teaching at a large school in a very affluent part of the city, and he helped me out by asking there if any kids wanted puppies. We found nice homes for all of them.

Chloe was different after that. She transformed from a lively young lass into a portly grandma almost overnight. Now, instead of lunging headfirst into the pool, she would just walk to the first step and wade there all day long, coming out only for meals and naps. She became a world-class napper after that.

I could have stood to sleep more myself. When I just drank and went to sleep at night, things went fine. Bad decisions would be confined to that one day or night. I might do something stupid, like hit golf balls through my picture window. I would never crash a car—or stick a needle in my arm. Or so I thought. But as I continued doing more and more coke so I could stay up longer and drink more, it began to change my thought processes.

Late one night I heard someone on the doorstep of the Edwin Drive house fumbling with keys. Cowering behind the door in my bathrobe, I tried to figure out what to do. My mind raced immediately to a dark, paranoid place. I ran and grabbed my twelve-gauge and threw open the door, the double barrels of the shotgun shoved in the face of the intruder. Only it was my brother Matt, who was trying to find the right key on his chain, his eyes now gleaming with fear, cursing once I lowered the shotgun and retreated backward into the foyer.

CHAPTER TWENTY-FOUR

✦ ✦ ✦

In the autumn of 1990, we booked our first gigs in more than a year. An eternity. We were going to headline two nights at the Rock in Rio festival in January 1991. When I was growing up, I never dreamed that I might one day have the opportunity to visit such exotic and far-flung places as a result of my music. Bakersfield maybe, but not Brazil. Those gigs now functioned like a lighthouse for me—a reassuring beacon twinkling on the horizon, something fixed and steady to steer toward through churning seas.

We also went into the studio that fall to record the songs for *Use Your Illusion*. When producer Mike Clink and I had pieced together the drum track for "Civil War" earlier that year, it was clear Steven was not going to be able to perform with us if he didn't turn things around. When we had played a couple songs to a huge crowd at Farm Aid in April, he was a mess onstage. After that, we thought we would scare him straight. We told him we were auditioning drummers and figured he'd snap out of it as soon as he heard that. When that didn't work, we hired a professional sober coach, Bob Timmons, who had helped Aerosmith get clean, to talk to him.

Bob took along Sly Stone—who had gotten sober—to Steven's house. Steven had met Sly at my apartment on El Cerrito.

"You know, man," Sly told Steven, "your band is worried about you. You've got to pull it together, Stevie."

Slash and I served as the voice of the band during Steven's last days with GN'R. But no matter what we said to him, nothing changed. We told him we were getting ready to enter the studio. Still no change. Finally, we suggested he get a lawyer. It was meant to scare him, but it proved convenient for Slash, Axl, Izzy, and me. In the end, we had our lawyer tell his lawyer that he was permanently out.

It sounded ironic to a lot of people for us to kick someone out of such a notoriously debauched band for drugs. The truth is we didn't care what drugs people did or how much they did. We cared only about our work and our ability to keep the band moving forward now that we finally had songs to record and shows to play. We didn't give a shit about cause, just effect. Drugs? Sure. But it could just as easily have been something else. Lack of motivation. Jail time. Death. For me, I always thought death and death alone could ever push me across that line when it came to this band. (I was wrong.) For Steven, coke and heroin proved enough to nudge him across.

It was heartbreaking, especially for me and Slash, but we had to find a replacement drummer.

When we booked Rock in Rio, we thought we would have plenty of time to find a new drummer. After all, the trip was months away, and we had lots of songs to record, too; we assumed that between rehearsing and recording, the new rhythm section could gel in plenty of time for those gigs. But the studio time kept getting pushed back further and further as we cast about for someone acceptable. The same thing that had made Steven an important part of our sound also made it difficult to replace him—his sense of groove. We tried out drummer after drummer. Things started to look a bit grim. Shit, maybe this would be the end of the band. Like Hanoi Rocks. Like Led Zeppelin. For those bands, losing their drummers signaled the end of the road.

Thankfully, at the very last moment we found Matt Sorum, who had been playing with the Cult. We had twenty-seven songs to record, and some of them—like "November Rain," "Coma," and "Locomotive"—were epic in length. Matt had to learn all the songs in rehearsals and make charts of them for the recording sessions. At the same time, he started to try to keep up with me and Slash on the drinking front. We recorded the first twenty-four songs fast. But between the volume of work, the volume of booze, and the pressure of recording with a band that was being treated as the biggest thing in town, Matt hit a wall. With three songs to go, he disappeared. I left messages begging him to come in and finish the last three songs. No answer. I told him I'd buy him drugs out of my own pocket. No answer.

He was renting my old place on Laurel Terrace during the recording sessions, so I went down there to look for him.

"Matt?" I called as I entered the house. "Where are you, pal?"

No answer.

I walked through the house.

In the bedroom, there was a deep walk-in closet. The door was closed, but I could hear someone in there. I opened the door tentatively and peered in, letting my eyes adjust to the darkness: there was Matt, cowering in the back of the closet with a pile of coke, just hiding from the world. He looked at me with no sign of recognition in his eyes. He was completely out of it and paranoid. I made him a very strong vodka drink to bring him down a bit from his coke high.

Matt pulled it together and nailed the last three songs. But by the time we started the process of mixing the records, something snapped inside me, too. There were so many songs to deal with. There was so much contention in the band over credits and everything else. I could tell there were subplots developing among the remaining band members, among management, among the label people. I looked around at how fame and a little bit of power and money had affected the guys I'd been in the trenches with.

Oh, really? This is how we're going to react to it all?

I was disappointed. It was a mess and I wanted nothing to do with it.

We—was it "we" anymore?—had finally made it to the threshold of another accomplishment. A record. Actually a double record. But I was no longer sure what it represented.

Is this why I moved to L.A.—for this? Is this what "making it big" meant?

I had already attained some of the things I'd wanted to when I left Seattle for California. Far more than I'd wanted. Far more than I could even have imagined. But as I looked around now, it was more clear than ever that things hadn't panned out the way I had expected. I wasn't living in a utopian punk commune with Donner and the gang. Friends were dead. Fans were dead. My marriage was dead. My band had lost a member and seemed to be either dying or transforming itself into something I no longer felt connected to.

Something else nagged at me, too, as Rock in Rio edged closer and closer.

Is anyone going to show up to our gigs in Brazil?

Sure, the promoter told us the gigs would sell out, but that was just his word. We had long since learned that a promoter's word wasn't always a solid piece of currency. Maracaña Stadium was the biggest *in the world*! Frank Sinatra had played there, Paul McCartney had played there, Pope John Paul II had played there. But us? We had played fewer than a half-dozen gigs in the past two years, and our one and only proper album had come out nearly four years ago.

Headlining two nights? In South America? Really?

I started to hit the bottle harder, which meant taking more coke, which allowed me to drink harder, which meant more coke . . . up to that point I had always thought I would address my drinking *someday*. Even if it had always been a lie, it exerted an element of control—there was a horizon. Right then, after recording the *Illusion* records, that horizon went dark. I lost all sense of orientation.

Then, on January 17, 1991, we boarded an American Airlines jet bound for Rio. This would be one of the longest flights I'd ever taken. A plane is a metal tube with no way out, and I have always been claustrophobic. Whenever I flew home to see family and friends in Seattle, I had to pay for someone else to come with me. Because of my panic attacks, I couldn't even contemplate heading to the airport alone. I self-medicated with whatever was available. For the flight to Rio, I took bindles of coke to snort in the airport lounge so I could stay upright and shuffle down the jetway. I was terrified. The flight, the gigs, the band. The flight, the gigs, the band. Fear. Doubt. Valium. *Stewardess. Vodka. Please.*

Out.

"Ladies and gentleman, this is your captain speaking."

Huh?

I looked out the window. Nothing.

"A little news here from the cockpit. I just received word that U.S. forces have begun bombing Iraq in Operation Desert Storm. America is at war."

What the fuck?

I started to worry about our reception in Rio. Would we be greeted as American warmongers? I was hoping just to get to the hotel and duck into my room unnoticed.

Again: *Is anyone going to show up to these gigs?*

Vodka. Valium. Vodka.

As we began our descent, I was exhausted from the constant to-and-fro of getting plastered and coming to again, from trying to get hold of huge quantities of alcohol from the flight crew to quell my panic without appearing panicked or out of control.

We taxied in and I staggered off the plane, bleary-eyed. I felt like a fucking Martian after traveling for so long and feeding my body with mind-numbing intoxicants.

What are all these people doing here? Why are they screaming?

A crowd of 8,000 fans greeted us at the gate. I was overwhelmed; they were overjoyed. We shuffled out to a van. Lots of security guys in and around the vans.

Machine guns, really?

Hotel. Nowhere near the famous beaches. Swank hotel, for sure, but perched just below the city's most infamous favela, a dense hillside slum called Rocinha.

Why here? None of the other bands are staying here.

Prince, George Michael, INXS—the other headliners—were staying elsewhere.

Why are we being kept apart from the other bands?

Next day. Rehearsal. Some shitty little space downtown. Guys with machine guns on our van again. A second van carrying more ex-military types with automatics. Following us everywhere. As we wound our way through the city, I had my first chance to see Rio's inhabitants in their natural state—which apparently was screaming "Guns N' Roses" at the top of their lungs.

During the next day there—a scheduled day off—I went to the hotel pool in my shorts and flip-flops to get some sun and drink myself into a stupor. The pool had a swim-up bar and was surrounded by dozens of toweled lounge chairs. Palm trees, exotic flowers, lush grounds all around.

No wonder there are so many gardeners.

People hovered around the periphery of the pool and gardens like flies.

Hang on—are those . . . I must be fucked up. Are those fans?

What I had taken for gardeners outside of the high fence surrounding the pool area were actually hundreds of fans. Now the security forces ran off the poor kids.

This city is on fire for GN'R.

Maracaña Stadium: 175,000 people and a river of sewage streaming right through the place. An actual river. Of shit.

People chanting, "Guns N' Roses, Guns N' Roses!"

The audience cried and sang along to every word as we launched into our set.

Fucking hell, there are a lot of people up here onstage.

We had two new keyboard players, backup singers, and horn players. The sides of the stage swarmed with crew and management and who knows who else.

Where my boys at?

I turned and looked toward the drum riser. Steven wasn't there.

+ PART FOUR +

I'D LOOK RIGHT UP AT NIGHT AND ALL I'D SEE WAS DARKNESS

CHAPTER TWENTY-FIVE

✦ ✦ ✦

The shows in Rio should have marked the triumphant beginning of a new phase in the history of the band, but instead it felt as if Guns N' Roses had somehow changed from a band into a traveling extravaganza in which we each just played a more or less independent role. We had added more people to the band, but there was much less sense that we were a unit of any kind, big or small. During that trip to Brazil, I sometimes felt completely alone and alienated even in my own band. I loved Guns N' Roses, I loved all the members of Guns N' Roses, including the new guys. But something still felt terribly wrong.

I drank every day prior to Rock in Rio, but I could still pull myself out of it at times and curtail my drinking. The shows in Rio were the beginning of a three-year headlong dive into drugs and booze—the darkest days of my life. For me, there was a difference between drinking a half gallon of vodka a day and drinking a quart or a liter. A liter was pretty good. Beginning in Rio, I drank half a gallon a day, every day.

Back in L.A., Mandy called me to say she was going to start dating. *Great, you should.* Her new boyfriend had a posse of friends. They showed up at the Rainbow one night and came up to me in the parking lot while I was waiting for my car. The boyfriend introduced himself, all puffed up and threatening.

"She's always fucking talking about you," he said, "and I want to let you know that I'm the guy now."

I didn't have a problem with that, I told him.

He confronted me a second time another night. Finally, the third time, at Spice club, I was drunk and pissed off that he kept doing this, so I said, "Okay, dude, you want to do something about it?"

We went outside through a side door. He had his friends and I had mine. He took a swing at me and I ducked. I got lucky—he missed. As I came up I swung and broke his nose. He went straight down.

I felt bad the next day. Someone called me and said he'd been taken to the hospital. I asked them to give him my phone number.

He called and said, "Hey, I can't afford this hospital bill."

"Listen, man, I'm real sorry about decking you," I said. "How much is the bill?"

"Four hundred and fifty bucks," he said.

"Well, I can help you out," I said. "How about I pay half?"

"That would be great, man, thanks," he said.

Then he added, "That was a great shot you put on me, by the way."

I told him to come up to my house to pick up the money, but warned him not to come with his dudes. Come alone. It took him a few days to swing by, but finally he showed up. I could see his mom in the car. Cool. I went out to the front gate and handed him an envelope with $225. At the same time he handed me an envelope and started running back down the street. Huh? I opened it. He had served me. He was going to try to sue me. For $1.25 million.

I had given my word that I would pay half his bill, I had apologized, and that's what I got. It pissed me off. I was paranoid, as usual, from all the cocaine. I called management and told them. In the end it went to arbitration and we settled for a few thousand dollars. From then on, I wanted to kill anyone who crossed me at any club or concert. In my mind I was still fighting for righteous reasons—not just to hurt people but to *protect*, to make bullies stop doing bad things. But it's pretty clear in retrospect that I was taking out aggression about the situation with the band. I would find offense in the stupidest little things and then I'd just flip and go street. Management quickly set up a security detail to follow me around all the time. Even so, out every night and for days on end, I

My brother Mark left for Vietnam when I was three years old. That's me bawling my head off with my mother and my brother Matt beside me. This is one of my first memories ever.

With all of my sibs, looking oh so groovy for 1972. That's me in the middle in the "UW" shirt.

Playing rhythm guitar with Ten Minute Warning in 1982 at the Metropolis in Seattle. *Photograph by Charles Peterson.*

With Ten Minute Warning in 1983. I had all of the hope in the world. *Photograph by Charles Peterson.*

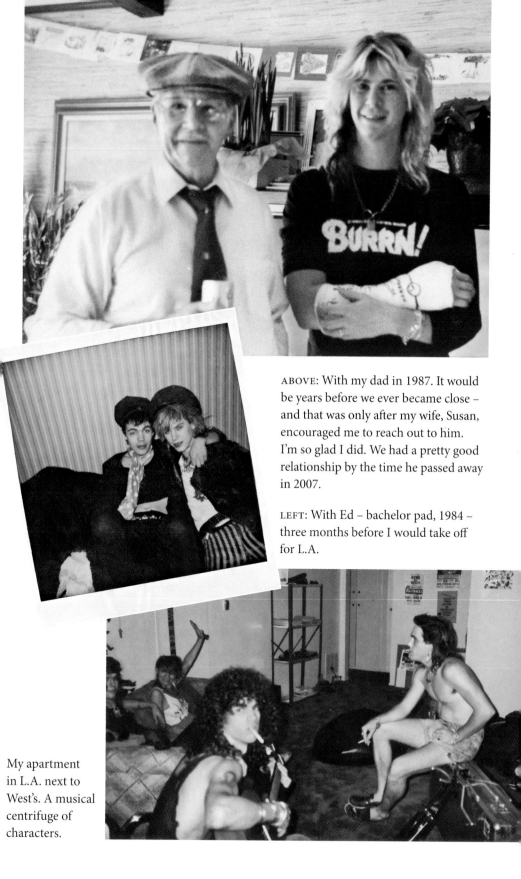

ABOVE: With my dad in 1987. It would be years before we ever became close – and that was only after my wife, Susan, encouraged me to reach out to him. I'm so glad I did. We had a pretty good relationship by the time he passed away in 2007.

LEFT: With Ed – bachelor pad, 1984 – three months before I would take off for L.A.

My apartment in L.A. next to West's. A musical centrifuge of characters.

ABOVE: The Vains – Chris, Andy, and me – gearing up for a show, circa 1979. *Photograph © Lance Mercer.*

RIGHT: Flyer for our 1985 show in Seattle: the first and only gig of the Hell Tour. The show ended up being shifted to June 12, and into the other (smaller) room at the same venue. *Photograph © Lance Mercer.*

GUNS and ROSES

Featuring:
ex-Ten Minute Warning
member Duff McKagan

with

FASTBACKS

plus 5150

SAT., JUNE 8

ROCK THEATER

5th & Jackson

Rare photos from the recording sessions for *Live Like a Suicide!* at Pasha Studio in Hollywood. *Photographs by Jeff Clark.*

RIGHT: Owning the right side of the stage with Izzy at an early Guns gig. He and I have remained good friends to this day. *Photograph by Marc Canter.*

BELOW: Onstage, 1986, with Guns. This is the bass that I got just before I moved to L.A. It's the one I wrote all the bass lines for *Appetite* on. *Photograph by Jack Lue.*

Now *that* is a rock and roll band. *Photograph by Marc Canter.*

They called us the
Rose Bros then.
Photograph by Jack Lue.

Slash's playing blew my mind from the first moment.
Photograph by Marc Canter.

ABOVE: Hair falling out and gloves on to protect my cracking hands. Puffy as fuck.

Bloated and hopeless, just before the fall.

LEFT: With Cully in the hills above L.A. Riding mountain bikes was a large part of my learning how to live a new life.
Photograph by Chris Hatounian.

BELOW: With Andy in 1995. I was one year sober, and he looks relieved.

RIGHT: In Hawaii. I think I just found out Susan was pregnant. Susan took this photo.

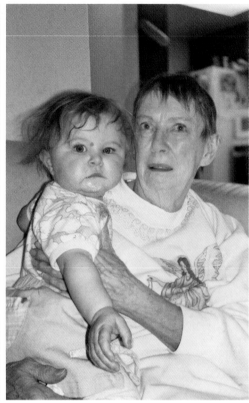

Susan and I with brand-newborn Grace. The beginning stages of me becoming a grown-up.

I was glad that my mom got to know Grace.

Teaching Grace to swim, under the watchful eyes of Barney and Chloe.

LEFT: Susan and I get married in Seattle! Grace was our flower girl.

BELOW: Grace and I backstage at a Velvet Revolver gig.

Baby Mae! In every picture I own of her as an infant, I am kissing those cheeks!

LEFT: Velvet Revolver at the premier of *The Hulk*. Our first ever band photo.

BELOW: VR at the El Rey in LA. Our first gig. *Photograph by Karl Larsen.*

Susan and I in New York on the way into a David Letterman taping of VR. *Photograph by Tina Marie.*

On tour with Velvet Revolver. Nice pants! *Photograph by Karl Larsen.*

Ah, the fog of a relapse.

Back in the saddle and sober again.

Hitting the dojo with Benny, my sensei, mentor, and brother.

ABOVE: Touring in Europe with Loaded for *The Taking* album. *Photograph by Afshin Shahidi.*

Love playing for our European fans – with Loaded in Lille, France. *Photograph by Afshin Shahidi.*

LEFT: The McKagan girls on vacation in Hawaii.

BELOW: The McKagans tour in London in 2010. We're a happy family!

BELOW: On stage in Buenos Aires just before I call my professor. "Duff *who*?"

managed to get into a few more scraps between Rio and the start of what would be our first-ever headlining tour.

As the first tour dates approached, Slash and I would periodically drive down to an industrial area in Compton to check on the construction of the massive stage set that would be our home for the next two and a half years. When it was complete, the set was moved to an airplane hangar over in Burbank where we commenced our full-production, full-set rehearsals. Lights. Monitors. Full PA. Full crew. All the additional musicians.

In May 1991, we had three warm-up shows. We were ready to go, but the tortuous process of mixing the *Illusion* records was still dragging on. We were forced to start the tour—a tour meant to support these albums—several months before there was even a release date for the records. Though I am sure it would have been better for our fans to know some of the songs we were playing, I found myself feeling that it was a very GN'R move. The *old* GN'R. *Fuck expectations. Fuck doing things by the book.*

It put us back in the position of having to win audiences over. And that played to our strength. That would draw us together, make us a team again.

We leased a 727 jet from the MGM casino to use for the entire length of the tour. Prior to setting off, we got to pick out our flight attendants from a sort of catalogue. We certainly had a nice-looking crew as a result. Stellar, in fact. The first thing I noticed upon entering the MGM Grand jet was a fully stocked bar that stretched from the door back toward the middle of the plane. Cream-colored chairs and bolted-down tables fanned out from the bar, creating the party room. To the left, running from the door to the cockpit, were big captain's chairs and a movie screen. I hardly went up there for whatever reason—it was too exposed and open. In the back were staterooms reserved solely for the band members—except Izzy. Izzy traveled on his own. He was still keeping his distance.

Each stateroom had a door, curtains, a fold-out bed, a dresser with a mirror, and a TV. As the plane taxied out onto the runway for our first flight, Slash and I repaired to one of the staterooms and smoked crack. I remember watching the smoke curl up into the air vent and thinking this just seemed logical. *Of course we can smoke on here, it's our plane.*

I looked at myself in the mirror in the midst of a rock-fueled rush: *This is going to be awesome.*

CHAPTER TWENTY-SIX

+   +   +

At Alpine Valley Amphitheatre in Wisconsin, my sense of anticipation for the first gig of the tour was overwhelming. Our intro music came on: the theme song from *The Godfather*.

The crowd roared.

Here we go.

My game face came on. I felt we represented something, something primal and animalistic. I felt that fire and anger—I was ready to kick someone in the head. All the background noise of life began to recede. We rushed the stage and I played the first few bass notes for "It's So Easy."

Total fucking bedlam. Tens of thousands of people absolutely losing their shit. I could see the first few rows of people. I could see how far back the masses of bodies went. Everyone was on their feet and the roar was almost louder than the band.

Again I thought: *This is going to be awesome.*

During the first month, we flew to amphitheatres and racetracks and basketball stadiums across the Midwest and Northeast. I did not have one panic attack aboard the MGM 727. It must have hinged on the fact that I had some level of control. With our own private jetliner, I knew I could go to the pilot and say, "Land, now." Of course, it didn't hurt that I also had ready access to as much booze and as many pills as I wanted, at any time.

But I soon realized this was *not* going to be awesome.

I'm not sure exactly which gig it was when Axl first showed up late to the venue, but it was very early in the tour. Don't get me wrong, I had never been a taskmaster about start times. I was as anti-establishment as the best of them, and going onstage right at the exact contractually obligated time wasn't on the top of my list of things to do each day. But as the fans became more and more upset about the late starts, it dawned on me that they were upset because they had to go to work or school the next day or had a babysitter at home watching their kids. Sometimes we came on so late that a significant percentage of the crowd had gone home.

A headlining band usually went on about 9 p.m. When we had opened for other bands in 1987 and 1988 and there had been any nervousness about us starting on time, the tour managers—the headliners' tour managers, that is—used to say, "I don't know when you're going on, but I know when you're going off." That was because most venues had 11 p.m. curfews and the headliners had to get their sets in by then. Curfews existed for any number of reasons: the venue might have a deal with its union workers or legal compromises with the surrounding residential neighborhoods; there were noise ordinances; the local public-transport schedule might play a role. Broken curfews often entailed a fine for the performer. Sometimes it was a set fee, other times it could be $1,000 per minute in overtime fees. In the most financially extreme cases, the band was on the hook for a huge fine *and* all the additional double-time wages for union stagehands and police and security. Obviously, unless you just loved to piss away your hard-earned money, you tried to wrap your show up within curfew times.

We kept going on later and later, and the crowds became restless and angry after our opener, Skid Row, finished and we failed to appear. Slash, Matt, and I ended up pushing our drinking and drug use to the extreme as the tour went on and things got worse and worse. Under normal circumstances, we were trying to get to the perfect level of buzz before a show started. When the shows began to start later and later, we ended up going way past that point.

Tension mounted within the band as we waited for Axl to show up and agree to go on. And because ticket holders also had to wait, tension mounted between the band and the audience. Some nights we would go on forty-five minutes late. Other times, one, two, or even three hours late. The only way I could bear the chants of "bullshit" from crowds of 20,000 people for an hour or two was to guzzle more booze. Inevitably, given the constantly changing amount of time I had to kill and the shifting magnitude of band strife and audience annoyance, I would drink too much. Then I'd have to do some coke to come up off the floor. Then, *oops,* too much coke, better drink some more. It was a vicious cycle.

I guess I hoped management would handle the lateness so we could avoid intraband strife. That's what I thought managers did, the very reason we paid them. But Axl had become a dictator before whom everyone—crew, promoters, even management now that Axl had switched us from Alan Niven to Doug Goldstein—quivered in fear. Doug seemed more concerned with the short-term goal of placating Axl than with making things run well for the long term. So I silently fumed at others, building up black resentment.

Izzy's sobriety functioned only if he traveled separately and stayed in different hotels from us. I had gotten used to not having him around, but it was still a blow to the band. From day one, Izzy and I had shared the right side of the stage. We had seen everything—from our rise through the L.A. clubs to these massive arena shows—from the exact same perspective. The perception in popular culture is that the singer and the lead guitar player are generally the artistic brain trust of any band. In our case, Izzy was probably the most significant force—without his initial vision and his songwriting cues, there would have been no Guns N' Roses. He and I still had our time together on the right side of the stage. But those moments made me think Izzy was extremely uncomfortable with the way we were treating our fans.

Still, I didn't have the self-confidence—or whatever—to do anything about it. Mostly because that would have meant looking in the mirror. I couldn't start calling people out—*that guy's always late, that guy's always high*—without eventually coming back around to my own drinking. So I just threw up my hands. *It's all fucked.* The situation made me angry, *really angry;* I've never dealt well with anger.

I began to have panic attacks all the time, bad ones. The attacks felt like being on a merry-go-round just starting up, then going faster and faster until it was too fast; then the ride turned into a Gravitron, where you are spinning so fast you are pinned to the walls and the bottom drops—you're unable to move, unable to make it stop, unable to get off. *I'm trapped.* The sugar in alcohol exacerbated panic attacks, as did cocaine. But drinking even more was the only way I knew to combat the attacks. It was a harrowing experience each time I arrived at a concert venue.

There were transcendent moments onstage. Some nights we were so "on" that it was otherworldly. A few nights we got into such a groove that we played three-hour sets. But we never aired what was bothering us about one another. Nobody ever stated outright to Axl how much we resented going on late or having him stop shows. Nobody told me I was drinking too much or doing too much cocaine. We were all kept separate and that is the way we began to like it. We each had our own security guards. We each had our own twenty-four hour limos picking us up planeside and taking us to the hotel and anywhere else we wished to go. We rode separately to and from the gigs. We had separate dressing rooms. A sense of band unity was evident only when we were onstage. Otherwise it was every man for himself.

Then came a gig at the Riverport Amphitheatre outside St. Louis on July 2, 1991.

The show started about an hour late—which by this point almost counted as on time. We played about an hour and a half, and were in the middle of "Rocket Queen" when all hell broke loose. For reasons that don't matter—they were immediately eclipsed not only by the coverage of the incident but also in the moment, onstage, as events unfolded—Axl dove into the audience to try to address something the house security had not. His foray didn't last long, and I helped pull him upright as he lunged back up onstage. He then strode to the mic and announced that because security hadn't done their job, he was leaving. He slammed the mic down and stormed off. We quickly followed.

For about ten minutes, we waited in the wings, unsure what to do.

Since we all had our own dressing rooms and staff and Axl had hurried off to his, we didn't know whether or not he was planning to return. We thought he probably would. The crowd seemed to think so, too.

Unlike a lot of venues, this one had a huge set of sliding doors at the back of the stage that could be closed and locked with chains. Most of the equipment not visible from the audience was already in a position to be locked backstage. After that first ten minutes, the tone of the crowd changed and people began to throw stuff at the stage. The crew started to shift some of the items in front of our set out of harm's way—guitars, amp racks.

Every time crew members went out now to grab something, all sorts of shit rained down. It was coming steadily. Most dangerous of all were the venue's plastic chairs with pieces of their metal frames still attached. Those were heavy. I could hear the thuds as they landed on the stage and bounced off the walls.

We had been in a riot once before, when we played the Street Scene festival in L.A. in 1986, opening for Fear. That day cops had come through on horseback and cleared the audience as we were about to go on. But we didn't lose any equipment, and nobody got hurt. We were shuttled over to a different stage at the festival and opened for Social Distortion instead. Just a fun story for a band like ours, another notch on the bedpost in a way. Now, scanning the scene from the backstage area in Missouri, we began to worry about the scale of what we were witnessing. Much of the venue was already in ruins. Were people getting hurt?

Axl re-emerged from his dressing room and we offered to go back out and play to calm things down. It was too late.

Security tried to push the crowd back from the stage with a fire hose. But the crowd got the hose and backed our entire crew, the house security, and all the local cops behind the sliding doors. The crowd now had total control of everything in front of the stage. Kids were climbing our hanging speaker towers, destroying our monitors, smashing lights.

We hunkered down backstage. We were lucky. In a lot of venues there is no chained door and the crowd would have taken over the entire venue.

Once the gates were closed and the kids had the stage, the crew did not go back out—there was no reason for anyone to risk opening a door and poking their head out to see what was going on.

But we could hear it all. Screams, crashes, the thunder of thousands of feet. *Boom, boom, boom, WHOOSH. Rumble, rumble, boom, AAAAAAAAAH!* Shouts, more thunder, the scraping groan of large objects being pushed around.

Another twenty minutes went by before forty or fifty police cars came screaming in and backup police stormed and retook the venue.

The band was shoved into a small van and told to get on the floor so we weren't visible. Slash's hat was sticking up. The driver asked him to take it off. When the van drove out of the enclosed part of the venue and into the parking lot, I could hear that the mayhem had spread outside. As we pulled out of the parking lot, I peeked out the back window—I could see speaker cabinets and pieces of our pianos. Kids had gotten tired of carrying them or dumped them when the cops showed. Clots of cops ran around with batons and pepper spray. Kids ran this way and that. Medics rushed around treating bloodied fans. Police had people in cuffs. It looked like a war zone.

Oh, no. Fuck, no. Fans hurt—again. Please don't let anyone die.

The van took us to our hotel, we ran in and grabbed our bags, and then we got back in and headed across the state line into Illinois to avoid any legal difficulties. We drove all the way to Chicago—management figured the cops would go straight to our plane if they were going to try to arrest us.

Every gig after Riverport, the threat of violence hung in the air—or at least it felt that way to me as I sat around stewing, waiting for our singer to turn up each night, listening nervously for the festive noise of the arena to transform into the low rumble of a big, angry crowd. A crowd could turn and you could hear it. I knew that sound now. I knew that if you were at the wrong end of that, it was scary. And I knew it meant more than a bit of property damage. It meant casualties.

CHAPTER TWENTY-SEVEN

+ + +

Once the crew was able to take stock of our gear in the wake of the riot, we canceled three shows. We flew to Irving, Texas, to put things back together, hoping to restart the tour with two shows in Dallas. The stage set itself was pretty strong and for the most part survived. Our crew called sound and lighting companies to try to reassemble the gear and we waited for things to come in. We also had to replace the two pianos.

We looked at venues differently now. In fact, a crew catchphrase came out of the Riverport riot: *Know your exits.*

We continued the tour the second week of July, in Dallas. The first night back, Axl wouldn't go on until two hours after we were supposed to start. But it's not as if I went to him and said, "Come on, buddy, let's go." I just grabbed another plastic cup filled with vodka and a tiny splash of cranberry juice. And another. And another. And so it went.

At the very end of July, we had a four-night home stand at the Great Western Forum in L.A. We also *finally* completed the mixing of the two *Use Your Illusion* albums at the same time we arrived back in L.A. We celebrated with a four-hour show the last night of the Great Western Forum run, August 3, 1991.

It felt awesome for a change. The records were a *band* accomplishment. *We* were moving forward together—even if only on vinyl.

The rest of the band took off for Europe after the L.A. shows. I stayed behind for my brother Matt's wedding. Robert John, our photographer, agreed to stick with me and help me make it through the flights, since I would have to fly commercial to catch up with our band jet in Europe. I needed to fly with a bro, someone who knew about my panic attacks. I gave the best man's toast and then had to leave.

Robert and I flew first to Paris and then had to take a smaller flight from Paris to Helsinki, Finland, where we were kicking off the first European leg of the tour. When we went to board the plane to Helsinki, the entire flight was full of schoolkids. Apparently in Europe whole school classes took field trips to other countries. So there we were—me and Robert, and a huge metal tube full of French schoolkids staring at us. I was so fucked up by the time we took that flight that Robert just put a coat over my head.

The fog cleared a bit as we drove from the Helsinki airport toward the band hotel.

Ugh.

So beat.

Stiff. I groan.

Where am I again?

The echo of all those kids' voices: *Là-bas! Oui, c'est lui!*

Starting to shake.

Drink, just need a drink. *A drink.* A big one.

Room service: a half gallon of vodka, please.

Uh, large bottle, extra-large bottle—*any* bottle.

And ice.

Off to a club. The Black Crowes? Why not.

Vodka.

Surely someone has lined up a coke connection here.

More vodka.

Too tired to sleep.

But then again.

Rehearsal tomorrow.

Pill.

The next night Axl walked offstage just as we started playing "Welcome to the Jungle" and disappeared for twenty-five minutes or so. That was the first show of this leg of the tour. At the fourth show, in Stockholm,

Sweden, he went to a street festival and watched fireworks before turning up to the gig three hours late. When you are an alcoholic, you need your intake or you get the shakes. You time your intake. We'd never go on at nine when we were supposed to. So I'd time it for, say, eleven, but when the wait extended longer and longer, it screwed everything up.

A few nights later, Axl's assistant called us in Oslo as we were getting ready for a sold-out show there. He said Axl was in Paris. He wouldn't be playing the concert.

I could see right then and there that Izzy wasn't going to last. The cadence of his walk was different now: I saw it as clearly as the lurch of a bicycle with a misshapen wheel. His face was drawn, his eyes blank, his body language exhausted.

He had made it with us, sober, touring. But he couldn't stand pissing off the fans and torturing the crew. He had to confront that reality sober. And at the same time he had to deal with Slash, Matt, and me trying to bury our own frustrations by obliterating ourselves with drink and drugs. It was only a matter of time now.

This cannot be happening.

Head down.

Bottoms up.

CHAPTER TWENTY-EIGHT

✛ ✛ ✛

I open my eyes.

Where the fuck am I?

Thirsty as a motherfucker. Vodka?

Vodka, vodka, vodka.

I sit up. Drape my legs over the edge of the bed. Elbows on knees. Head in hands. I groan.

Vodka.

Fumble for the phone.

I clear my throat and spit on the floor.

Into the phone: ice.

Where the fuck am I?

That sound, that ominous sound.

Schiesse!

Scheisse, scheisse, scheisse.

Not a good word. The change in tone.

The bad rumble of a stadium of fans becoming foes. Again. *Not again, please.*

I throw my full cup onto the floor of the stage. *No!* I turn around and glare toward the wings of the stage. I hold my thumb and pointer finger far apart and thrust my hand toward my bass tech, McBob. Then I pinch them almost together and gesture again. *That much vodka and that much cranberry.*

I spit on the hotel carpet again and rub my eyes. Knock at the door. Thank fuck: ice.

I pour a tumbler of vodka over the fresh ice cubes.

Back in the jet, snort some more coke. Vodka. Vodka, vodka, vodka. *No, Izzy, man. No, it's not going down like this. But no.*

The whole room is vibrating. With anger. From within and, more ominously, from without.

Scheisse, scheisse, scheisse!

Mannheim, Germany. Last night. Maybe several nights ago now. Nights not slept.

They're here for us. They hate us. They're here for us. I can't stop shaking. Give me another drink. I hold my thumb and pointer finger far apart and thrust my hand toward the caterer. Then I pinch them almost together and gesture again. *That much vodka and that much cranberry.*

Fuck, not again, Axl. There's no going back from this.

I see the line. I'm standing with my toes right on it. Time for a line. Another sort of line. Sober up. I disappear behind a stack of amps.

Flying like an aeroplane. Feeling like a space brain.

Get me to my airplane.

Get me the fuck out of here. Wembley? Vodka. Only an hour and a half gone by since the openers. On we go. I can stand. I can see.

Izzy, man, this was *your* band. This was *our* band. *Our gang.* This is a fucking war of attrition.

CHAPTER TWENTY-NINE

✦ ✦ ✦

When Axl left the stage in Mannheim, Germany, another riot looked inevitable. We had gone on really late again. The venue was huge, an outdoor stadium packed with twice as many people as even the biggest of the basketball arenas we had played in the United States up to this point.

Matt Sorum tried a novel approach when Axl left; maybe to a "new" guy it was the obvious thing to do. He went to find Axl and confront him. He was turned away by Axl's security detail.

The promoters—not the band members, not the managers, not the entourage—saved the day. Their threat that Axl would be arrested if a riot occurred might not have worked on its own. But they had also locked us into the venue.

Axl returned and finished the show. Izzy disappeared as soon as the houselights came up. We still had one final show left on that leg of the tour, at Wembley Stadium on the last day of August 1991. I knew now that Izzy was definitely going to quit, but nobody knew for sure when he would actually leave us.

Izzy didn't walk away and force the cancellation of the Wembley show. He stayed and played one last gig to draw the curtains on this leg of the tour—the last show before the release of the albums we were ostensibly touring.

Axl arrived on time.

We played spectacularly well, as fierce and inspired and *together* as ever before. If not for the additional people and gear onstage, it could have been mistaken for one of our club shows.

When the show was over, we limped back to L.A. and had about three months off before we had to set out on the next leg. My brother had since moved out to a life and family of his own and nobody from the band wanted to see the other members. I was alone.

I needed a tumbler of vodka and two lines of coke just to get off the mattress when I woke up. Alcohol and drugs I now bought in bulk. I wanted to have a sure supply around all the time. I was alone in my house and had no one and nothing to stop me from ingesting bad stuff whenever I wished. Panic attacks had been coming daily at this point, and they didn't stop once I arrived home. I always took a bottle of vodka with me if I was going anywhere outside of my comfort zone, which is to say anywhere outside a ten-block radius of my house.

In late September, *Use Your Illusion I* and *II* finally came out and went to one and two on the album charts. In October, ousted drummer Steven Adler initiated a lawsuit against the band. In November, Izzy officially quit.

Ever since I was very young, I would just shut down sometimes. As if I were in a trance, sitting silently. Despite growing up in a huge and social family, I never knew how to talk things through with others very well. I probably thought it was a sign of weakness, a transgression against a false concept of manliness I held. Manliness was something I obsessed over after my dad took off. Now I was trying to deal with so many things without talking to anyone about any of it. I was also letting what I did define who I was as a person. *I am the punk-rock torch carrier! I wear the Sid Vicious chain! I am in the biggest, baddest band in the world! I am a party animal celebrating all my good fortune!*

One morning, I found myself in my walk-in closet with a loaded shotgun. I had the barrel in my mouth and my right thumb on the trigger.

As I sat in my darkened closet with the twelve-gauge in my mouth, I thought about my waterskiing accident and the glimpse I'd had of the other side—the warm embrace, the blissful calm. How peaceful death seemed, a simple and beautiful way out. *Take me down. Take me home. Paradise* . . .

My surroundings came flooding back in—the closet, the house, the hilltop, the buildings and beings sprawling out in every direction. And a thousand miles away on the distant horizon, my mom. I pulled the gun out of my mouth.

What has happened to my life?

CHAPTER THIRTY

✦ ✦ ✦

We had only a few weeks to find a rhythm guitar player for the next leg of the tour, which started the first week of December 1991. We hired Kill For Thrills guitarist Gilby Clarke to replace Izzy. Billy Nasty took good care of my dog, Chloe, when I was away, but she still looked sad when I packed my bags to head out on the next leg.

After two shows in Massachusetts, we played three nights at Madison Square Garden. The first night, Axl showed up late. I hated listening to the crowd chanting "bullshit" after the first hour's delay. We had three more hours of that. I drank more and more to deaden the angry sounds. I was fucking wasted.

By this point, the security guys were supposed to keep me from getting cocaine. They didn't care about my drinking, it was the drugs they worried about. Actually, the problem wasn't really the drugs, but procuring them: management wanted these security agents to keep me from getting arrested on some dumb-ass attempted drug score, as GN'R was their golden goose and they needed to keep us on the road. Truck, the security agent assigned to me, was charged with keeping things around me to a dull roar. Axl's guy, Earl, also spent most of his efforts on me, too, as Axl wasn't making drug runs. These guys were very good at their jobs, but the drug addict in me just got craftier and wilier as I was backed into a corner.

Gilby was under less scrutiny—and he was the new guy. I pulled him aside right before we finally went on at Madison Square Garden.

"You have to find me some cocaine."

Gilby didn't even do coke. This was typical of the bullshit I was putting people through. But he scored some for me.

I stayed in the pocket onstage. As long as my performances didn't suffer, I knew nobody would hassle me too much.

These days tours are run with an iron fist. The smallest possible crew, no private plane; the idea is to come out with as much profit as possible. The philosophy was completely different back then. The idea was to promote record sales and make money from the band's cut of those sales. By the end of the various legs of the *Use Your Illusion* tour, about seven million fans had come to see us in concert. But even though we were playing stadiums, we weren't making any money.

The tour staff sometimes approached one hundred people. Not only were we carrying backup girl singers, a horn section, and an extra keyboard player, but also chiropractors, masseuses, a singing coach, and a tattoo artist. Each of us had bodyguards and drivers. Money—and this was band money, not individual money—poured into nightly after-show theme parties. There were gambling nights and toga parties; in Indianapolis the theme was car racing. The party staff was part of the paid entourage, too. The parties would go into the early morning hours. The guys in the band didn't actually go to many of the parties. And neither did much of the crew. But the money was spent whether or not any of us showed up.

In theory, we each absorbed our own costs. Axl's posse would do things like rent helicopters to fly over this or that city. Fortunately nobody could touch the band's money for that sort of thing. If anybody brought someone on the road—clairvoyant, porn star, whatever—it was all fine, but we each paid out of our own money, not the band's. If I wanted a suite at the hotel instead of a room, I paid the difference. Guns was a partnership where people had to sign off on anything above the standard costs. But Axl couldn't absorb the costs his lateness caused at a place like Madison Square Garden—overtime for cops, vendors, all the union dock loaders. We were going on at 2 a.m., racking up tens of thousands of dollars in overage fees. That came on top of the crew salaries, per diems for the staff, hotel rooms for everybody, and cuts for the agents and managers.

The upshot was that we were paying to play MSG. This was not a part of the good ol' days I longed to revisit. Paying-to-play sucked at the lowliest clubs and it sucked at the world's most famous arena.

From New York we went to Philadelphia ahead of two shows on December 16 and 17, 1991. I had a jones going by the time we reached the Ritz-Carlton from our plane. I didn't even bother going into the hotel to check in. Instead I told Truck I was going to the pizza place across the street. In my mind at that point, virtually everyone was doing drugs. Yeah, if I just asked some likely-looking hood at the pizzeria to help me score, I figured I'd surely get lucky. It must have been glaringly obvious that I was one of the guys in Guns N' Roses—even if someone didn't recognize me from one of our videos then monopolizing MTV, I had two GN'R tattoos to cement the deal. As luck would have it, I did indeed find a guy at the pizza joint.

Every major city had its shitty high-crime areas. In America, there were areas a white boy like me drew attention—not only from residents but from police patrolling the areas. I was always so fucked up during this era that those societal constraints seemed only for other people. Not for me. When our guy said he could get me some drugs out in West Philly, I didn't think twice. We got in his car. As we drove farther west, I realized the streets were getting sketchier and the buildings lining them more dilapidated. At red lights, the dude driving merely slowed down for fear of a carjacking. Now, even in my benumbed state, the hatred-filled glares from the inhabitants of West Philly got my attention. I vaguely remembered this was the neighborhood where the police had dropped bombs on a house of black activists a few years prior, killing several children and destroying dozens of nearby buildings, but my need for drugs overcame any fear that may have welled up about my safety.

When we pulled up to the row of houses where my guy had a contact, eleven- and twelve-year-old kids were peddling and delivering drugs all along the street. I guessed their adult employers—perhaps even their own parents or relatives—were inside. There were kids with baseball bats and tire irons, and in an instant I suddenly realized I was in over my head. Then my guy just got out of the car—and took his keys, leaving me in the backseat, stranded and exposed. For a minute that seemed like a week, I thought this must be some sort of setup and that I would be robbed and killed. I could see the headline of the following day's newspaper clearly in my head. I thought it was rather pathetic that I was going to die on a stupid drug run with some fucking scumbag I didn't even know.

Stupid!

How could I be so fucking stupid!

Ah, but before I could make up my mind about what to do next, my man showed back up with a coat pocket full of drugs. In an instant, everything was suddenly okay. Great, in fact. I took out a cigarette, pulled some tobacco out of the end, and shoved in some coke. This was an invention I called "the smoker," sort of a cross between a blunt and crack. I was proud of that technique—unlike crack, which necessitated a pipe and created a telltale scent, I could smoke one of these *anywhere.*

When I got back to the comfy Ritz-Carlton, I knew I had been lucky. But I stood casually at the hotel bar and puffed on another smoker before heading up to my room to really dive into that bag of coke and gulp down some pills with a glass of vodka. Fuck, why not? It was a day off and the night was very young.

Truck was pissed off. What did I care? I got what I wanted and had a tale to tell. Rock and fucking roll. Guns N' fucking Roses. After that, Truck and the rest of the security guys tried to keep a tighter leash on me and clamp down on my drug-scoring activities.

On New Year's Eve, we had our first stadium headlining gig in the United States at Joe Robbie Stadium in Miami. I flew out Ernie C, the guitarist for Body Count. After the show, we went to a club owned by Luke Skyywalker of 2 Live Crew. I was the only white dude in the club, dancing with a bunch of girls. I must have looked too crazy for anybody to care.

The tour continued until early April, until we found out Axl would be arrested on charges stemming from the Riverport riot if he remained in the United States. So we canceled the last few U.S. dates and flew to Europe ahead of another leg of the tour there.

On April 20, 1992, we participated in a Freddie Mercury tribute show at Wembley Stadium. Guns played a couple songs, and the band sounded fiery and tight. Then there was a long break before all the performers united for a grand finale sing-along of "We Are the Champions." Backstage I let it go too far—I was too drunk to talk, too drunk to walk. Elton John literally carried me to the side of the stage, propped me upright, and helped maneuver me out onto the stage where almost 100,000 fans awaited the showstopper. About fifty performers lined up in a chorus line with Liza Minnelli singing lead. I remained upright through the song—no doubt using the sets of shoulders on either side of me—then I had to be carried again back to my dressing room, unaware of what was happening around me.

We are the champions! That's right: Duff McKagan, king of beers, viscount of vodka, count of coke. Champion of the world. Asshole.

In May 1992, we had a gig at Slane Castle in Ireland. It was the first time I'd ever been to Ireland, and the day before the show about a hundred people from various branches of my family, people I'd never before met, threw a big barbecue for me. First they took me on a pub crawl—we stopped at every bar between my hotel and the family reunion, and there were apparently quite a few bars along that stretch.

At some point along the way, an old lady—a great-aunt or something—pulled me aside and grabbed my cheeks.

"You drink too much," she rasped. "I've seen you on the TV, and you drink too much."

I looked around. All these fuckers were drinking.

I drink too much compared to these folks? Really?

That would be bad. But it also seemed hard to believe. I only drank so much to get to the same place other people got off on one cocktail. I wasn't falling down. I'd get too drunk sometimes, sure, and that's when I would disappear and do a little coke to sober up. No problem.

Maybe she was onto something, though, as a few days later I woke up in Budapest, Hungary, and looked incredulously at my passport. In it was a stamp from the Czech Republic. We had played a gig in Prague. I couldn't remember having been there at all.

Memory always amounts to a form of negation—you exclude most of what you experience and retain only the sensory impulses that your brain deems important, that help you make sense of the world, that allow you to track the plot of your own story. The situation on tour, however, had become so intolerable that I no longer had anything left after that process of negation—and I made sure of that with booze. There was no way to make sense of a situation in which we traveled the world antagonizing our fans with late starts or shows cut short. Very little else had any importance; the arc of my own story had been reduced to this single, painful plot line: my band was making the people who loved us most, hate us. Or so I thought.

Of course, blacking out also stemmed from fear. When it comes to your values and personality, you are what you do in adverse situations. My inability to alter this plot line did not fit with the way I defined myself. But of course, it defined me. No, I wasn't "the guy." I was a mess. The solution was to expunge those moments of fear and self-loathing from the record.

CHAPTER THIRTY-ONE

✦   ✦   ✦

Because of the sheer scale of our stage set and the complexity of juggling open dates in such big venues, there were many weeks when we played only two or three shows. That gave me way too much time to fuck up. As a means to keep myself busy and push back the hard-core drinking for a few hours, I rented studios sporadically during the tour and recorded my own songs. I had a few I knew wouldn't work stylistically for GN'R, and I figured maybe I could still make a record like Prince, playing all the instruments. Not that I pretended for a second I was anywhere near as gifted as Prince—I would play a sloppy, Johnny Thunders–style version of all the instruments. But still. I had recorded one song, called "The Majority," just before we left on tour, with Lenny Kravitz on vocals. I had become friends with Lenny before he blew up—I'd had a demo tape of his first album that ill-fated summer in Chicago.

Since I recorded on the road, I was able to get some other guest spots from bands opening for us and from musicians who lived in towns where we played. Sebastian Bach, Snake Sabo, and Rob Affuso from Skid Row played on a few songs, Jerry Cantrell from Alice in Chains added a guitar track somewhere along the way. Slash, Gilby, and Matt helped me out. On June 6, 1992, GN'R performed a pay-per-view concert in Paris and lined up Steven Tyler and Joe Perry from Aerosmith, Lenny Kravitz, and Jeff Beck to make cameo appearances. In the end, Jeff had to cancel because his ears were damaged during rehearsals, but he offered to play on a couple of my songs. I couldn't believe it.

After the Paris show, Guns had some days off in London and Jeff and I arranged to enter a studio there. I had invited my mom to meet me in London, too. She had never been to Europe. She had never really been much of anywhere, as she had been too busy and too broke raising eight kids. Mom was a huge Agatha Christie reader and loved all things quaintly English as a result. My mom also loved to be around me when I worked. I arranged for a friend of mine, drummer Slam Thunderhide of the band Zodiac Mindwarp, to have my mom over to his flat for a proper English tea and then to bring her down to the studio where Jeff and I were recording. Jeff had already been playing for a little while when my mom arrived. He's a virtuoso, and watching him play is like seeing musical butter melt.

After Jeff had played some blistering passes at one song, my mom said, "Jeff, you play really nice guitar."

My mom was not aware of Jeff Beck's iconic status—she didn't know about the Yardbirds or his influential albums like *Wired* and *Blow by Blow.*

Unfazed, Jeff answered, "Oh, well, thank you so much, Marie. I thought I messed up that last pass pretty good. Did you like it, then?"

That guy will forever be my hero.

On June 21, 1992, Guns N' Roses had to pay to keep the public-transport system open late in Basel, Switzerland. The only way back into town from the soccer stadium was a tram line that normally closed long before we finished—maybe before we even started.

Almost every night we heard the crowds get antsy and then ugly. After about an hour of waiting, kids would start to chant. Then they would start to throw beer bottles and rocks and whatever else they could find. Everyone on the crew knew not to walk around in front of the stage equipment—not to make themselves a target. From backstage it was difficult to know whether people had started or would soon start to try to scale the security fences or rigging—that is, break into full-on riot mode. But the thumps of flying objects and the angry chants sounded threatening enough to fill my soul with foreboding, dread, and embarrassment. *Know your exit.*

We shared our plane with U2 on this leg of the tour, with the MGM 727 crisscrossing the skies over Europe to tote each band to its next location. Everything had scaled up. We often flew from our hotels to the venues in helicopters, plural—even massive double-prop Chinook helicopters. We rented yachts the size of oil tankers for outings on off days. We went on private shopping sprees at designer boutiques and spent entire days racing go-karts on tracks reserved exclusively for us. Everything had become outsized. Everything. When McBob and his brother started slugging each other at a club late one hazy night, Harry Connick Jr. pulled them apart. We had celebrities breaking up the fistfights between our crew members.

On Tuesday, June 23, in Rotterdam, I stewed backstage after the Dutch police told us power would be cut at 11:30 p.m.—fans had already waited two hours since opener Faith No More finished playing, and our set would not be finished by 11:30 p.m. I feared another riot. Onstage, Axl told the crowd about the police threat, and basically invited the audience to tear the place down if the show was stopped. The power stayed on. We closed out this leg of the tour about a week later in Lisbon, Portugal, then flew home.

I was so used to being in hotels—and I acted like an animal in hotels—that I woke up in my own bedroom and spat on the floor and tried to call room service. During the break between that European leg and the launch of a co-headlining tour with Metallica in late July, I got married to Linda Johnson, a Penthouse Pet and an enthusiastic co-conspirator in drug use. At least I think it was then. I don't remember the wedding. I think we got married on a boat at Lake Arrowhead, which was still party central—all about cocaine and debauchery. We were drinking with a bunch of friends; I woke up a few days later and we were married. I guess boat captains can marry people.

That I could do all my coke—even crack—in front of her was pretty much the basis of our bond. And now we were *married*.

It was obvious even to me that my life was unraveling. I was married to a drug buddy. How much worse could it get?

In July 1992, we started a co-headlining tour with Metallica at RFK Stadium in Washington, D.C. In some cases, such bills are plagued by disputes over who gets to play second. Not this bill. Metallica graciously insisted on taking the stage first. It was smart: they wanted to play and get paid, whether or not Guns turned up on time.

Less than a month into the tour, on August 8, 1992, we stopped in Montreal. Metallica front man James Hetfield inadvertently stepped into the plume of one of his band's pyrotechnics pots at the show and had to be rushed to the hospital with extensive burns. The other members of Metallica came back out onstage after James had been whisked away, explained what had happened, and apologized for suspending the show. We could have saved the day by going right on and playing a long set. It would have been a great gesture to the fans and to the guys in Metallica. It would have been the professional thing to do, the right thing to do. And we were capable of an epic set—we had played for four hours in L.A. the night we found out mixing was complete on the *Illusion* records.

But no.

The same shit happened in Montreal as elsewhere, us going on late—more than two hours after Hetfield was rushed to the hospital—playing to pissed-off fans. Our own fans, pissed off at us. I sat backstage monitoring the sounds drifting in from the arena, drink in hand, and could feel the crowd's mood change. The rumble of tens of thousands of people beginning to get angry is a deep, low sound that penetrates walls and vibrates the fundaments of buildings, where dressing rooms are located. It's a horrible sound, and the panic and embarrassment and frustration in my own head was compounded by that rumble. After letting the crowd reach its boiling point, we finally went out and started playing. Then, forty-five minutes into our set, a microphone stand hit Axl in the mouth. He threw down the mic and left.

This time the riot didn't start near the stage. We didn't even see it. The crowd blew up back at the concession areas and merchandise stands, and then spread outside into the streets. In fact, our crew did their normal teardown of the set, oblivious to the riot already raging out of view. Only when our buses pulled out of the parking enclosure did we see the full extent of the situation—cop cars turned over, vehicles on fire, lots of broken windows. Once again there looked to be a lot of injuries. Once again I felt anguished and heartbroken. This time I also felt deeply embarrassed, a feeling that managed inexorably to worm its way into my vodka-numbed psyche.

It didn't have to be like this.

CHAPTER THIRTY-TWO

+ + +

It's time.

Step up.

Fix this.

Let's get everything out in the open. Get this weight off your chest.

It's time for a band meeting.

This could get ugly.

Don't worry. Slash and Matt and Gilby are in.

Still, could get ugly.

You can do this.

Where to start? *Listen, we're drinking ourselves into oblivion . . .*

These backstages all look the same, another drab locker room that the wardrobe people have draped with the same old tapestries they carry around in a trunk. *The vibe room.* That's what the crew calls this. And the same old big-screen TV. Shit, did we pay for that? Is it always a new one, or do they tote around the same one to every venue?

Don't lose focus.

Just stay cool. You can fix this.

Listen, none of us likes conflict, but there's stuff we need to talk about. The lateness is a big problem for us. Personally. Hearing the chants. I mean, look, I'll take responsibility for drinking too much, but . . . and,

well, also, I know we're not exactly businessmen, but I don't think you
have any idea what it's costing us . . .

Okay, here comes Axl.

Close your eyes, take a deep breath, gather your thoughts.

Everything goes black.

I open my eyes and reflexively spit on the floor. Huh?

I grab for the vodka on the nightstand.

Fumble for the phone.

Room service: ice.

Okay, when's this meeting?

Shit.

There is no band meeting.

Shit.

You're not the man.

You're a mess.

Pen.

Scrap paper.

Drink.

A couple of lines:

I have often wondered what my
Life really means to me
Wasted days and broken dreams
Let it all slip away from me . . .
And why'd this dream fade so fast
And why am I lookin' toward
The past to set me free

I spit on the floor.

Refill my glass with vodka.

A couple of lines.

Jesus, that burns.

Shit, no band meeting.

No meeting.
No understanding.
No change.
Spit.
Drink.
Snort.

CHAPTER THIRTY-THREE

+ + +

Truck and Earl still kept a close watch on me. So in San Francisco for a show in Oakland on September 24, 1992, I decided to arrange for a hooker to come to my room at the band's swanky hotel. There was nothing wrong with that as far as management—and Truck and Earl—were concerned. If anything, a hooker might keep me in for the night, keeping me away from drug connections.

That's exactly what I was betting they would think.

I had my L.A. friend Billy Nasty in town that night and planned to party. And I knew any hooker would have a coke connection—probably her own pimp. I found a number for an escort service and dialed it.

When the woman showed up, she took one look at me and my friend and I could see her doing calculations—how much for a double-back, or whatever they called that. When I explained to her that all I wanted was drugs, and that I would still pay her for her services all night, it was on. Her pimp was indeed a coke and pill dealer. Bingo!

The last date of the tour leg with Metallica, October 6, 1992, we played a homecoming show—for me, anyway—at the Seattle Kingdome. My brother Bruce was living back in Seattle at that point. He called me at the hotel the day of the show.

"What do you say tomorrow we go out for a round of golf—the McKagan brothers."

"I don't really know how to play," I said, "but I'll hang out with you guys, I'll ride along and drink some beers."

"Okay," Bruce said. "I'll pick you up."

That night Axl was on time. It was out of respect—he knew the gig meant a lot to me.

The next day, Bruce picked me up at the hotel as planned.

"We're going to stop by Mom's place and pick up Jon," he said as I climbed into the car. It made sense. I knew we would all be going there for dinner later, so my brother Jon was probably helping to get the place ready.

When we got there, Bruce had me come in with him. When we went inside, my whole family was there, all seven of my brothers and sisters, including Matt, who lived in L.A.

Wow, I thought, *they've thrown me a fucking surprise party.*

But nobody really made eye contact with me. Then the one person there I didn't recognize stood up. Everyone else sat down. She introduced herself as Mary. She turned out to be a doctor.

"I'm from a rehab center," she said. "There's a van down the street that will take you to a facility where you can dry out." Blah, blah, blah.

This is a fucking intervention!

"Sorry, Mary," I said. "This just isn't your business."

Rage coursed through my body. Of course I had a drinking problem, but this wasn't going to work.

This is bullshit!

"I love all of you," I said, "but this isn't any of your business. You can't just spring something like this on me."

The band had a bit of time off before we headed to Venezuela for a South American leg, but I would never abandon my band midtour, whether or not we had a few weeks to kill. This was not happening.

My brother Matt—who, it turned out, had not agreed with the idea in the first place—started talking.

"This isn't the right way to do it," he said, directing himself to the rest of the people in the room, rather than to me. "You don't know what he's dealing with."

I edged toward the door. Jon was standing near the front door, anticipating that I might try to bail. He blocked my way. I made it clear things would get ugly if he didn't move. Jon stood his ground.

"Dude, don't fucking do it," I said.

I knocked Jon out of the way. I ran out the door. Matt came after me. He pulled his rental car around and we hightailed it back to the Four Seasons, where the band was staying. From there we went to Sea-Tac and flew back to L.A.

CHAPTER THIRTY-FOUR

✦ ✦ ✦

Back in L.A., I called everyone in my family and said pretty much the same thing to each one.

"Look, I've been on the road and you can't be certain what I'm doing. I'll sit around and talk with you, but not like that."

I assured them I was going to try to get better.

We kicked off the South American leg of the tour in Venezuela with an open-air show on November 25 in Caracas. The band left the next day for Colombia on the MGM 727. Cargo planes would follow us with the gear and crew once the teardown had been completed.

When we arrived in Bogotá, Guns N' Roses was the lead story in all the local newspapers. When we asked what all the headlines were, someone translated for us. A fourteen-year-old Colombian girl had committed suicide after her father refused to let her attend our upcoming show.

Jesus. Another person whose life we touched . . . gone.

That night, more news: a coup had been launched in Venezuela. An air-force pilot named Luis Reyes Reyes and his co-conspirators were able to wrest control of most of the country's air bases by the morning of November 27. Our cargo planes were grounded. McBob and the rest of the crew were stuck.

The next morning a bomb went off near our Bogotá hotel.

Then Colombian drug lord Pablo Escobar told the press that we were his friends and that he was supplying us with a bunch of cocaine. He was already in hiding then as a result of American pressure (we never met him), and I guess he was just sticking it to the U.S. government, using us to have some fun. I was already annoyed at the political questions fired at us at press conferences—just because we sold some records didn't mean people should suddenly care what I thought about Bill Clinton or Boris Yeltsin. Now we had become inadvertent political pawns in a grand international game.

Great.

At some point that next day, I went to leave my hotel room. Outside my room stood a machine-gun-toting soldier. He motioned me back inside. I was—we were—under house arrest.

Oh, shit.

I didn't know what to do. I spent the day stewing.

What are we going to do now?

At least there was booze.

That evening there was a knock at my door. I opened it. The hallway was dark. The soldier was gone. Instead there was a guy in a suit—also carrying a machine gun.

"*Yayo?*" he said. I had learned this was slang for coke in South America. "*Yayo?*"

I slammed the door and locked it.

Shit.

I'm being set up.

I just know it.

I picked up the hotel phone. Who did I know who could help? Who could call somebody? I didn't want to scare my mom. Then it hit me: my dad. He'd been a fireman. *He must know people at city hall in Seattle.*

I dialed my dad. It went through.

"Dad, I don't know who else to call," I said. "It's all gone terribly wrong. I'm in a hotel room in Bogotá with an armed guard out front. I don't know if they're going to let us out. I don't know if they're going to let us play the show—if our planes even get here. And I don't know what will happen if we don't play the show. I'm really worried. Is there anyone you can call?"

I have no idea what my dad did, but the U.S. consul soon showed up on the scene. The atmosphere lightened. The armed guards disappeared.

Eventually our planes were allowed out of Caracas after the coup in Venezuela sputtered. The crew arrived and began to feverishly set up for a delayed Bogotá show. Then, after a huge rainfall, pooled water on the roof collapsed the stage. The crew started over with what was left.

The day of the rescheduled show arrived. It rained and rained. It continued to rain during the show. Then, as Axl played the opening chords of "November Rain," the sun broke through the clouds. Everyone in the audience crossed themselves. After the song, the rain began again.

This was shaping up to be some tour leg.

We had a guy who flew ahead of us and greased customs agents' palms. I don't remember customs people ever boarding our plane, though our hotel was raided in Chile. Not that there were any stupid motherfuckers among us—we didn't smuggle drugs from one country to another. We could always get whatever we needed locally.

Axl tried to reach out to me a few times. One time in São Paolo he called me from his hotel room. Stephanie Seymour was visiting him; Linda was with me.

"Hey," he said, "why don't you come down to our room and we'll have dinner? We'll just have a nice time."

We had a relaxed dinner and acted like adults. I thought we might be creating grounds for getting things together again. *If it stays like this,* I thought to myself, *maybe I can dig myself out. I'll have people I can depend on.*

Half an hour after Linda and I left the dinner, Axl was throwing chairs in the lobby of the hotel and trying to fistfight some guy.

We started 1993 in Asia, then came back to the States for yet another leg. I was using so much coke by this point that I needed more and more things to counteract it when it was time to take the edge off a coke high. One night when I couldn't get my hands on any pills and someone had some China white—powdered heroin—I snorted that instead. It did the trick: edge dulled. I found that smoking the brown tarlike heroin on tinfoil—as I had tried once in Amsterdam with Izzy and Slash—also did the trick. I never lost my fear of smack enough to shoot it with a syringe, but I soon started smoking enough of it to get twinges of withdrawal. It didn't take much, that was for sure. Fortunately I never came to enjoy the effect of heroin for its own sake, but floating away on a silk pillow was infinitely nicer than grinding my teeth in a drunken, paranoid stupor at the end of a coke binge.

Sorum suddenly got sober. I don't know what happened, but there was a moment that changed things for him, an epiphany of some sort. That left just me and Slash from the toxic trio. Then Slash and I kind of separated, each spending more time with our own little groups. We were tired of manning each other's line, which at this point—especially now that I, too, was dabbling in heroin—meant checking to make sure the other one was still breathing.

On the American leg of the tour, I went looking for trouble with Dizzy or Gilby. I remember landing in Fargo for a show in late March 1993, at the Fargo Dome. We got into town, looked around, and thought, *Oh, god.*

Dizzy and I hopped in a limo and decided to cause a stir. We drove to the local rock radio station and went inside unannounced. We went on the air and people started showing up at the station's office. Then we went to the local mall, looking for drugs or action of any kind.

Onstage in Sacramento on April 3, a bottle came flying out of the top tier. I saw it out of the corner of my eye. It hit Matt's floor tom and careened off. Then everything went black.

The bottle had hit me right in the temple and knocked me out. The show ground to a halt. I was rushed to the emergency room. From the hospital I returned to our hotel in Lake Tahoe—the next night we had a show in Reno and our managers deemed the Four Seasons in Tahoe the only hotel in the region worthy of our business.

Gilby and I had arranged for our dads to attend the show in Reno. Despite all my dad's fuckups, I figured he was still my dad. And he had bailed our asses out in Colombia. Maybe I was also thinking about my mortality, dotting *i*'s and crossing *t*'s. I flew him to Tahoe, where he saw all the chicks swarming us at the fancy hotel. We all drove together from there to Reno for the concert.

Gilby's dad was a retired fireman, too, and he tried to engage my dad about fireman's shit. My dad never told stories about saving this or narrowly avoiding that. I'm sure house fires were harrowing to witness, and he never talked about them.

Gilby's dad went on talking, reliving his glory days in the hopes of engaging my dad in conversation.

Finally he said, "You know, Mac, I always say if I had it to do all over again, I'd do it exactly the same. Wouldn't you?"

My dad looked at him. "Hell no," he said. "I'd do what this kid did here."

He had never supported my music career until I started making money. This was his way of showing approval, I guess, though he never apologized for not supporting me earlier.

At a gig in Mexico City later that April, we called a band meeting. Slash, Gilby, and Matt agreed we had to confront Axl about the lateness. Somebody had to start the conversation.

"Listen," I said to Axl when everyone was assembled, "we're drinking ourselves into oblivion, waiting three hours listening to our fans chant 'bullshit.' We've been working hard to keep this thing together . . ."

I paused and looked around for support. The other guys looked away and shrank down in their seats a little.

That was it.

Later, at the show itself, I was too fucked up—and I knew it. I could hear myself babbling incoherently backstage, the guttural sounds spilling from my mouth between gulps of vodka and cranberry barely resembling words. Then we took the stage. I finally stumbled across the line I had always held sacred: I found myself falling behind.

Stay in the pocket. *Stay in the pocket.*

Just play.

You can always play.

Always.

Just stay with Matt.

I tried to hold it together. I stared at Sorum banging the drums and tried to stay with him, concentrating. He exaggerated his strokes to help me. He nodded. His shoulders rose with the beat. *Come on, man.*

Still not getting the fingers on my left hand to the right spots in time. Still not moving the pick fast enough.

Pick it up.

Pick-me-up.

We had hidden rooms below the stage, so I staggered into one at the first chance to get more coke to sober up. Not happening. I could barely bend over to snort without tipping over. I righted myself. No time. Back out onstage.

Struggling.

To stay.

In sync.

With.

Sorum.

Pick it *up.*

Can't quite.

Come on.

You fuck.

Fuck.

CHAPTER THIRTY-FIVE

✦ ✦ ✦

In the middle of May 1993, we headed back out for another summer swing through Europe.

For the first five nights—in Israel, Turkey, Greece, and at two shows in England—Izzy rejoined the band to fill in for Gilby, who'd broken his hand in a motorcycle accident just before we left. Crowds stopped the show for minutes on end to chant Izzy's name. It was great. Greek teenagers seemed to understand something we had lost track of to some extent: this was—or had been—first and foremost a band of friends who believed in our music and in one another.

Izzy and I had started out as neighbors who would take a city bus to get to a gig where we were the fourth band on a bill of four bands, just happy to be playing a gig with a band we believed in with everything we had. And we saw it through. Now I looked at Izzy and recognized the clarity he had, the sense of purpose behind his decisions. Izzy had his feet beneath him and could walk away—which he did again after those five shows. My feet felt stuck in cement. Or quicksand. I wanted what he had, but had no idea how to get it. Though I guess I didn't want sobriety badly enough to go to Izzy and ask him for help. That would have put me in a situation where I would have had to either follow through or fail.

With Izzy gone and Gilby recuperated, we worked our way through soccer stadiums in Scandinavia, Germany, Austria, Switzerland, Holland, Belgium, Italy, Spain, and France. Izzy's departure triggered a realization:

perhaps the simplest explanation for what was going on with Guns N' Roses was that the band members had stopped needing one another. Sure, we wanted to continue to make a living playing music, and these record sales weren't going to go on forever. But we no longer needed one another to write ourselves out of poverty through our songs. Guns didn't start out about money, but once we all had houses and cars, we just needed one another less. The layers of infrastructure and the assistants, bodyguards, and drivers were fine: we could afford not to deal directly with one another anymore. Pissed off? No problem, I have my own hotel room, my own home. Not working on new songs as a band? No problem, I'll rent a studio on my own. Shit, we had a management team: *Oh, we'll take care of this, we'll take care of that.*

On this last European leg of the tour, we sometimes weren't all together in the same city except for the performance itself. On a few occasions, we weren't even in the same country. Our plane could drop some of us here and others there.

On July 5, 1993, we all rendezvoused in Barcelona for a huge outdoor show at the Olympic Stadium. Axl came in from Venice. I returned from a visit with Linda to the Spanish island of Ibiza. Slash was already in Barcelona.

After Suicidal Tendencies and Brian May had played their opening sets, our manager, Doug Goldstein, sent an oddly formal request to see me and Slash before the show. This was unusual.

When Slash and I arrived at the vibe room, one of the tour managers was sitting there waiting for us. The guy was clutching some papers. He put a slim stack of pages down in front of each of us. I leafed through it. It was a legal document giving Axl the right to continue to play as Guns N' Roses even if either Slash or I—or both of us—were not part of it. Though it didn't affect our status as shareholders in the operation, Axl and Axl alone would control the name if we signed this agreement.

"What the fuck?" I said.

"Look, man," the tour manager said. "The truth is, you guys are not in good shape—you know that yourselves. If one of you dies, nobody wants to have to spend years in court battling your families or whatever."

That was not what it said, however. There was nothing about death in these documents.

With the crowd outside already getting rowdy, the guy then implied Axl wouldn't go onstage that night unless we signed the documents.

I pictured people getting hurt if a riot started—at least that was my fear. And I was so *fucking* exhausted—it felt as I though I'd been dragging a house around behind me for the last two years. Besides, at the time I never thought GN'R could possibly exist without us. The idea seemed ridiculous. And in that case, maybe the documents didn't need to be fixed?

Fuck it.

I signed. So did Slash.

Guns N' Roses—the trademark now owned by Axl—took the stage.

The next day, I grabbed Doug Goldstein on the tarmac at the airport. I had woken up really upset about what had happened the previous night. Slash and I shouldn't have signed those papers. But management wouldn't let the whole thing go forward anyway. Right? I shouted at Doug, saying he needed to fix things.

"Look, Duff," he said, "you're a smart guy. I manage Guns N' Roses."

"Yeah, I know, Doug. And that's why we have to—"

"No, you're not getting it. I manage Guns N' Roses."

"Are you trying to tell me you manage the *name* Guns N' Roses?"

I was still a member of the band. Not a paid hand. Slash and I still had the same equity stake as before. We had just relinquished control of the name.

Doug looked at me with no expression.

"You manage the guy who owns the name Guns N' Roses—is that where you're going, Doug?"

He shrugged. That *was* where he was going.

I was apoplectic with rage. I couldn't even speak.

We boarded the plane.

Only five more shows in Europe. Five. More. Shows.

You can make it.

After twenty-six months, the final concerts of the *Use Your Illusion* tour appeared on the horizon. We had tacked on two shows in Argentina at the end of the European leg, and then it was over. Just two more flights to go now: Paris to Buenos Aires, Buenos Aires to L.A. The finish line had come to seem like a tangible, physical threshold—I could practically see it out the window of the plane as we floated toward Argentina in mid-July 1993, for those last two shows.

By this point, the members of the band had long since stopped showing up for sound check, so the crew would play our instruments, test the equipment, and set levels without us. For this, the crew had assembled a shadow band and even developed a signature tune: "Crack Pipe" by an Atlanta act called the Coolies. The song was from an album called *Doug,* a spoof rock-opera about a skinhead who bashes a gay chef, steals his cookbook, and becomes rich and famous. Of course, there's a downfall— it was an opera, after all—and "Crack Pipe" came during that last section.

On the night of the very last show, three hours elapsed after the opening band finished. No Axl.

Please, can't this end without any more people fucking getting hurt?
Please.

Audiences in South America tended to throw a lot of rocks, and with no sign of GN'R, things were getting ugly. Our production manager gathered the guys who formed the crew band.

"Get up there," he said. "You're playing."

A huge scream went up from the audience as the crew band jogged out to their places and the entire stage set sprang to life. The band launched into a tune. The lights pulsed. Then the jumbotron video screens lit up and showed McBob and the rest of the guys rocking to "Crack Pipe."

Suddenly 50,000 people started shouting what must have been obscenities.

Then Axl arrived. There would be no riot.

When we finally took the stage for that last show in Argentina, I peered out at the crowd.

This could be it.

Remember this moment, remember this scene, this stadium, these fans.

We limped back to L.A. and quickly went our separate ways. Back into our private lairs to lick our wounds. Except me. For me it was straight off to rehearsals. Geffen had released *Believe in Me* while Guns were still in Europe, and now I was off on my first solo tour.

That's when Axl called me, telling me I was crazy to go back out.

"It's what I do, Axl."

Besides, I wasn't going to sit still.

Keep moving, keep moving.

After the incident a few months before with my coke dealer and his pregnant wife, I had quit coke. For the most part that had stuck so far. It would be easier to stick with it on the road. I just had too many drug connections in L.A., and my life there was intertwined with coke. *Keep moving.*

The tour started with three showcase appearances in clubs in L.A., San Francisco, and New York. And it started badly. I had switched from vodka to wine, but immediately found myself drinking about a case a day. Wine, wine, wine. And blood.

Blood in San Francisco when my wife, Linda, got into a scrap back-stage and traded punches with another woman until teeth started rattling to the floor. Blood in New York as fistfights broke out in the audience. Then we flew to Europe to join the Scorpions' tour. A fistfight broke out between a couple band members in an airport. Blood. Our lead guitar player pulled a knife on the bus driver in England. Talk of more blood. Blood, blood, blood. And wine. I often had to travel alone to get to the next town early to do publicity. I showed up at a record signing in Sweden swilling wine from the bottle. Got skewered in the local press for that—a lot of young kids in line for autographs.

We played some inspired shows, but there were also times when I shouldn't have been up there playing, times when I let it go too far and my performance suffered. There I was in huge venues, playing with my own band, under my own name, not bringing my A-game.

What's your excuse now?

At the end of that leg, I needed another guitar player. Couldn't keep the guy who stabbed our driver. I called Paul Solger, my old bandmate from Ten Minute Warning back in Seattle. I hadn't spoken to him in ten years. He was sober. *Want to tour with my band?* He said yes.

On to Japan we went. Bottles and bottles of wine each day. My innards burned. *Tums, I need Tums.* Sloppy onstage again. *What the fuck are you doing?*

Home to LAX, a long, long commercial flight. *Oh, fuck.*

We had a break before heading back across the Pacific for a tour of Australia.

I just can't do this anymore.

I felt sick, really sick, the worst flu I'd ever had.

Are you going to be that guy—a quitter?

I picked up the phone and dialed the tour manager.

I'm out. I can't do it anymore.

I was that guy now.

No tour, fine. But I needed to keep moving.

Seattle.

Seattle.

I have a house there. That's where I'll go.

March 31, 1994, at LAX, there was Kurt Cobain, looking as lost in the lonely, jagged maze of his mind as I was in mine. Then he was gone. *Man, I really wish I'd asked you to come over to my house that night when we landed. I'm sorry.*

May 10, the paralyzing pain. The unbearable pain. The pain, the pain.

I'm going to die. Here. Alone.

Andy.

Please let him come upstairs. I don't want to die alone.

Dr. Thomas.

Demerol. Nothing. Demerol. Nothing. Sheer panic.

Emergency room.

"Kill me."

I begged over and over.

"Please, kill me. Just kill me. Kill me. Please."

+ PART FIVE +

A GOOD DAY TO DIE

CHAPTER THIRTY-SIX

+ + +

As I was pleading with the ER doctors to kill me, they brought in an ultrasound scanner so they could monitor my burst pancreas. My childhood doctor, Dr. Thomas, was in charge of assessing the ultrasound images they kept taking at regular intervals in preparation for emergency surgery.

Landing in the Northwest Hospital that day didn't surprise me. In fact, the surprise was that I was alive at all in May of 1994. I had long thought I would die by the age of thirty—and I had just reached that milestone in February of that year.

You knew this was coming, I thought.

All you ever wanted to do was leave your mark on the world.

Get in, get out.

You've done that.

I figured as part of Guns, I'd left a big mark.

What else do you have left to live for anyway?

Then Dr. Thomas suddenly said, "Hang on a minute."

My pancreas had expanded and then burst. But now it was starting to contract again. Once the expansion stopped and the blood started to coagulate, they decided not to perform surgery after all. I just might be able to survive with my organ intact—no dialysis necessary. Instead of wheeling me down to an operating room, they continued to monitor me in an intensive care unit.

They put me on really high doses of morphine and Librium. At first I had buttons to push to self-administer them. For the first two days, it was constant. Pushing the button, pushing the button. Then, at some point on the third day, I realized, *Wow, I didn't push the buttons as many times this hour.* By the sixth day, they took the buttons away from me—because I was a full-on junkie. They switched me to drip doses.

I started to have withdrawal from the morphine.

I'll never forget when my mom came to the hospital to see me. She was in a wheelchair, from Parkinson's disease. There I was, her youngest son, with a morphine drip in my left arm and a Librium drip in the other arm for the shakes from alcohol withdrawal.

I saw myself in the hospital bed with tubes in my body and her in the wheelchair.

The order isn't right here—I should be taking care of her. It's not right.

You're a fuckup.

You're a fuckup.

CHAPTER THIRTY-SEVEN

✦ ✦ ✦

The old adage about addiction is that the first thing you have to do is to admit you have a problem. In my case, I already knew I had a problem; the key for me was admitting how selfish I was being. *Look, you're hurting your mom.*

I didn't know whether I would survive during those first few days in the hospital, but I felt strongly that if I did live, I would be prepared to change. When I was released from the hospital, Dr. Thomas asked me to come talk to him in a consultation room.

"I've arranged for you to enter a drug and alcohol rehab facility near Olympia," he said. "We can transport you directly there."

I thanked him for all his help.

"I think I can do it on my own," I told him.

I saw the look in his eyes change. Instead of expressing a helpful glint, they now betrayed skepticism hardened by experience. Frustration crept into his tone.

"Duff, if you have one more drink you will die."

I thanked him again. "Two weeks alone here in the hospital has done as much for me as any rehab could possibly do."

I believed that. The mental work had started as soon as I saw my mom in her wheelchair forced to tend to me, to worry about me—anxious she might have to grieve for me. I was done. Now that I had been granted this reprieve, it was time to turn my shit around.

When I got to my house, my yellow lab, Chloe, was waiting faithfully

at the front door, just as she always had been whenever I came home between tour legs. I had brought her with me when I flew up from L.A. and
Andy had taken care of her while I was in the hospital. Chloe seemed to
sense my fragility; she stuck close to me at all times and nuzzled me even
more than usual.

Thanks to the Librium, it had been a kind withdrawal from alcohol—
at least while I was in the hospital. They juiced me pretty good in there.
When they sent me home, they gave me a two-week supply of Librium
pills. And there was a prescription—you know, take two pills six times a
day, then two pills five times a day, and so forth, with the number of pills
diminishing each day.

That was my first challenge. But I did it; I did exactly what the prescription said. Still, I was shaking all the time. During the first few weeks,
I shook so badly from alcohol withdrawal that I was afraid to drive my
car. I was sure I would crash it. I found an old steel mountain bike in my
garage and started riding that instead.

One of the first things I did was to go to the grocery store to buy food.
It was a novel idea at the time—it had been years since I really shopped
for food. Now here I was, thirty years old, an adult with a credit card, a
checkbook, and an ATM card. I could buy whatever I wanted in the store,
but I had no idea where to start. I thought everyone was staring at me—I
was sure my shaking was freakishly visible. It had also been so long since
I had been anywhere sober that I didn't know how to act or how to deal.
It was like being on LSD. The lights in the store were glaringly bright and
I could swear the music was playing hidden messages. I grabbed some
milk, barbecue sauce, and cigarettes, and that was all.

I looked at the girl at the cash register.

"I give you this money, right?"

My shirt was drenched in sweat and I was having a full-blown panic
attack.

She nodded nervously, barely able to disguise her disgust. She gin-
gerly took the money from my hand, trying to avoid actually touching me.

Something I failed to realize was that simply functioning in life again
was going to be my biggest hurdle. I guess I always thought that avoiding

bars and drug dealers and cravings would be the biggest impediments to sober progress. Yes, those things would be a challenge, but first I had to figure out things like what time to go to bed and what to do with my waking time. *How do I talk to someone on the phone now? Who do I call? Should I tell people that I'm sober? Should I just go away somewhere and disappear? How are people going to view me after a crisis like this? What the fuck should I do?*

Those questions reverberated until the fragile web of my existence shook. How was I going to play music again? Could I do it sober? Guns N' Roses was a shambles, and the dynamic inside the band—if you could even call it that—had changed. Was there anything there to salvage, and if so, could I do it in a completely new and unfamiliar state of mind?

Initially I rode my heavy old mountain bike just to stave off the shakes, but I quickly realized riding made me feel better. And it was something to fill the time. Those first few days I just rode around aimlessly and only realized I'd been out for a long time when darkness gathered. Without ever thinking about it, I soon found myself riding around for eight hours a day—slowly, in flat areas, but all day long.

My muscles ached each morning. I hadn't exercised for years. But the soreness lifted my spirit. Not spirit as in mood, but my actual spirit—my body was so wrecked from abuse that my spirit was the only thing keeping me afloat, all I had left.

After about a week of long flat rides, I began to challenge myself on the bike. Seattle is hilly and I had no trouble finding steeper and steeper climbs to test my endurance and my tolerance for pain. These increasingly hard rides came to represent a form of self-flagellation, a way to punish myself for all the damage I had done to myself and others. I could feel this healthy new kind of pain searing every muscle fiber and neuron in my body. I was on fucking fire—and I liked it.

As the weeks passed, my endurance started to increase and my mind started to clear. It was like I hadn't been alive for a long, long time. I was smelling the grass and trees for the first time in years. Smell is the strongest sense we have, and my long-dormant olfactory system was triggering memories that I had thought lost. The whiff of newsprint reminded me of riding in the backseat of my sister Joan's car, delivering newspapers along my paper route one morning in middle school when she saved me from doing it on my bike in the rain.

The smell of Lake Washington evoked memories of swimming and fishing with my brother Matt. Rain on fresh-cut lawns took me back to practices when, from ages eight to fourteen, I played pee-wee football. Our team always had the smallest players in the city league, and our coaches compensated by putting a premium on physical conditioning. The hope was to run other teams into the ground. The practice field ad-joined a steep hillside. Anytime someone screwed up a block or jumped offside, we would instantly hear our coaches say: "To the hill, gentlemen!" This was the cue to run wind sprints up and down the muddy incline. It was intense and I got sick frequently, but we weren't allowed to stop to throw up—we just kept running. The coaching staff always said such suf-fering built character.

Like that, biking for entire days hurt but also felt somehow positive—as if the aches might represent a moral victory of some sort. And for the first time in years, I thought I might actually have a chance at survival. I started to feel *human*. My kidneys no longer ached when I urinated, and my stomach hungered for actual nourishment.

Eddy came over to my house with a book on nutrition, outlining a diet suited to the reduced capabilities of my body's digestive system in the wake of the damage to my pancreas—lots of fish and greens. He told me he had decided to go on the diet with me.

Those first few weeks out of the hospital were probably the most im-portant in my entire life. People say things happen for a reason, and if I hadn't been shaking so badly, I probably would never have hauled that rusty bike out of my garage. And if I had never straddled that old frame and cranked those creaky pedals, I might never have held it together in those early days—I simply had no idea what else to do.

Of course, I was still in a band that was trying to make a new record. At some point, I would have to return to Los Angeles and that thought terrified me. The only hope I had was to get a mountain bike down there. It would be the first thing I did, I told myself.

Not long after I got out of the hospital, Axl came up to Seattle to visit me. He was the only member of the band who had called me in the hospital, though McBob and Adam Day from the crew also called. I think from afar it must have sounded to Slash like just another brush with the line—and besides, he was dealing with an addiction of his own. Not that anyone owed me a call in a situation that was of my own making, but Axl's concern still touched me.

Axl and I talked about Guns. The challenge was to figure out how we were going to make a new record and what direction we were going to go musically. Obviously the trust and understanding within our band—the sense that we had one another to rely on like a family—had been tainted, perhaps irrevocably. A lot of wedges had been driven between us. Looking back now, it is all so fucking clear. But at the time I couldn't wrap my head around the fact that people we were paying to facilitate the business side of our band seemed willing to exacerbate all the personal problems among the people who made up the band—that they could be so selfish and moneygrubbing and shortsighted.

Now, however, I was doing sober things with Axl, riding bikes and eating healthy food, and, once he returned to L.A., talking with him on the phone about productive musical directions. Maybe he, too, had changed. Maybe there was something to salvage in Guns N' Roses. Axl and I decided we should regroup and start writing the next album.

Fucking hell, I really have to go back down to L.A.

How was I to avoid my old ways in the city where I had almost killed myself? How would I keep the drug dealers from stopping by my house? Or all the friends I partied with?

Fucking hell.

CHAPTER THIRTY-EIGHT

✦ ✦ ✦

When I got down to L.A. in June 1994, I was five weeks sober. Before even going up to my house I stopped at the Bike Shack, a cycle shop in Studio City. One of the first things I noticed in the shop was a sign-up sheet for a long-distance cross-country mountain-bike race in Big Bear, California. The race would take place in seven weeks. There was a beginners category. I had never entered a race or done any sort of individual sport before. I found the thought of it a bit daunting and alien, but what the fuck? I was on my bike all the time and every day. I might as well train for an event. I figured someone at the bike shop could give me some tips. Besides, if I entered this race, it would give me a concrete reason to stay sober until a certain date—a goal.

I registered for the race.

I had never felt so alone, yet now I also felt strangely invigorated. Next I picked out a new mountain bike. Though I had been using an old no-name steel bike, I decided to splurge on what I thought was a pretty nice bike—a Diamondback. After all, this was my thing now and I wanted a good bike.

I knew I had a lot to deal with. For one thing, I had to cut it off with my wife, Linda. She was not understanding about the situation. How could I have expected her to be? Our relationship was based on getting fucked up together.

Aside from my dog, I was very much alone in Los Angeles, as I felt it prudent to throw out my black address book filled to the brim with the names and phone numbers of people I partied with—and who would probably like to keep on partying. No one likes to drink or drug alone. A fence encircled my house, and I kept the front gate shut. I didn't drive Laurel Canyon anymore. I took different roads so I didn't have to pass my dealer's house and all my party buddies' places. People tried to come around sometimes, people from the past, but word got around that I wasn't going back to that world. For the most part, it turned out, addicts were pretty respectful—*oh, he's gotten out of the game.*

I had no program, no Alcoholics Anonymous, no community around me. I had Eddy, who was sober, but he was in Seattle. Izzy was sober, too, but I'm sure he still had doubts—*is Duff really sober?* Ed and I continued to talk almost daily on the phone. He gave me tips on things to eat and on books to read—things to feed my mind. He flew down and stayed with me as I went through the initial divorce papers and struggled with the realization that I was a two-time loser in the marriage department. He helped me to understand that my idealized vision of love could never have been attained in the fucked-up state I had just come out of.

With the Big Bear bike race on the horizon, I spent a chunk of every day riding hard on the steep hills near my house. On one of my first rides, I went through Fryman Park, intending to cut through it to familiar trails in Wilacre Park, farther down the slope. But I ran across a trailhead in Fryman Park I'd never noticed and took it. As I rode up one section, something caught my eye in a gulch next to the trail. *What the fuck is that?* I stopped the bike and peered over the edge for a better look. Below sat a grotesquely misshapen heap of metal—the wreck of an old car. It turned out this was the point directly below Dead Man's Curve. I had found my trail of choice.

Mornings I was still panic-ridden. I felt myself gasping for air after what seemed like an eternity dunked underneath a thick green film of pond muck. I was sober, but thirsty. My mind had almost atrophied from lack of stimulation. Now that my life had taken a turn for the better, I felt that I needed to read. I wanted to experience the things I had missed out on, all of the books high schoolers were required to read. It's not as if I was nostalgic for the days of high school, but I was curious.

F. Scott Fitzgerald? Shakespeare? Melville? Where do I start? Fiction, nonfiction?

Someone gave me the Ken Burns Civil War documentary on VHS. I would go to my bedroom early each night, around nine, and pop in one of those videotapes. I was enthralled. I could not get enough. So I started to read books about the war. Then other wars. I went from the Civil War to the First World War to the Second, back to the Revolution, forward to Vietnam.

When I happened upon a book by Ernest Hemingway set during the Spanish Civil War, it dawned on me that I had yet to delve into my initial plan: to plow through some of that required reading. For me, that book, *For Whom the Bell Tolls,* was the one that suddenly unlocked the world of literature. Hemingway's descriptions blew me away. They were sparse but beautiful. When he wrote of hunger or pain, I felt sudden pangs of soreness and dread. And when one of his characters talked about alcohol addiction, I cringed: "Of all men the drunkard is the foulest. The thief when he is not stealing is like another. The extortioner does not practice in the home. The murderer when he is at home can wash his hands. But the drunkard stinks and vomits in his own bed and dissolves his organs in alcohol."

I went straight from there into *The Sun Also Rises, A Farewell to Arms, Green Hills of Africa,* and *The Old Man and the Sea.* Hemingway's writing woke me to the rhythms that could make a phrase or paragraph dance or saunter. I read his poems. I read his short stories. I plowed through two huge Hemingway biographies—even though one was unreadable.

In my new and lonely world of desert-island sobriety, I was at last connecting with something. If I was not yet finding my place in the world, I was at least finding places and ideas and people I could relate to, despise, or aspire to in these great books. As I moved on to other writers, working my way through literary classics alongside my steady stream of nonfiction, the authors also gave me confidence to use my own voice when speaking and to use intelligent words, as opposed to a raised voice that had really only masked fear—fear of how to deal with uncomfortable or incomprehensible situations.

The space between the covers of these books became my place of solitude. Reading continues to represent a meditative haven for me to this day. At the end of every day, whether on tour or at home with my family, I always take time alone at night to read. It has become a time to arm myself for trials to come. And with Guns N' Roses in 1994, there were definitely trials to come—and soon.

CHAPTER THIRTY-NINE

✛ ✛ ✛

As the weeks leading up to the bike race passed, I cleaned up my house and bought real food at the grocery store. I had to throw out a lot of my clothing and bedding—my broken body had left bloodstains everywhere.

Truck, my former bodyguard, came over one day to check in on me, and I was in the middle of doing laundry.

He opened the dryer.

"You know you have to clean out the lint trap, right?" he said.

I smiled. I knew that by now. I appreciated the fact that he was trying to look out for me.

I went to bed early every night and woke up at the crack of dawn. I read Gavan Daws's *Prisoners of the Japanese* and pondered my solitary life. Though it was only two months earlier that I had landed on this deserted isle, it now seemed like a whole other lifetime ago. I was alone for the first time in a long time—except for Chloe padding around the house—and the isolation felt wholesome. It was not the type of isolation I had felt when my band was on top of the world and I was in a fishbowl, gasping for a breath of fresh air and praying for a friend to pick up the phone. *Please pick up, Mom—God, I hope you're home. Please pick up, Andy or Eddy or Brian or Matt or Joan or Claudia or Carol or Jon.* That kind of isolation made it seem logical for me to give the keys to my house to a drug dealer so that someone would be there when I came home on breaks from the tour. That kind of isolation made me invite entire clubs of derelict partiers up to my house at closing time. That kind of isolation made me start suicide notes countless times, only to stop because I couldn't do that to my mom. At least not in such a direct way.

No, I was alone by choice now, and I was dead set on starting a new life for myself based on solid ground. I was in uncharted territory and had no idea how to do what I wanted to do. I trained hard, drank plenty of water, and watched the booze weight fall off me. I lost fifty pounds in the first three months following my acute pancreatitis. I prayed to my training hills and found deep faith in the physical suffering of the present and the mental suffering of the past.

The race had come to represent much more than a nineteen-mile bike ride. Making it through the race would mean I had successfully navigated the first stage of a totally different course, too—one out of a previous life and into another, one out of despair and into hope. Preparing for the race at Big Bear was a fight for survival and sanity and maybe, just maybe, a chance to overcome. The nineteen mile markers of the race would collectively represent the first mile marker in my sobriety.

Meanwhile Guns was trying to happen. If the band was going to work for me, it was going to have to work with me sober. We booked a rehearsal place. The first day Axl didn't show up. The next Slash failed to show. After a week of that, I stopped going down there unless one of them called me to say he was actually walking out of his house.

Slash was beyond the heavy nodding, but he was still using heroin. Still, that posed no immediate problem for me. When I saw him ducking out to fix, I wasn't thinking, *Oh, that looks good.*

Axl had demonstrated a lot of compassion over the years—and especially in the wake of my pancreatitis. That's what also drove me crazy. He knew that I'd changed my life around, that I got up early and went to bed early, that I was doing whatever I could to stay alive. And yet, right at this point he made a big switch and became a night person.

One night he showed up at the rehearsal studio as I was packing up to leave.

"Sorry, man, but I have to go," I told him.

"What do you mean you have to go?"

"Dude, it's four a.m., and I've been here all fucking night. I've got to get home."

"Fuck that, man!"

What made dealing with Axl maddening was the fact that he and I were also in agreement on a lot of things. One of the points of contention between Slash and Axl was a batch of songs Slash brought to the table. Axl thought it was Southern rock—not Guns N' Roses material. I backed Axl.

Slash and I started trying to write new stuff with other guitar players added to the mix. This was the first time we'd written without Izzy to bounce ideas off of and to bring ideas of his own.

Zakk Wylde, who played with Ozzy Osbourne on and off for years, brought energy and enthusiasm that was lacking within Guns at the time.

"We can build on the legacy," he said excitedly. "We can make something great. Listen to this."

He saw a piano against the wall and sat down and elegantly played it. I had no idea he could play piano at all, much less like this. We recorded a few demos with him, but nothing panned out.

Then Axl wanted to bring in a guy named Paul Huge.

"You want to bring in your old buddy from Indiana?" Slash said incredulously.

"Look, he'll just jam with us and maybe it'll work out," Axl said.

"No," both Slash and I said.

"Yes," said Axl.

This wasn't some wedding band you could just bring friends into. If I wasn't going to bend for the sake of one of my best friends—Slash, and his Southern-rock songs—I sure as hell wasn't going to let a stranger come in and fuck around with Guns.

"Fine," Axl said. "How's this: you guys try him out on your own, give him a few days."

We let him come in. Gave him a couple of days. It was hopeless.

We told Axl.

"Fuck you guys," he said.

That was pretty much it for Slash. After that he concentrated on his solo band, Slash's Snakepit, and eventually released a record under that name early the next year.

I started to get calls from our manager, Doug, and from Ed Rosenblatt, the president of Geffen Records, pleading with me to somehow get the band back into the studio. I suppose in their eyes they finally had a sober and clearheaded member of the band who could somehow pull everything together. But Jesus, I was only just sober, and if they knew how fragile my sobriety was at that point, maybe they would never have called. I still didn't know if I would stay sober for the rest of my life.

Sure, I could say I was done. But I still had urges. The urge to grab a bottle of vodka and take the edge off when these motherfuckers called me, for instance. *Goddamn it, I can't have a glass of wine to take the edge off?* Maybe *urge* is the wrong word. Perhaps it was more a sense of disappointment: disappointment that I had used up all my chits. *Really, fucking never?*

Then again, maybe they would have called even if they thought it might imperil my sobriety. If anyone entrusted with the care of the band had actually given a fuck about the health of any of us, Guns would have been pulled off the road and put into therapy years ago. This was not lost on me as the phone calls became more and more frequent. These trusted professionals were after the gold and I was only a means to an end. They could all go fuck themselves. *Hey, band manager, why don't you stick your neck out and actually manage the fucking band instead of worrying if you'll get fired for saying what needs to be said? There will be no band to manage if you keep on being a pussy and passing the buck!*

If I was going to "save" my band, it would be for us, not for them. We had already made a lot of money—and I had reached the seemingly unattainable dream of making a living from playing music. But for the people calling me now, it felt like their lone concern was making *even more* money, regardless of how. Money hadn't been my motivation to get into music in the first place, and money wasn't now going to motivate me to get dragged back into a situation that I hadn't yet figured out how to fix—or even whether I wanted to *try* to fix.

Besides, I had a bike race to ride.

CHAPTER FORTY

✦ ✦ ✦

From my days up at Lake Arrowhead, I knew altitude adjustment could take a couple of days. The Big Bear race course started at 7,000 feet and climbed to 8,500 feet. I found a bed-and-breakfast up on Big Bear Mountain and stayed there for a few nights prior to the race.

Slash's guitar tech, Adam Day, had started riding with me in the run-up to the race, and on race day he showed up to cheer me on, a sign of friendship I will never forget. As I took my bike off the rack on the back of my truck, I had to laugh at myself. I suddenly realized just what a neophyte I was. Of the thousands of people I saw getting ready, I was the only one wearing high-top sneakers, cutoffs, and a backward baseball cap. Everyone else had on proper bike shorts, click-in riding shoes, and aerodynamic crash helmets. The bikes themselves were slick, light racing machines made of titanium or carbon fiber with front and back shocks. My Diamondback had no suspension whatsoever. I looked like a hick. My teeth started to chatter audibly. Oh well. I had trained for this and I was not going to back down now. I consoled myself with how far I had come in such a short time.

When the starting gun blasted, a mad rush of bikes crushed me, knocking me over, and I scrambled to get back on my bike and back into the race. The first part of the course climbed a brutally steep incline. This was my zone. Hill climbs were my chosen place to suffer; suffering was my gateway to serenity. I dug in and started my climb, my race. I was soon passing the guys who had knocked me down in their fancy costumes on their fancy bikes. I rode and I climbed and I passed even more riders.

My mind cleared and I even started to enjoy the scenery. I realized I was lucky to be here. The race was becoming fun and relaxing, and after fifteen miles, I had spaces of open fire road all to myself and could spot the finish line a few miles down the mountain.

I smelled the baked earth and aromatic shrubs. The sun-saturated air itself seemed to have a scent. Maybe the stifled feeling of being inside a fishbowl had been only partly imposed from without—maybe all along part of my disconnect from the full spectrum of life had been the result of my dulled senses. Now I heard birds screech, dried leaves rustle, pebbles skid out from under my tires. And even though my pulse was racing with the exertion, the pounding in my chest didn't fill me with dread and paranoia the way it had when my whole being seemed to shudder sickeningly with every frenetic beat of a coke-fueled heart.

The course veered from the crest of the ridge, and as the last few downhill miles clicked away, I realized I would finish this race. There is no way I can express how exultant I was at that moment. I knew my life was truly in my own hands, that I could dictate its course, and that whatever crazy way I had figured this thing out without the help of a treatment center or rehab, it was working—for now. I finished the race in fifty-ninth place out of the three hundred riders in the beginner class. A fucking miracle.

Once I finished the race, I milled around at the stands set up to cater to riders and spectators. Bike manufacturers had brought in their sponsored pros to man their displays. People could get autographs. But I didn't know who the pros were.

Then a guy said to me, "Hey, dude?"

"Yeah?"

"Hey, you Duff?"

"Yeah."

"All right, man, I'm Cully."

I realized the posters behind him had his face on them. Cully turned

out to be a former world champion named Dave Cullinan. He was drawing wide-eyed stares. I was new to the game and hence had no idea at first
of the magnitude of his accomplishments. Of course, I did notice he was
drawing a lot of attention, so I played it cool and sort of pretended like I
knew the score.

Cully was a music fan. He had recognized me in the crowd. Sure, I
had long hair and a few tattoos, but I am sure the dumb shorts and high-
top Chucks must have made me stick out much more than the ink. None
of which, of course, was my intent. In fact, I was so damned scared just to
enter the race that sticking out was the last thing I wanted to do up there.

"I was in Japan earlier this year for a race," Cully said, "and I bought
a copy of your solo album."

"Oh," I said, "so *you're* the one."

He laughed.

We started chatting and hit it off right away. We exchanged phone
numbers and he said he had some downtime and that maybe we could
ride sometime.

Outside of the United States, bicycle champions are celebrities, almost as famous as our major-league heroes here. Cully was a huge star.
He had won the 1992 downhill mountain-bike world championship and
he earned big dough from both his winnings and his many sponsors. Not
that any of this mattered to me. He was just a nice guy who welcomed me
into this new world.

About three weeks later, Cully came up to my house and we went
for a ride. We swam in my pool afterward and then went to get chicken
burritos at Baja Fresh. A big day out for me. In fact, the biggest day of
socializing of my sober life so far. Still, as the hours ticked away, I couldn't
help wondering why Cully was able to spend so much time with me—the
mountain-bike racing season didn't end until October.

Finally, I asked him.

"Why aren't you racing right now?"

He told me. It turned out an aortic valve in Cully's heart had burst as
a result of a hard fall at the end of a recent race. Luckily for him, the race
was in Phoenix and he had been rushed to a branch of the world-famous

Mayo Clinic in nearby Scottsdale. The doctors there saved his life. But at the same time they told him that between the titanium replacement valve they had installed and the blood thinners he'd have to take, he would not be able to compete at a professional level anymore. Then, when Cully got back to his home in Colorado, his place was empty—his wife had left him once his career was in jeopardy. He moved to Los Angeles.

His life was in as much disarray as mine, and he, too, was struggling to put his back together. He and I started to ride together and hang out.

I could tell from riding with him that Cully was still faster and stronger than most of us on this planet, titanium heart valve notwithstanding. Here was a guy who had always been an athlete and who had reached the top of his sport. He had not planned for anything else in his life and never expected his career to be cut short. He remained undeterred by doctors who told him there was no alternative to the titanium valve—and that it meant no more racing. Cully refused to accept that as the last word.

"Shit," he told me, "racing is what I do. I don't want to go flip burgers."

He'd set out to learn everything he could about the human heart and how it worked, and during the time we became friends he began to pin his hope on getting a nonmechanical replacement—either a human transplant from an organ donor or a valve from another mammal. Apparently this could be done, but the chances of failure were high. Failure in a heart operation meant death, but Cully preferred that risk to living as anything less than he was in his head and spirit.

My social life had now expanded big-time: instead of just me, there was me and Cully. I had someone to get lunch with now. He also began to bring some of his buddies over for our rides and before I knew it, I was riding with some of the best mountain bikers in the world. These guys had no idea about drinking or doing drugs—they were pro athletes. Sometimes they would come over to my place before or after rides. *Hey, wow, nice place—oh, you're that Duff, wow.* My first new friends were X Games jocks. I was starting to believe I could craft an enjoyable life without booze, without drugs, without parties.

Adam Day caught the mountain-biking bug, too. He and I started to do a daily grinder in the brutal hills below my house. Soon Adam joined

Cully and the gang as well. What was amazing for me to see with these pro bikers was just how hard they trained. It took genuine suffering to get good at this type of sport. It also struck me that self-discipline wasn't the only byproduct of all that painful work: humility seemed to accompany it. There was always someone better, and always something you yourself could do better. The other eye-opener for me was the way they viewed food first and foremost as fuel—fuel for their bodies that should be kept as clean burning as possible.

One Sunday morning I went out to the house of one of Cully's friends to watch some football with a crew of professional mountain bikers. There were some empty beer bottles around.

One of the bikers said, "Oh man, I'm so hungover."

"What did you guys do last night?" I asked.

"We partied like rock stars!"

"Huh," I said. "What does that mean to you?"

"I drank a six-pack by myself," said the hungover guy.

I chuckled.

Cully nodded in my direction and said, "Oh, don't fuck with this guy."

Cully knew. I had talked a lot with him since we became friends. Now I told the rest of them. I told them how much I drank, I told them about the blow, the rocks of coke I'd shove up my nose, about having no septum, about throwing up and drinking the throw-up because there was alcohol in it. The whole thing. And their faces dropped.

"Yeah," said the guy, "we partied like mountain bikers last night."

CHAPTER FORTY-ONE

✦ ✦ ✦

I still did not go out at night. I was too scared, to be honest. Besides, nothing out there held any interest for me. Go hang out with drunk people? No thanks. Go see a band? No, I had spent the last fifteen years touring and playing live shows. Go see a movie by myself? I was much more interested in books at this point. I was living the life of a monk. I even decided to cut out sex for a while.

How could I start a relationship if I didn't even know who I was? There was another aspect, too: I was scared to death of the opposite sex at this point. Not because I had two failed marriages. Because I was sober for the first time in my adult life and had no experience dating sober. No, I would hold back on that for a while.

Though I continued my daily rides on the steep hills surrounding my house, with the race at Big Bear a few weeks behind me I began searching for another challenge. I thought I had pushed myself pretty hard on my mountain bike, and the race had given me added confidence. When Cully and I did our hard rides, up steep grades, pushing the pace, I found any negative thoughts I had in my mind at the bottom of the hill disappeared by the time we reached the crest. We were so tired and so hungry at the top that we forgot about any demons that might have been plaguing us at the bottom. My system would get so taxed I'd vomit. I called it "throw-up cardio." In fact, eating enough and keeping it down became one of my biggest problems. The new misery—burning, physical pain—helped cure me of the old.

I wanted more. More pain. Something equally physically exhausting to add to the mix. Something that could drive so much out of me that my demons must surely follow.

Someone suggested I try working with a weight-lifting coach named Louis, who operated out of the Gold's Gym in North Hollywood. Once again I didn't know what to wear. I thought Converse All-Stars *were* cross-training shoes. I figured all the biking had raised my cardiovascular fitness, but I soon found out that when it came to strength conditioning, I was sorely lacking. I was thirty and hadn't done anything outside of an occasional push-up and sit-up since I was playing sports—and that ended at fourteen, more than half a lifetime ago. This was something totally new and different and taxing. I hurt every morning when I woke up, but that pain let me know that I was alive.

I went every day except Sunday—and that was just because the place wasn't open Sundays. Louis kept on me about a clean diet. I started to eat the same thing every day: melon for breakfast, a salad with grilled fish for lunch, and barbecued chicken with corn and beans for dinner. Simple fuel. He also taught me to drink even more water. I did not drink any water whatsoever in my twenties, thinking it a total waste of time and stomach space—time and space better devoted to vodka. I now realized the source of one of my earlier health problems: my hands had cracked from *dehydration*. Aha.

I started to feel at home in the gym, and soon I confided in Louis about my still-constant dilemma: *I don't know what to do tomorrow, or even tonight after the gym closes; I don't know what I'll do when I get home.*

"There's somebody you should meet," he said. "You know the fighters who come in here?"

On a few occasions I'd seen kickboxers come into the gym. These guys were usually getting ready for professional matches. In the mid-1990s, mixed martial arts and Ultimate Fighting had yet to appear—kickboxing attracted the baddest of the badassed. When I watched them work out, I was in awe. Not only were they capable of amazing physical feats, but they all seemed to share a sense of calm and confidence. It all seemed so mysterious.

"I want to introduce you to their trainer," Louis said. "Their *sensei*. His name is Benny the Jet."

I gasped.

Benny Urquidez was famous in the Valley. This was the era of Jean-Claude Van Damme and Steven Seagal; Benny had been the opponent in two of the most famous fight scenes in Jackie Chan's illustrious career. But Benny was no action-star wannabe. He was a champion ring fighter. He had helped introduce full-contact fighting to the United States and had founded his own martial-arts discipline, called Ukidokan. Just months before, Benny had come out of retirement to defend his twenty-year undefeated run as a professional kickboxer against a young Japanese fighter who said he would not consider himself to hold a true world-champion title until he had beaten the legend. That is, Benny. It ended up being the fight of a lifetime: Las Vegas, fifteen complete rounds, the forty-year-old veteran versus a twenty-four-year-old champion in his absolute prime. I have since watched the match on video dozens of times. It seems impossible neither of the men was permanently damaged—or worse. Benny won, and at the time Louis suggested I meet him, so close on the heels of this epic battle, his star burned brighter than ever.

It turned out Benny's House of Champions was just down the road from Gold's Gym. It occupied a storefront on Laurel Canyon near the corner of Oxnard—part of a row of nondescript buildings probably thrown up in the 1960s as suburban sprawl pushed out across the Valley. But there was no entrance onto the street, and you wouldn't realize it was there unless someone pointed it out. They weren't seeking foot traffic. It wasn't that type of place.

I will never forget the first day I entered the House of Champions. It was a hot Indian-summer day in September 1994. Louis took me into an alleyway and in a back door. I steeled my nerves. I took a deep breath. And we walked in—to a tanning spa. *Aha.* Running a dojo is not a lucrative business, it turned out, and House of Champions sublet part of its space.

Then we walked down a hallway and into the high-ceilinged gym. The front wall was the storefront. One sidewall was bare cinder block.

The other was Sheetrock. And the back wall was covered with mirrors. The place was completely bare-bones: an open area with floor mats, a couple punching bags, a ring, and a section with wood flooring where people could jump rope. There was a desk at one end where they sold hand wraps and gloves and other odds and ends.

And there stood Benny the Jet.

Benny was about five foot five, with brown hair and intense, deep-set eyes. If other fighters I'd seen seemed coolly confident, this guy was a glacier. As he made his way over to us, I noticed that he walked absolutely silently. Like a ninja. If I wasn't already humbled by my stay in the hospital, I most certainly was now as Louis introduced me and I went to shake Benny's hand.

Benny looked me straight in the eyes and smiled.

"It's nice to meet you," he said.

It wasn't the words that really mattered, and in fact Sensei Benny spoke only when altogether necessary. There was something else about him that made the moment so memorable—you might call it an aura. He didn't create this presence with any trappings or regalia; he was wearing ordinary gym shorts, tennis shoes, and a T-shirt. I wasn't really sure what it was about him that struck me so, but I immediately knew I wanted to receive whatever wisdom and mentorship Sensei Benny was willing to offer me. My band wasn't doing much of anything at this point, so I had the time to fully commit myself to something new.

There were still a lot of toxins in my body. Stuff had been oozing out of me ever since I started flinging myself at hills on my bike; boils crusted my skin. As far as I was concerned, only brutal physical exertion could rid the system of that shit. I suppose time might accomplish the same thing, but I was type A about it and wanted it out *now*.

I also knew by now that if I were to remain sober, I would have to do some deeper and much more serious work—work on my soul and on my psyche. The demons that lay hidden just beneath my skin were still alive and kicking and so far I was only just tamping them down. To survive, I would have to make this my way of life. Little did I know just then that the word *ukidokan*—the name of Benny's discipline—was Japanese for "a way of life."

Benny took one look at me and knew how to set the course. I could just tell. And I could tell one other thing: all the work I had put in on those hills and at the gym was about to be rendered mere child's play. You've got to go to hell if you want to face the devil, and Benny was going to be by my side all the way there and back.

CHAPTER FORTY-TWO

+ + +

Sensei Benny knew without my telling him that the first order of business was to exorcise my body and soul of the dark and sticky drug remnants in my system. The first phase of training with him was pretty much boot camp. I was in the dojo twice a day, six days a week. And in the middle of the day when I wasn't at the dojo, I rode my bike.

None of my fellow students knew I was some dude from GN'R. I had cut my hair short and I trained all day and every day—how could I be in a working band? The guys training at the House of Champions treated me as an equal—a position I earned by working hard, showing respect for the dojo, and keeping my mouth shut.

At the start, though, I was still self-conscious. Benny understood. He led me up a set of stairs at the back of the main gym. In a brutally hot loft with no a/c was an empty room with a few punching bags. There might be one other person training up there at any given time, but it was out of the way. During the first few weeks, it got as hot as 115 degrees upstairs, and I found the heat cleansing. Benny *did* know me. This space became my temple.

For the first few months, I worked upstairs with Benny, just one-on-one. Before learning any of the fighting techniques, I had to improve my basic fitness and work on some essential skills. The movements of Ukidokan are smaller than the big kicks of Tae Kwon Do and not as flashy as kung fu, but they are very demanding—especially for a gangly guy like me (I'm six foot three), starting from scratch. I needed to improve my sense of balance, for one thing, and my footwork was awful—I constantly tripped over my own feet. First I learned to jump rope, which was pretty comical. I was that guy with two left feet. At least that is what I let my head tell me.

A typical workout would start with a series of three-minute sessions of jumping rope. Instead of allowing me to rest between rounds of jumping rope, Benny sent me to the bottom of the staircase and had me leapfrog back up. Sometimes he would have me carry another fighter up the stairs. Then I'd do push-ups. Then back to jumping rope. I threw up in the corner of the room a lot, especially during those unseasonably hot weeks in September when I started.

After jumping rope, there was a heavy stretch. I would be shaking by this point. Benny would stretch me—and sometimes that would be the rest of the workout. He could tell when my body had been pushed far enough. He could also pick up on stress during the stretching sessions. He looked in my eyes and gauged the tension in my muscles and could tell what was going on inside me. That was how it must have been, because I never said a word about anything happening then in my life. In fact, I typically never said anything beyond "yes, sensei!" when I worked out with Benny. He talked to me when he sensed I was receptive to his lessons, but it wasn't a conversation. I remember during one of the first weeks I had to deal with a lawyer about what was turning out to be a protracted divorce process. Still stretching me, Benny began to talk.

"Sometimes we have to face things, face people, face situations in life that we don't like to deal with," he said. "It can feel like everybody is out to get you. That's when you have to refuse to succumb, make people realize you are a force—but you also have to give and take in these situations."

I felt like crying.

Other times he would simply intensify the workout when he picked up on stress. That worked well for me, too.

After the stretching, the workout would continue. We would do kicks without holding a bar, kicks with my fists not moving off my jaw, low kicks, mid kicks, high kicks, all without putting my feet down between sets. Then I'd hit the punching bag—close the gap, kick, and hit. Then handstand push-ups. Then various types of sit-ups.

Often at the end of these workouts, Benny would bring out a device he had invented to aid his training regime. It consisted of a waistband with rubber straps attached to it. Two straps went under your gloves and around your hands. Another pair went around your feet. He could swap in straps of varying tension—thick bands, thinner bands. I then had to kick and punch through these restraints. By the end of a workout, I'd be empty and just dry-heave.

"Place pain in a steel box and let it float away," Benny would say. "Pain will always be there—it's how you deal with it that matters."

Benny pushed me to do things that I would previously have thought physically impossible for me to do. But in order to move on to Ukidokan kickboxing—and to advance within the discipline—I simply had to do these things. I quickly realized my body wasn't going to break from the stretching or from those last few reps of whatever we were doing that day. It was just pain. I could feel the value of this pain, its transformative power.

My fight training started with learning all of the defensive moves and blocks and parries. Anyone can throw a punch and hurt someone else. That is the easy part. But defense is particularly important, especially in the ring. Benny drilled that into me day in and day out. He still does, for that matter—I guess I'm a slow learner. A lot of moves in Ukidokan looked pretty daunting when I first saw them demonstrated. But I slowly began to trust my body and my strength. One of the best and most simple edicts in Benny's teachings was his definition of confidence: "Knowing you can do something even before you try it." Imagine that. Imagine being asked whether you can run a marathon and answering yes even though you have never done it. Ukidokan was about having full confidence that you were capable of anything.

Of course, that confidence depended on more than being able to parry a punch. The draining workouts served as a prelude to daily attempts at meditation, with Benny teaching me to build a mental safe-house, a place where I would always be able to go to collect myself, renew myself. My progress in this department was not nearly as steady—or as easy for me to recognize as it was during the physical workouts. Benny talked me through this, but I had no idea whether I was succeeding as a student.

Benny, who is part Blackfoot Indian, also liked to quote the famous Sioux warrior Crazy Horse, who defeated George Custer's cavalry forces at the battle of Little Bighorn in 1876: "Today is a good day to die." The first time he said this, it sounded like a macho throwaway line expressing a sort of I-ain't-scared-of-nothing ethos. *Gnarly,* I thought. But the more I considered it, the more I knew there must be something else to it. Benny wasn't macho, and he never threw out vacuous lines. Despite my inability to pinpoint its meaning, I decided not to ask him about it. *This must be part of my mental training.* I'd have to figure it out.

After every workout, I would remove my gloves and Benny would take the end of the cloth wrap around my fists and have me back away from him to unravel the wrap. When the wrap had completely unraveled, I held on to my end and the two of us remained connected, Benny holding one end, me the other. As I backed up and then held the taut wrap, Benny made me recite the five rules of fighting:

1. Never move back in a straight line.
2. Never set.
3. Redirect.
4. Fight your opponent as he fights you.
5. Place your opponent where you want him.

But Benny never went in order. It was like a quiz, testing me at my most exhausted.

"Three," Benny would say.

"Redirect," I would answer.

"One."

"Never move back in a straight line."

"Four."

"Fight your opponent as he fights you."
"Two."
"Never set."
"Five."
"Place your opponent where you want him."

CHAPTER FORTY-THREE

+ + +

In my twenties, there were two things I never really had to come to grips with: taking responsibility for my actions and thinking about what I would do besides playing music. I just didn't think that I would be around to deal with that shit. Now, as I began to figure out the first of those two things, I also had to grapple with the possibility that I'd have to solve that second question at the same time. With only Axl, Slash, and me left of the original Guns and progress toward a new record at a standstill, what if the band imploded, as was looking more and more likely?

I still struggled to fill my time, and one day when I was poking around in my basement, I found a crate filled with Guns N' Roses financial statements. I opened the crate and pulled one out. Then another. And another. I realized I had no idea what they meant. For all I knew, I could have been getting ripped off during all those hazy years of world tours and record-breaking album sales.

My bandmates and I were streetwise, though, and we knew what a shark looked like. I still remembered telling the accountants that I wanted their home addresses. But then I had kind of lost track of the money side of things pretty quickly. Shit, there were weeks when we were out on the road that I could barely remember my own name, much less follow where all our money was going.

One of my older brothers, Mark, was a financial guy at Boeing who really knew the nuts and bolts of investments. I asked him to have a look at the financial statements.

"These are hard to follow even for me," he said, "and I have an MBA. More than anything else, they're misleading."

This was not good. I needed to pay attention to this stuff. And I also needed to find places to invest some of the money I'd made. I couldn't just leave it sitting in a checking account.

Once I got engaged in trying to figure things out and Mark and I started talking, he helped me find an investment guy in Seattle. We started going through basic public information available about companies whose stocks interested us, information like a company's annual report. You could read how the company viewed itself and what—at the most rudimentary level—it planned to do in the future. It sounds like simple stuff, but it turned out that just reading those sorts of things and deciding whether they made sense put us ahead of most people.

I bought some forward-thinking equities. Everybody in Seattle was buying Starbucks because you could see it growing. It hadn't turned up on every street corner yet, but it had a foothold in L.A. and San Francisco, and there might have been a couple storefronts in New York. And there were lines at their coffee shops. People were going there. We thought it might be a short-term investment, but at that time it didn't look as if they were expanding too fast. I also bought Microsoft. A little later, I got in early on Amazon, another Seattle stock. It was cool to start investing in the 1990s and have a connection to Seattle. There was an excitement in the air about some of those companies, and they just happened to be in my hometown. They also just happened to be some of the hottest stocks of the next decade or so.

In late 1994, Axl called and we talked about plans for the band, trying to figure out what to do. The conversation went on for more than an hour. We started to talk about GN'R's accomplishments—something that none of us had ever acknowledged or discussed together prior to this. We talked about our creative success, about our collective vision, about why that vision had resonated. We talked about how the band had represented a family, how that family had started a business, how that family business had gone global. We had come a long way from the days of Gardner Street.

"We've never sat down and said, 'Look what we did,'" I said. "I know we're not the type of band to high-five or whatever, but we never even went out to dinner and just shook each other's hands."

"You know," said Axl, "you're right. But we still could."

It took getting sober and contemplative about the whole situation, but now it struck me as sad that we hadn't stood face-to-face and congratulated one another—alone, without management or minions around. At this point, it would have been just Axl, Slash, and me, but there would still have been value in doing it. It could have led to something else we needed to do: to take stock of where things stood, to take a step back and remember that despite the centrifugal forces driving us apart now, we had started the band as friends.

"We should never lose track of that fact," I said.

Axl was definitely behind the idea, but I never set up any kind of meeting. Somehow it was already too late. This was right around the time the movie *Interview with the Vampire* came out, featuring a cover of the Stones' "Sympathy for the Devil" credited to Guns N' Roses. Guitar work by Paul Huge, Axl's childhood friend, had been added to the track and Slash was more furious now than ever.

There was something else keeping me from acting on it, too. My panic attacks had finally subsided, I was getting comfortable in my own skin, gaining confidence, becoming an adult; I had lost all that booze weight, was feeling good, feeling calm, feeling centered; I had been sober for a good chunk of time. I liked the person I had become. I had made it through—or so it seemed. It dawned on me that perhaps I had let people's perceptions of me define who I was. In other words, I had believed the hype. I wasn't Duff-the-king-of-beers anymore. So was I Duff–from–GN'R or Duff-the-punk-rock-guy anymore? I didn't have to be. These definitions now seemed a bit adolescent. Maybe I was finally growing up, glad my turbulent teens and twenties were a thing of the past. And despite my protectiveness about Guns, it hit me: the band was no longer the most important thing to me.

I decided to spend a quiet New Year alone in Hawaii. I didn't take my bike with me, but I wanted to continue to exercise. So I decided to go running. I headed out to the beach and started to run. At some point, I became aware of the padlock and chain—that I'd worn around my neck since Guns got signed—clanking against my chest.

Bam, bam, bam.

Damn, it was heavy.

Why did I wear this thing anyway? As a tribute to Sid Vicious? To carry his torch and safeguard punk? Was that how I needed to identify myself?

Bullshit.

I found a guy who was taking care of the lawn at the complex where I was staying.

"Hey, man, you have any bolt cutters?"

"Sure," he said. He motioned for me to follow him.

He led me to a maintenance shed. He rummaged around inside and emerged with a set of bolt cutters.

"Can you cut this off?" I said, pulling at the chain around my neck.

He shrugged. With a quizzical look on his face, he grasped the chain between the blades of the bolt cutters. I craned my neck in the other direction and he snipped the chain in half with a forceful jerk of the handles.

I'd like to say I heaved it grandly into the Pacific and watched my former identity recede into the depths, but I didn't. I threw it into the dumpster next to the maintenance shed, said thank you, and finished my run.

CHAPTER FORTY-FOUR

✦ ✦ ✦

Back in L.A., the House of Champions was in constant motion with kick-boxing pros getting ready for fights in the United States or abroad. Once they saw that I was dedicated to training and wasn't some pampered rock star, they began to help me with my workouts with Benny. I started to do technique-only sparring with some of these guys and saw the speed at which I would be expected to compete. Okay, note taken.

Sensei Benny was like a father figure to me, and I never called him by anything but his title in or out of the gym. Not because he demanded it—in fact, he specifically told me I could address him less formally outside the dojo—but because I felt that strongly about his role in my life. He was a teacher; he deserved a different level of respect. I continue to this day to call him "sensei." After a few months of one-on-one workouts with Benny, we started to work out together with another guy at the gym named Michael Morteo. Like Benny, Michael was strikingly calm. He had been a martial artist since age five. Michael, too, was a sensei; when he walked through the dojo, students turned and bowed to him out of re-spect. But Michael was my age and the longer we worked out together, the more I came to think of him as a friend. Even so, I rarely shared personal things with Michael, either—all he cared about was the work. Everything was about that day, that moment, that punch or kick.

Benny would sometimes have me and Michael spar in the room up-stairs with one of my legs bound to one of Michael's. I still had a strong fight-or-flight instinct at that time, but tied to my opponent I could not possibly run. So I had to fight, to deal with the challenge at hand. I got tired, I got hit, I wanted to fall over. Michael connected with some good punches—though this was technique sparring and the blows were not full strength or meant to hurt. Still, getting hit helped bring home the lessons I'd been trying to master. After taking a few smacks in the face, I found it easier to remember to keep my right hand up in a defensive position when not punching.

Sparring exposed any lack of focus; I got a lot of black eyes.

The shakier and more exhausted I was after these sessions, the better able I was to focus during my meditations afterward. With my mind still and clear after a throw-up-inducing workout, my mental safe house began to take shape. In my head, it was an actual house. The main room resembled the dojo, with one wall covered in full-length mirrors. I began to furnish the house with the things I thought I would need: a suit of armor, vials of cleansing potion, amphoras of pure water, and an arsenal of weapons—hey, life was tough, so, yes, there were swords in my safe house.

The hope, Benny said, was to reach a point where I would no longer need to be physically exhausted to find this place; I would be able to go there whenever necessary—like when I felt a panic attack coming on or when I had to deal with a threatening person or tense situation and felt somewhat unsafe.

Benny placed a lot of importance on honesty. "Start every day with a clear conscience," he said. "You should be able to wake up, go to the mirror in your bathroom, look yourself right in the eye, and say, 'I didn't lie to anyone I encountered yesterday,' 'I didn't skirt an issue yesterday.' If you lead an honest life, there are no regrets."

At first I would actually do that—look in the mirror. I started sleeping really well. Then, concentrating, deep inside my mental safe house, I began to raise my gaze and look myself in the eyes in that full-length mirror in my mind. Maybe getting so loaded all the time had just been a way to avoid dealing with unpleasant truths about myself, a way to flee the consequences of speaking and acting honestly, a way to dull the heavy burden of living with dishonesty?

I looked at myself in that mirror: *Consider yourself checked, McKagan.*
"Today is a good day to die," I heard Benny say.

Huh? I still didn't get it.

The next big step for me would be fighting in the ring, which I had yet to do. Fighting represented the coming together of all the skills I had begun to develop—the physical, the technical, and the mental. I would have to connect my footwork to the other movements, and I would simultaneously have to play the chess match in my head—move my opponent, anticipate, deflect. And then, of course, there was the cardiovascular test of ring fighting. No matter how many reps you did on a bag, punching and kicking nonstop for a three-minute round in the ring was a completely different ball game.

Without warning, one day Benny took out two sets of headgear and put one on my head. I felt panicked in the headgear—my claustrophobia kicked in—and Benny saw it in my eyes. Or rather in the fact that my eyes were darting all over the place, looking away, looking down. He helped me calm down, concentrate, and work around it.

I also had to get it together because I now knew I was about to spar with someone in the ring—there was no other reason to wear headgear. I had seen people freak out after taking their first real punch in the ring. One huge guy had gone into shock and started weeping. A lot of emotions were released in the gym. I wasn't sure what to expect from myself.

Sensei took out a jar of Vaseline and daubed some under my eyes. Then he did the same to his face. No. It couldn't be. He was going to be my first sparring experience? The world champion? I recognized the look on his face from videos I'd seen of him in the ring.

As the bell rang to start the first round, all my technique vanished in a rush of fear and I started to swing wildly. I probably threw some of the worst kicks ever thrown in that dojo. A few minutes into the second round, I saw for an instant the back of my sensei's head hanging in the air above me and I suddenly woke up on the ground with my head cradled in Benny's arms.

I had been knocked out by a jump-spinning back kick to the liver. Apparently, a sudden shock to your organs can and will knock you out.

This was Benny's signature kick. An air strike. Like a fighter jet. Aha. Right. Benny *the Jet*.

Sensei admonished me for not using my defense. I was still on the ground, still sort of waking up. He said that I should have parried the kick and thrown a counter.

"Yes, sensei."

He asked me how I felt. To my own surprise, I was actually fine. Getting knocked out wasn't so terrifying after all. It was like falling out of a chair onto a soft rug. No big deal.

CHAPTER FORTY-FIVE

+ + +

One year after my pancreatitis, I went back to see Dr. Thomas in Seattle for a physical. He just couldn't believe my metamorphosis. Not only the changes in my outward physical appearance, but more important, in my organs and blood. He could see no discernible damage—except, of course, for the hole burned through my septum. At the end of the exam, he had a look of amazement on his face.

"To say I didn't have much hope for you when you left here is an understatement," said Dr. Thomas.

Hmm.

"I didn't expect you to live more than six months," he continued.

Don't sugarcoat it or anything, Doc. I guess alcoholics who reached the stage of acute pancreatitis didn't often turn their lives around. I got the point. And it gave me a shot of adrenaline.

Perhaps more striking were the internal changes even Dr. Thomas couldn't see—the changes in my mind.

I did have one question for Dr. Thomas, however.

"Why does my nose still run so long after I stopped snorting coke?"

"Quitting is just the beginning of the process," he said. "Your body is still trying to slough it out."

In other words, my body had become so accustomed to ridding my sinuses of foreign substances that it hadn't turned off the spigot yet. And that would take much longer than I anticipated—much, much longer.

Soon after I returned to L.A., Cully got the heart-valve transplant he had been dreaming about when we first met. He took six days off from riding after the surgery, then started training for a return to professional racing. I went to his first race back on the World Cup circuit. Being back at this level of competition was a major triumph.

Then Matt Sorum called to see whether I'd be interested in playing rhythm guitar for a Monday-night show at the Viper Room with Steve Jones—the original Sex Pistols guitar player—and John Taylor of Duran Duran. It was tempting. Slash was out touring with Snakepit, so there wasn't anything happening on the Guns front. And shit, Steve was a personal hero of mine. Still, it would be a big step for me because up to this point I had not played a live show sober. In fact, to the best of my knowledge I had never played sober in my entire life. I always took at least a couple of pulls off a bottle before a show, even at my earliest ones. The myth of being glamorously wasted for gigs was something I guess I had bought into from the beginning. All of my idols were that way, right? Keith Richards, Iggy Pop, Johnny Thunders—and Steve Jones, for that matter. I was terrified at the prospect of playing sober.

Of course, a few years earlier I had witnessed how Iggy could still flip a switch in the studio or onstage even after he got sober—he blew me away with his ability to reach that special place with no substances at all. And Steve Jones was sober now. Matt Sorum and John Taylor, too, so I would be in good company. I decided to go to a few rehearsals. Before I knew it, gig night had arrived and there was a line stretching down the block of Sunset Boulevard in front of the Viper Room.

This was June 1995, and back then the tinfoil-lined Viper Room was Hollywood central, filled with all of the hippest and most judgmental people on the planet. Fortunately the crowd that night also included Cully, Adam Day, and McBob. But still.

Can I do this?

I couldn't shake the feeling that people were just going to be staring at me. Could I get out of myself without some sort of inebriant to help me? If I had learned nothing else during my career to that point, I did know that if I was too self-aware, I was going to suck. And if that was going to be a nightly occurrence, then I might as well just give it up. But I wanted to try, despite my fear.

It all came down to that old dilemma: fight or flight.

As we got near the little stage, something suddenly took over. I felt that anger. That healthy rage. I wanted to attack the gig, the people there, myself.

The show itself was a bit of a blur—which was good. But I still wasn't confident about my performance. Sure, I knew I had played the notes correctly. But I didn't know whether I had been any good. As soon as I could, I went out to find Cully.

"Dude, how'd I do?" I asked him.

"What? How'd you *do*? Are you *kidding*? You guys killed it."

He looked at me and I could tell what he was thinking: *We've made it back.* Cully and I often seemed to know what the other was thinking, so I'm pretty sure he heard me silently add: *Together.*

CHAPTER FORTY-SIX

✦ ✦ ✦

At the time of that Viper Room show, I had been out of the public eye for more than a year and no one really knew anything about how I had been spending my time. My life was super-private as I recovered and trained. I guess I never noticed that I'd undergone drastic physical changes. Of course, Axl, my doctor, and my brothers and sisters and mom had noticed the changes and made encouraging comments. But I wasn't prepared for the response following that first concert at the Viper Room.

Matt Sorum called me the day after the show.

"The rumor is you got liposuction and a face-lift!"

"What? No way!"

"Yep, that's what everyone is saying."

The extent to which my path diverged from the typical Hollywood path was never so clear as it was through those rumors. Actually, I took them as a compliment.

Another thing happened that night that hadn't happened in my life for a while: I interacted with women. Some of them even showed interest in me, even went out of their way to make it easy for me to talk to them, I could tell. But I looked at everything differently now and wasn't quite ready for any of that. I still had more work to do. Besides, what would I do with a drunk girl or someone who was a scenester or club kid? I really had absolutely nothing in common with these people. My life was all about literature, martial arts, healthy food, and mountain biking. I was a stone-cold nerd. I was only in Los Angeles because I was still trying to work with GN'R. The nightlife ethic there was something I now saw as shallow.

I went home alone that night.

Now that I knew I'd be able to continue to play music, it rekindled an incredibly strong urge to do it right away. I looked forward to a string of gigs Matt had lined up in September and October of 1995. I really liked the guys in the band, too—Steve Jones even started mountain biking with me.

The Viper Room was jammed with beautiful women every time we played. John Taylor proved to be a total chick magnet. After a while I thought maybe I was ready to try again. The first girl I started hanging out with was also sober. She started talking a lot about "the program." At first I had no idea what she meant, though it was clear that I was supposed to know. Turned out she meant AA.

"I don't know about that stuff," I told her.

She started leaving clothes at my house. I would gather them up and put them in a pile. *No, no, no, be honest.* After a few weeks, I took the clothes back to her.

"I'm still trying to figure everything out," I said. "But one thing I do know is that I'm not ready for a girlfriend."

My old friend West Arkeen started to call me more often around this time, too. He had struggled with crack and heroin addiction since the day I met him in Hollywood back in 1985. For many years I felt helpless to do anything to straighten him up—despite pleas from his various girlfriends, I was just too fucked up myself to possibly play a role in addressing other people's addictions. I realized in retrospect just how bad off he must have been if people around him had called me, of all people. Of all people! I was constantly putting myself in harm's way to get hold of drugs and drinking myself toward organ failure, and compared to West I had my shit together. Really? Wow.

As I talked to him now, it seemed as if West was serious about cleaning up, and I felt that I also now knew some things that might help him—even if I didn't yet feel equipped to help anyone with sobriety myself. So I invited him to join me down at the dojo. One of the teachers at the House of Champions, Sensei Anthony—a world-champion *eskrima* stick fighter from Australia—took a particular interest in West's case and soon agreed to train him. Anthony seemed undaunted by all the scarring on West's body from needle marks and abscesses. Anthony studied up on the ins and outs of drug withdrawal. It was a war; Anthony took it upon himself to help West fight it. West proved a dedicated student and poured himself into his training. After a few months, I figured West was out of the woods. I figured he had found what he needed in martial arts, just as I had.

But drugs and addiction always lingered in the shadows and crept up on you if you failed to look them off. The moment you think that you have a little breathing room is the exact moment you need to redouble your vigilance. I already knew this to be true for me. Soon I found out it was the case for my friend Eddy, as well. Ed had slowly slipped back into his old ways and I was too far away in L.A. to see it. He went all the way in and found himself hanging in very dark places. Luckily Andy got wind of what was happening and called me. We set up a drug rehab for Eddy. Then we both called him. He agreed to go into rehab that night.

If I was going to avoid those pitfalls, I was going to have to further steel myself mentally. The only way I knew how to do that was to push myself even further physically. I started sparring as often as I could alongside my workouts and bike rides.

Despite all the training at bobbing and weaving, when I climbed into the ring I often forgot everything as soon as I took a blow to the head. That was the biggest shock—getting punched or kicked in the head, especially in the nose.

I'd hear someone yelling in my corner and recognize the words: "Bob! Jab!"

But it just didn't sink in. When I got hit I tensed up and shut down.

When I wasn't mentally focused, my head got treated like a punching bag, bobbing back and forth as I took blow after blow. But once I got used to it, it became no different than being punched in the shoulder. I was able to relax despite taking a shot to the head. Soon I found taking a good punch in the face oddly satisfying.

Pain is good.

Then I began to actually *like* getting hit in the head. Or kicked in the head. Anything. I started taking shots I saw coming and could have parried.

Pain feels good.

Benny snapped at me when he realized I was taking unnecessary blows.

"I didn't train you to be that guy. The impact is what we try to avoid. Start playing chess, not checkers. This is a chess game. *Life* is a chess game."

I had to learn to distinguish between good pain and bad pain. Of course, what I was experiencing when I threw up in the gym was different from the pain in my sinuses as coke had burned away my septum. But the ache from getting hit was not the same as the ache from hard work either. Let *good* pain float away. *Honest* pain.

Never move back in a straight line.

Never set.

Redirect.

Fight your opponent as he fights you.

Place your opponent where you want him.

One day Sensei Benny told me I was ready to get in the ring again.

"It's your time," he said.

I trusted Sensei Benny with my life by now, and so when he said I was ready, then ready I was. I didn't blink.

I don't know if Petey "Sugarfoot" Cunningham remembers the three rounds we went inside the ropes, but I sure do. Petey was the world middleweight champion at the time and was tuning up for a title defense. I was just another sparring partner, mere fodder. But I was fast.

Petey was faster. Much, much faster.

In my first round with him, I knew I was watching a showman at his best. He was known for his high kicks to the head and his lightning-fast axe kicks to the shoulders. I had fairly solid defenses now for anything around my head, but the axe kicks happened so fast that pretty much every one of them landed. By the end of the second round, and all through the third, my arms were useless. My shoulders had taken a beating the likes of which I'd never felt before. But I did not get knocked out—or even knocked down. I did not panic or get flustered. I knew my sensei had put me in there to learn and to prove once and for all that I would and could protect myself.

When the final bell rang and we were finished, Petey came up to me and said, "You can go home and tell your friends you lasted three rounds with the world champion!"

I am not sure whether he was bragging about himself or surprised that I had hung in there. It didn't matter.

I went to see a Red Hot Chili Peppers concert with Axl not long afterward. When I left after the gig, two dudes started shouting at me:

"Fucking faggot! Short-haired faggot!"

In the old days, that sort of thing would ring in my ears, and if I walked away I'd feel like a pussy. Two years earlier I would have been like, "Fuck you, I'll fuck you up." Now I had a hard time picturing why I would have been offended. If someone thinks you're gay or is dumb enough to think that calling you gay is an insult, who cares? And if someone is ignorant enough to say it in public, they're probably just drunk. I just laughed to myself as I kept walking. It didn't matter at all.

Benny had talked to me about the confidence to walk away. I had also seen guys from the dojo who I knew could literally kill someone just walk away and smile when someone tried to antagonize them. What was it to them?

Having that same sort of reaction now to the two guys yelling at me confirmed that Benny's lessons were indeed sinking in: I had gone to my mental safe house and realized I didn't need a sword. Confidence was a weapon.

All this fight training, it turned out, was designed to enable me *not* to fight.

PART SIX

YOU SHINED A LIGHT WHERE IT WAS DARK, ON MY WASTED HEART

CHAPTER FORTY-SEVEN

+ + +

After appearing as Kings of Chaos, Mr. Moo's Futurama, and Wayne Neutron, Matt Sorum, Steve Jones, John Taylor, and I ended up calling our unintentional "supergroup" Neurotic Outsiders. It was funny to hear it described as a group at all, much less a supergroup. The whole thing was totally casual—our live shows were nothing more than punk-rock parties, a couple of dudes playing loads of cover songs—Clash, Pistols, Damned, Stooges—with lots of our friends jumping onstage to join us for a song or two. But after we played a string of Viper Room gigs and a few national gigs through February 1996, record companies started pursuing us. I was dumbfounded. We were just having a laugh, after all. In the end, Madonna's label, Maverick, gave us a million-dollar advance. This was four times what Guns got! From our perspective, the deal had an element of a heist to it, and the whole thing—especially with Steve Jones a part of it—reminded me of *The Great Rock 'n' Roll Swindle*.

John Taylor chuckled about the weird contours of the music business. He was living in an apartment in Venice Beach while we worked on the Neurotic project. He told me cautionary tales about his time in Duran Duran.

"I thought I was just fabulous and that it would never stop rolling in," he said. "I owned places in Paris, London, and New York. I flew everywhere in private jets. And one day I woke up and it was over. The money was gone."

The bands I'd been in never talked about business. For most of them, of course, there simply had been no business to discuss. There was plenty of business whirling around Guns N' Roses, but we were afraid to talk about that stuff for fear of betraying our ignorance. Now, failing to acknowledge the business of being in a band seemed to me like a sort of cowardice, or at the very least a failure to deal with reality: professional musicians may be reluctant businessmen, but we are businessmen nonetheless. To pretend otherwise, or to ignore the obvious, felt dishonest. Now that I knew I was going to live and that I was going to continue to play music, I decided that at some point I should try to figure out how the commerce side of things worked.

But first, Neurotic Outsiders had an album to make. We went into NRG Studios in North Hollywood, recorded the songs we'd been playing live for the past year, and by the end of the summer of 1996 we were preparing to release our self-titled debut album. Even though we had told all the labels pursuing us that we weren't willing to mount a full-scale tour, we did line up a string of gigs in September to promote the record. I was going back out on the road.

A few days before the album came out, we played New York City's Webster Hall, which had been one of the launching points for my ill-fated solo tour. This time it was actually fun. Next up were Boston, D.C., and Toronto. Then came September, 13, 1996, and a show in Pontiac, Michigan. We did press at each stop, and here, outside Detroit, I was slated to talk to a writer named Jon Stainbrook, a contributor to the skateboard magazine *Thrasher.* Stain was a longtime ringleader of the Toledo punk scene, and he had interviewed me several times over the years. He brought his tape recorder to my hotel room. I was glad to see him again.

After the interview, he said, "Hey, man, I know you're sober now and that you're not into model chicks and all that shit. But there's this girl, friend of my family. We've been friends since we were kids, she's really cool, she's been modeling in Milan and Paris. She just moved to L.A."

I wasn't sure what he wanted, and just said, "Yeah, sure, man, I can show her around or whatever when I get back."

"Great!"

But instead of giving me her number, he reached for the phone in my hotel room and dialed her number.

"Her name is Susan," he said as he waited for her to answer.

He quickly told her about me and then just handed me the phone. We exchanged pleasantries and agreed to meet up at some stage when I got back to Los Angeles in October. She sounded nice.

After that, Stain and I left the room to get coffees, and as we walked past a newsstand he pointed to a magazine cover.

"That's Susan there," he said.

"Oh!"

Call me shallow, but I was much more interested once I saw that photo. She had long brown hair and dark almond-shaped eyes. Fucking beautiful. She was nearly naked in the shot, too, and her body was absolutely slamming.

"Yeah," Stain said, reading my mind. "She's the real deal. I didn't want to say it, but the photographer Steven Meisel gave her the nickname 'the body' after a shoot."

"What's the body's last name?"

"Holmes."

I called Susan Holmes again the next day. We talked for a long time. I called her again a few days later. We started talking a lot. I still had a few dates to play in Europe, but by the time I was ready to fly home from Germany at the end of September, we had agreed she would pick me up at Burbank airport.

When she approached me at the airport, it was marvelous to be able to look her in the eyes without craning my neck: she was five foot eleven. At six foot three, I appreciate tall women.

I wore a ratty tank top for the long flight. It was comfortable, of course, but I also had a clever plan. Susan and I were supposed to go out to dinner when I arrived.

When we climbed into her car, I said, "Listen, why don't you just come up to my house? I can shower and change . . ."

Susan wasn't having it. She suggested we go to a supercasual sushi place instead and hang out there.

Wow, she has morals. This was getting interesting.

She had no real idea of what I had gone through beyond rumors and the little I had already told her about what I had been like once upon a time. When she ordered a sake to calm her nerves (of course . . . I am a stud!), I was not bothered in the slightest. I was beginning to get comfortable in situations like this. The Neurotic Outsiders tour had helped a bunch. I was no longer "gripping" every time I went to a bar or spent time around people who drank. Socializing with "normies"—people who function normally rather than abusing alcohol—helped me see just how screwy my life had been and how bad an alcoholic I was. Being around normal drinkers actually started to make me feel more secure in my sobriety.

I soon learned that when Susan got together with her girlfriends, they often had a glass of wine or a cocktail—the stuff normal people do. Susan wasn't a big drinker, though. Not even close. One glass of wine was almost too much for her. I always found this amusing. Back in the day, a *bottle* of wine was like taking a sip of water or chewing a piece of gum for me. It didn't affect me.

I was sober and honest, so the first few weeks with Susan were emotionally intense. A month together felt like a year—in a good way. Without the bullshit, we got to know each other quickly and built a solid foundation. And when Susan did finally come to my house, Chloe took an instant shine to her.

I called Cully soon after I started hanging out with Susan.

"Holy shit, I hit the lottery," I said.

"You sound fired up, bro," said Cully.

"Yeah, I can't tell you how excited I am," I told him.

It was all well and good to share this with one of my best friends, but I should be open about my feelings with Susan, too, I thought.

"I am so happy," I told her.

This was life without regrets.

And that's when it hit me.

Today is a good day to die.

I think I just might get it.

If something were to happen tomorrow, my last thought wouldn't be, *I wish I had told Susan how I felt about her.* I'd done everything; I didn't *want* to die, but I could be proud of not having left anything unsaid or undone. That's what it meant to wake up with a clear conscience, to be honest.

Maybe that Crazy Horse quote wasn't morbid. Maybe it wasn't even about death. Maybe it was about *life* and how you live it.

CHAPTER FORTY-EIGHT

✦ ✦ ✦

A press release went out in late 1996 announcing that Slash had officially quit Guns N' Roses. It barely registered with me—I had long since come to grips with the fact that he was done. And anyway, it wasn't as if Guns was active. He left behind an empty studio being paid for by an entity that itself barely existed.

Neurotic Outsiders finished its live obligations and drifted apart again. The friendships remained but we stopped playing regularly.

One afternoon I went down to the House of Champions and walked in while a class was taking place.

The sensei leading the class said, "Turn and bow."

The students turned toward me and bowed.

This was a huge and totally unexpected rite of passage. An organic show of respect from the people who trained and taught here was the highest praise I could imagine. It held far more value for me than any belt or diploma—though I did feel as if I had somehow graduated.

In December 1996, Susan and I decided to make plans to go away together for New Year's. We booked a room at the Hilton Waikoloa on the Big Island in Hawaii.

We were alone together and in love. Things went great. Until one morning when Susan woke up feeling sick. We called the front desk about seeing a doctor. No problem, the hotel had a doctor on-site and we could get an appointment that same day.

Its tropical decor made the doctor's office feel unusually friendly. A nurse checked us in and then escorted us to an examination room. She asked Susan to describe her symptoms. The woman wrote everything down, smiled broadly, and gave a sort of silent-movie wink. She said the doctor would be right in, and walked out.

"What's up with her?" I said.

The doctor came in, all chipper and whistling. He asked Susan to give him a urine sample. She did. An exaggerated grin spread across his face and he went back out.

"Weird," Susan said.

He came in again a few minutes later.

"Well, congratulations, Mr. and Mrs. McKagan, it's just as I suspected. After all, Hawaii is where love happens."

"Sorry?" I said.

"You're going to have a baby!"

I just about fainted.

Here's the deal: we weren't yet a Mr. and Mrs., we had been together for only a few months, and neither of us had ever before been in a situation where "congratulations" would accompany a discussion of pregnancy.

We went back to the hotel room and didn't say much to each other. We had talked about having kids—*someday*—from quite early in our relationship. Now all the things we had said to each other would be put to the test.

The timing couldn't have been better, though. Susan was done modeling, so there were no career concerns for her. Once we got over the edge of that first day, all the things we had worried about melted away.

The next step was to get the skeletons out of the closet. I told her all my sordid stories. It took a while. She told me hers.

This was not the way I planned things in my new life. But I realized my idealized notions of a perfect life were nothing more than a mishmash of unattainable images from Frank Capra movies. Those old dreams of mine were too passive. Outside forces didn't dictate romantic success any more than they dictated the course of other parts of life. I had to take ownership, dictate the course myself—or rather, together with a partner who was also willing to work toward the same goals. Yes, we would have to work at it. Shit happens; life would always be unpredictable. It was up to me—and us—to rise to every occasion.

At long last, I felt ready for this. Those dark hours and days and weeks and years fell by the wayside there in Hawaii as Susan and I discussed our next move. We would be a team, come hell or high water, and it was going to kick some serious ass.

Confidence is knowing you can do something even before you try it.

Could I be a good father?

Yes.

CHAPTER FORTY-NINE

✦ ✦ ✦

When Susan and I returned to L.A., we started to do all of the typical things an expecting couple did. We bought stacks of books on childbirth and parenting. We found a prenatal doctor. We enrolled in child-birthing classes. Of course, until you actually have a baby, there is nothing that can prepare you for having a child. It's all sort of make-believe until the baby comes. But we sure were floating on puffy white clouds of excitement and swooning over all things newborn.

Susan never really got sick. As the weeks progressed, she settled into a comfort zone. She and I worked on some meditation techniques I had learned from Benny. The techniques had helped me conquer many of my gravest fears. Susan got into it.

It had been over two years since I made my first investments in 1994, and while those tentative investments were by no means huge—my initial outlay was less than $100,000—some of the stocks had split and continued to grow. I felt pretty savvy when I considered those results. But I came down to earth anytime I examined my GN'R financial statements. No matter how long I stared at them, the paperwork never made sense. A few years earlier, I would have looked at those things and fallen asleep. But there was a carrot out there I was chasing now. That carrot was knowledge. And I was now in a frame of mind to accept what a good teacher had to offer.

One day I drove down to Santa Monica Community College to register for a class on financial accounting. I immediately encountered a problem.

"I'm sorry, sir," the registrar said, "but you have to be able to prove you graduated from high school to take a college course."

That could be tricky. I had never graduated from high school. It wasn't that school had been so hard for me as a kid. When I was in third and fourth grade, I was determined to become a doctor. My mom was secretly psyched—her brother was a doctor. My grandpa had been kicked out of his house in Ireland when he was fourteen and got on a boat to America, where he fought for the United States in World War I, worked in mines on the East Coast, started logging and moved out west, and then, during the Depression, worked on Ross Dam in the northern Cascade Mountains. For his child—my uncle John—to become a doctor was a perfect American success story. Uncle John even attended a Jesuit school, Seattle University, pleasing his Irish Catholic family. It seemed like the path I wanted to follow when I was an elementary school student. By junior high I was in gifted classes with all the brainiacs. It was so easy that I stopped paying attention—and I got into rock and roll and girls and drugs. Before long, school started to pass me by and I began to get into trouble. Eventually I got kicked out of my junior high for pulling a knife on someone. I was sent to another school, where I didn't know anyone.

By high school I started playing in bands. Beginning sophomore year, I was playing out-of-town gigs. I went to my mom and said I couldn't do both, and music was what I wanted to do. I transferred to an alternative school called Nova, which had been founded by hippies in 1971. There were no classrooms, just a lot of beanbag chairs and nerdy kids. Being in an alternative school meant I wasn't really going to school at all. In theory, you did your work on your own. But I didn't; I rehearsed and played gigs. You had to have somebody at least eighteen years old as an off-campus counselor who certified your work. Kim Warnick from the Fastbacks became mine. The only other requirement at Nova was to show up at school for half an hour every two weeks. After a while I didn't manage to make those appearances and got thrown out. That was the end of my school career. It was 1982.

Now, fifteen years after my last classroom—or even beanbag—experience, I wanted to head back to school. Fortunately at eighteen I had taken a GED test. I did well—scored a 97. I even received a letter of commendation from the governor. My mom had kept that along with the paperwork from my various schools and a copy of my GED. I returned with copies of all of that and Santa Monica Community College gave me the all clear to take a class in the summer term. But that turned out to be just the first hurdle.

For my first class, I purposely dressed low-key. My hair was still short. But people still knew who I was immediately—this was L.A. After that first class, people were hanging out in the parking lot to ask me for my autograph. From then on, though, it was fine. After that, I had only to deal with class.

The professor was cool. He'd had a hand in bringing the *Power Rangers* TV show to the United States. He taught because he loved to, not because he needed to work. Things he covered in class quickly became clearer, but I found I didn't know how to study on my own. I would call my brother Matt and ask for help. Eventually I hired a tutor—an assistant professor from USC. We met at a library. Before I could pose any questions about the classwork, the guy had questions for me.

"Tell me about the chicks," he said. "How many girls have you had?"

What? We're in a library, and I'm looking for help with my class.

"Come on," he said. "Let's talk numbers."

Still, I made it through the class, and by the end I was able to see GN'R hadn't gotten ripped off. *Hallelujah.* Guess all those threats about wanting to know the accountants' home addresses had paid off.

From my experience, once you were pegged as a rock guy, people just assumed that you were either brain-dead or off high-flying on a private jet with hookers and cocaine. (Or both.) While I had definitely been guilty of both of the aforementioned clichés, in that classroom I found—don't laugh—a love of academia.

I earned an A in that first course.

And I was totally hooked.

CHAPTER FIFTY

+ + +

West Arkeen suddenly stopped coming to the dojo. Sensei Anthony called him and drove to his house on multiple occasions—but was unable to make contact. I called West once or twice, but then my old defense mechanisms quickly went up when I figured he must be using again.

You fucked me, man!

I was filled with a searing black anger I hadn't felt in a while.

West started to call my house again. I sat idly by, listening to his voice messages and not picking up the phone. He wanted help.

Yeah, I gave you help and you fucked me. You can forget it now.

I had yet to learn the art of forgiveness. I couldn't yet feel compassion when someone like West didn't follow through.

Then, at the end of May 1997, West Arkeen was found dead in his apartment, his body badly burned from a crack torch and riddled with track marks and bruises. His drug buddies had robbed his apartment and made off with all his musical equipment while he lay dead nearby. They also stole tapes with demos of all the songs he had written.

I felt I had let West down. Maybe there was something more I could have done. Maybe I could have at least been there at his apartment in his last minute—if for no other reason than to let him rest his head on a friend.

I loved you like a brother from the day we met and started playing guitars together and telling jokes. I am sorry, West.

I began to think more and more about getting the hell out of L.A.

Susan and I went for a drive one day to look for a lake I'd heard about in Malibu. I still had a waterskiing boat up at my cabin on Lake Arrowhead, but it was so far away that I rarely used it anymore. I thought instead of having a place right in town and one far, far away, maybe we could find a house to live in full-time where we'd be close enough to town for work but could also use the boat.

Though I'd ostensibly lived in L.A. for more than ten years at this point, I wasn't around for much of that time and had never gotten to know the surrounding areas very well. We drove around aimlessly until I saw a pickup hitched to a boat on a trailer. The rig was stopped on the shoulder of the road. I pulled over.

"How's it going?" I said. "Hey, we're looking for the lake around here. You on your way there?"

"Uh, no," he said. "I'm on my way up to Lake Arrowhead. I was just fixing a flat."

"Do you know where the lake around here is?"

"There's something called Malibu Lake just a couple miles up the road," he said, "but it's nothing more than a pond."

He hopped back into his truck and pulled away with a wave. We kept driving on Mulholland—the same road that runs along the top of the ridge through the Hollywood Hills—and came to a narrow body of water that had to be Malibu Lake. The guy was right about it. Still, I pulled over, we climbed out, and I scanned the surroundings. As I looked across the street I saw a sign: FOR SALE. Up a hill, set back off the road, was a house—or rather a mansion. A huge place. There was a phone number on the sign. For some reason I called it.

After our initial conversation, the voice on the other end said the place was in foreclosure, owned by the bank.

"Make an offer," said the voice.

We chatted a little more and I arranged to take a tour of the house. I was curious what a place like that looked like on the inside; Susan and I could have some fun and take a peek.

At the top of the hill, the driveway circled a grand fountain. Outside were an Olympic-size pool and a tennis court, and inside eight bedrooms, seven bathrooms, and 7,500 square feet of living space. The place was straight out of a hip-hop video. But it wasn't in what you would call move-in condition. The couple who owned it had gone through an ugly divorce. The man moved out and the woman had trashed the place.

Waterskiing in the nearby lake was out of the question, but on a lark I put in an offer on the house for significantly less than a million dollars. For a place this size, my offer would have been a steal in Fargo, North Dakota. This, of course, was Malibu.

The next day my phone rang: offer accepted.

What? No way!

Susan and I decided to rent out the place above Dead Man's Curve and move into this new place as soon as we had it repaired. It turned out the damage was just superficial and the house was soon ready.

Moving out of the cliff-side house on Edwin proved more emotional than I had expected. But I reminded myself of the best rationale for moving out: Where could a little kid play there?

CHAPTER FIFTY-ONE

✦ ✦ ✦

As the August due date for the baby drew nearer, I began to think I needed to move on from GN'R, or what was left of it. Guns had been paying rent on studios for three years now—from 1994 to 1997—and still did not have a single song. The whole operation was so erratic that it didn't seem to fit with my hopes for parenthood, for stability.

I told Susan I wanted to quit.

"Don't leave Guns because of me!" she exclaimed. "I don't want that ever to come between us."

"I'm not, and it won't," I said. "Trust me."

As far as I was concerned, the truly amazing time for the band was from 1985 to 1988, a three-year period that had ended almost a decade before that conversation with Susan in August 1997. It didn't get more important the bigger we got, it just got bigger—and more bloated. A lot of people in GN'R's extended social circle had never moved on in their lives. Maybe they didn't even want to. I knew now that I could move on. And I wanted to.

I called Axl when my mind was made up. We went to dinner and I told Axl, my good friend and business partner, that I was done. We shook hands and that was that.

Despite the anger I felt after the late gigs, there was another side to my relationship with Axl that trumped all of the unpleasantness, and that is the side I choose to remember and hold dear. Axl can be the most tender and thoughtful of friends. Was he the ideal bandmate and business partner? Actually, no. He was stubborn, moody, arrogant, and greedy. But to be fair, was I any better? Instead of stepping up some time in 1991 or 1992, I fell deeper and deeper into my stupor. I am sure I was arrogant and moody and difficult myself then. Make no mistake, Axl pushed my trust and friendship to the brink many times with his reckless disregard for others. When, through Doug Goldstein, he demanded ownership of the Guns N' Roses name, I probably should have written off all of the sacred moments of friendship we had shared to that point.

Still, when it came to leaving the band, it wasn't about Axl. I just had new challenges on my mind.

Unfortunately for both me and Axl, more than a decade passed before we ever spoke a single word again. It's sad, but the history of GN'R is so fraught with barbs and accusatory hand grenades that complete separation seemed to be the one and only answer for a while—for such a long while, in fact, that it seemed we might never meet again. I was just too damn exhausted from living on a razor's edge for so many years. I didn't regret the choice I made, but I eventually did wish we could still have been friends and have gotten together once in a while.

Susan and I went to see our doctor when she was two weeks overdue. He said he was going to make us an appointment to go into the hospital the following morning so they could induce labor.

Whoa!

Okay. We'll just go home, pack some things, and get a good night's sleep before we go and have our child the next morning. Yeah, right. We packed our stuff just fine, but the sleep part did not happen. We were way too excited. And ridiculously nervous.

When doctors induce labor, they introduce a drug called Pitocin into the mother's bloodstream. Of course, they have to use the right amount at the right time to get the best results. In Susan's case, however, they must have used too much because she went into sudden, acute labor.

Okay.

Shit, no doctor yet? No epidural? No spinal block?

Time to practice what we had worked on for the past few months: the meditation.

"Just look into my eyes, babe," I said, "and stay with me."

Easy for me to say.

Susan showed me through fifteen excruciating hours of labor that she owned the warrior spirit of ten men. She powered through all that pain and confusion. I know she was more scared than she had ever been in her life, but she never quit and never cried.

And then it happened.

Our daughter.

My daughter.

My baby girl.

I have a baby girl?

I have a baby girl!

We named her Grace.

Now life made sense. This was why I had survived my pancreatitis. This was why I had survived my waterskiing accident. I was here to be the father of a baby girl, and I was, at last, ready for it.

CHAPTER FIFTY-TWO

✦ ✦ ✦

Susan and I basked in parenthood. I learned to swaddle Grace, and I came to relish soothing her on my shoulder during those cool autumn nights in our quiet new surroundings.

Our dog, Chloe, had not only settled into the new house but had quickly made a new bed right underneath Grace's crib. Just as she had gone everywhere with Susan while she was pregnant, Chloe now stuck close to the baby all the time. As Grace grew into a toddler, Chloe would gently play ball with her. It was astounding to watch them interact.

I decided to take another course at Santa Monica Community College—an intro-level business class. My decision to continue to take classes thrilled my mom, whom I was talking with even more now that Susan and I had a baby. Mom and I had excited discussions about the possibility of my going to college—not for a course or two, but for a degree. Her Parkinson's disease greatly limited her physically, but her mind remained smart as a whip. My uncle John had told me many times that my mom was the smartest kid in the family, and that in another era she would have gone off to college and become a doctor or lawyer herself.

Thank God I didn't have much work to do just then, because school ate all my nonbaby time. I didn't know how to use Word or Excel. I had to learn rudimentary computer skills on the side. And I still didn't know what the fuck I was doing at the most basic level. I would read everything, I would write down way too much, and I would take notes on all the wrong things in class. I didn't know how to filter through my notes to get what I needed. I would go to the library and wouldn't know what to look for. When I went back over texts I had read, practically every sentence was highlighted. I knew the material when a test came, but it was overkill. It would take me literally ten times the amount of time to prepare as the other students.

I had to relearn the learning process. I kept at it even when I felt I wasn't getting any better at studying. I knew I could do it. And the process of formal education sparked me. Suddenly the world of finance became a fascinating, living thing for me. Again I got an A. And I immediately signed up for another class—introductory economics.

By early 1998, I began to record music again, too. I poured myself into it, working every day. Despite my departure from Guns, our old label, Geffen, remained supportive of my solo career.

"We're backing you, Duff," I was told at a meeting with Geffen staff. "This album will be our top priority for the first quarter of 1999."

Despite my songwriting and recording, my latest class, and my work-outs, Susan and I managed to find time to constantly shuttle back and forth between L.A. and Seattle—it was great to be able to share Grace's first year with my mom. During my teenage years, my relationship with my mother had really blossomed when I quit taking drugs after my first panic attack. We had sat down over tea together nearly every day back then, and I had been able to come clean to her about some of the things I'd gotten into—like stealing cars—while struggling to find my way. It had been like that since my pancreatitis, too, and now, in 1998, we were becoming even closer as I learned to be a parent. I wanted to be around Mom as much as possible.

I was also beginning to think I really did want to attend a proper university. By the middle of 1998, I had completed three different business classes with a 4.0 GPA. I figured any school would most certainly see that I was a genius, right? Shit, with those grades I thought Yale and Harvard would fling open their doors.

Then I remembered: there was a grand old university situated atop

Capitol Hill in Seattle, the school my uncle John had attended, Seattle University. When I was very young and still doing well in school, my mom would have liked nothing better than for me to have followed her brother to Seattle U.

A plan was starting to take shape in my mind.

By fall, I had an entire album done, which Geffen planned to release as *Beautiful Disease* on my birthday, February 5, 1999. An index of some lyrical themes explored on the songs:

Number of lines about getting kicked in the head: 2
Number of veiled references to GN'R breakup: 2
Number of drug deaths mentioned: 2
Number of songs about a person whose drug habit imperils his
    or her ability to parent: 1

By the end of 1998, promotional copies of *Beautiful Disease* had been sent out to magazines and the press campaign was in full swing. I ducked into Tower Records one afternoon and saw my album on their big list of upcoming releases. Cool. I formed a band in anticipation of touring the record. This group became the first incarnation of Loaded, the band that's been a constant in my life ever since.

For most of the press interviews, I would go to the Geffen office and talk on the phone with writers planning to cover the album. One day in December, I headed over to the office for another round of phone interviews. When I walked in, everyone was in hysterics, crying.

"What's going on?" I asked.

"We were just bought. There are going to be mass layoffs."

A few days later, I went to the office again—this time to meet with an executive of the new corporate entity. I was ushered into a conference room. He came in and shook my hand.

"Here's the story," said the exec. "I'm going on a ski vacation and I'm going to listen to all the upcoming releases with my kids. We'll decide whether they have a future with the label or not. When I come back I'll let everyone know. I'll have each artist into my office to tell them personally where they stand."

I never heard what his fucking kids thought of my record. In fact, I never heard from the guy again. On my birthday—the day of the album's supposed release—an intern from the label called and left a message on my answering machine to say it wouldn't be released that day or any other day.

I subsequently offered to buy the album back from the label so I could release it some other way. After all, I had put a lot of work into it and was proud of the results. I said I would pay all the recording costs—about $80,000. They said no, sorry, we will only sell it at a profit. You can have it back for $250,000. Otherwise we'll just keep it in the vault.

Fuck this, I thought.

This was just another test, another challenge.

Rise above.

I rented a van and Loaded did its first-ever tour, punk-rock style, playing the songs from the unreleased album up and down the West Coast for a few weeks. I wanted to stay in motion rather than sitting around and stewing over the severing of this last tie to the past.

That tour reminded me of one of the reasons punk was so great: the interaction with the audience. The fans weren't in Row 600. They weren't behind a barricade. They were right in front of our faces. Obviously, if they were at our show, we shared musical interests; the sweaty intimacy of these hastily organized, small gigs amplified that feeling of camaraderie.

Still, once I was back in L.A., I began to think.

Fuck this business.

Fuck this whole fucking town.

You've been itching to go back to school. So let's fucking do it.

I pictured myself up at Seattle University, following in Uncle John's footsteps. I pictured my family living in our place on Lake Washington, far away from L.A.'s bullshit. I pictured being able to visit Mom every day.

We were already shuttling back and forth to Seattle constantly. I asked

Susan what she would think about moving there full-time. We started talking about marriage, too. It felt like the right time, so I proposed to her. We started to plan an August wedding. We sold the place in Malibu. And along with our toddler and an aging yellow lab, the soon-to-be Mr. and Mrs. McKagan moved to Seattle.

CHAPTER FIFTY-THREE

+ + +

Those first few months in Seattle in 1999 were an exciting time. Grace had just passed eighteen months and was building up a vocabulary. I started counting the words she used and quickly hit one hundred. We saw my mom nearly every day. Together with Mom and my uncle John—my mom's brother, a doctor, and sober since the early 1980s—I tried to figure out what I wanted to study when I started at Seattle U—which now felt like an inevitability. Finally I decided on my goal: the undergraduate business program at Seattle University's Albers School of Business and Economics.

Then one afternoon in April 1999, I was driving to my mom's place with Susan and Grace. We had just stopped to pick up some lunch for her at Taco Time. My phone rang.

Mom had died.

What? I just spoke to her this morning! This can't be!

Mom had been battling Parkinson's for a long time, but the doctors thought she had a lot of life ahead of her. Anyone who has lost a parent knows the huge and bottomless hole left yawning in the lives of the children. For a while at first, it was tough to curb some habits—I would instantly reach for the phone to call her every time Grace used a new word, for instance. *Mom, guess what Grace just said . . .*

My mother's death had a huge impact on me. Her sage advice and calm demeanor helped not only me but dozens of my friends—and even kids who were random strangers to me. I'll never forget coming home on various occasions after I'd left the family house to find bedraggled punk kids sitting with my mom, talking over a cup of tea about whatever was eating at them. That sort of generosity of spirit was important for me. Always had been, and I hoped it always would be.

Her well-lived life informed and influenced all that I did in my own life, and I'd been striving to hew closer to her ideals as I'd put my life back together in recent years. While I was devastated, I could at least take consolation in the fact that she'd witnessed my determination to start a new life, to form a family, and to get an education.

After Mom's death, Uncle John became the patriarch of the McKagan clan in addition to his own side of the family; his sons and daughters and grandchildren shared him with us. He helped me focus on the goal I had set for myself most recently—getting an education. The undergraduate admissions guidelines at Seattle University included categories for transfer students, international students, and "other students." That was me. Or so I thought. As it turned out, even the "other" category didn't have a slot where I would fit—it was for kids who had been homeschooled or had previously been booted from Seattle U, or adults who already had a BA and were seeking additional enrichment without working toward a degree.

Finally I talked to a staffer at the admissions office and was told I could apply. He instructed me to write an "admissions essay." Admissions essay? What about my perfect GPA? I thought the doors would open instantly for me, a hero returning from the battlefields of life, scarred but alive. No. None of that. It instantly became clear that the school saw my junior college "achievements" as just sort of cute. And all I had to show from high school was a GED. You can't get into Seattle U with a GED. Reality was setting in.

I hadn't written an essay since I was in junior high, twenty years before. Thank God for Dave Dederer. I'd been friends with Dave since the last time I'd written an essay. By the mid-1990s, he was best known as the guitar player in Presidents of the United States of America, who had huge hits with "Lump" and "Peaches." But I also knew him to be a well-educated man: he had majored in English at Brown—an Ivy League college—and had worked as an English teacher before his music career took off. He and I had a little side band, an acoustic duo called the Gentlemen, and we had been playing tiny gigs around Seattle ever since Susan, Grace, and I had started coming back regularly the year before.

"I don't remember how to write an essay," I told Dave.

Dave showed up at my house with a gift that I use to this day: Strunk and White's *Elements of Style*. It became my go-to book on the ins and outs of the English language, and in its pages were the blueprints for the structure of an essay.

Next I asked Dave the obvious question.

"What do they want me to tell them? Do I just pick a random topic and write an essay on it?"

"No, Duff, tell them *your* story," said Dave. "Tell them everything. Tell them about growing up in Seattle and playing in punk-rock bands and moving to L.A. Tell them you were in Guns N' Roses, tell them you were a drunk, tell them you did cocaine and a lot of it. Tell them about your success, about getting strung out, and about your fall. Tell them about your redemption and getting sober and your martial arts and mountain biking. Tell them about Susan and your new baby. Let them know you are of the here and now and exactly how you got here."

Whoa. I was skeptical.

But the admissions office liked the story. They invited me in for an interview.

"The next thing to address," the admissions adviser said, "is your academic record. All we have to go on are a few classes at a community college in California. I'm sure you can understand how difficult it is for us to assess that. You don't have any track record whatsoever in math, for instance."

Shit. The essay was all well and good, but it was merely a starting point for a rigorous university like this.

"Here's what we propose," he continued. "See if you can gain admittance to Seattle Central Community College. If you can, here's a list of classes we'd like you to take. Get all A's and come back to us and we'll consider your application at that time."

The course list was like nothing I had ever done—college-level math, history of western civilization, a survey of English literature. But a challenge had been issued and I was at the exact point in my life to face it. I was fueled for this. With Susan and Dave and Sensei Benny and my uncle John firmly planted in my corner, I could rise to this occasion.

This time I took my GED and commendation from the governor with me when I went to the community college—I got into Seattle Central right away. Then I had to take placement tests. I scored low in math. I just couldn't remember anything. The classes themselves interested me—even the math, in part because it was such a challenge.

At the end of the fall semester, I returned to Seattle U with my community college transcript in hand. I had straight A's—Mom would have been proud, and I wished I could have shown her the transcript before I took it to the admissions office.

"That's great," I was told at Seattle University. "Now we want you to take this list of classes and get all A's."

Come on!

I ended up spending an entire academic year at community college. Throughout that year, there were indicators that let me know my mom was still around. One time, two-and-a-half-year-old Grace turned to look at me and Susan and we both froze—we were looking at mom's crinkled-up seventy-six-year-old face, just looking at us and smiling. It stayed there for a few seconds. I guess such a strong connection based on love and all-encompassing trust doesn't disappear overnight.

Early the next summer, in 2000, after submitting another slate of A's from Central, I received a letter from Seattle University.

Dear Mr. McKagan,

Congratulations! We are pleased to inform you that you have been selected for admission to the class of 2004 at Albers School of Business and Economics.

That same summer, on July 14, 2000, Susan gave birth to our second daughter, Mae. She was a big, round Buddha baby, but Susan's labor was much shorter and easier than it had been with Grace. And for her part, Grace took an instant liking to Mae and doted on her little sister.

For a middle name, we gave her Marie, after my mom.

CHAPTER FIFTY-FOUR

+ + +

When my first semester of classes at Seattle University kicked off in the fall of 2000, I quickly realized the year at community college hadn't helped me much as far as studying was concerned. The classroom situation was different, too. At Seattle U, the students knew they were there for the next four years. This was it. They weren't just trying things out; they would be there, seeing one another, every day, for years. I had the same basic plan in mind, but I went home to a family every night and was closer in age to the professors than to my fellow undergrads.

Still, the kids were pretty respectful—they could see I was serious about it. They could see I wanted to learn. Early on, a few classmates brought in their copies of *Appetite* for me to sign, but that stopped as soon as they saw I really was just another student—one taking notes so voluminous they could fill a dumpster. I was up on campus all the time and got to know some of the kids in my classes. They were so smart. About half were from elite schools in and around Seattle, and the rest were academic studs from farther afield, including a good number of international students. It seemed everyone had taken AP classes or college-level courses while still in high school.

Learning to study was the key. At first, I probably spent eight hours studying what these whiz kids could cover in an hour. After a while I began to be able to filter better—I wasn't trying to skate by, I just got better at picking out the important stuff. Susan and Dave Dederer taught me how to write, editing me—"hey, what about moving this part up to here?"—and fine-tuning my use of hyphens, semicolons, and other grammatical minutiae. Of course, by then I was reading a ton, too, so writing was somewhat intuitive once I got rolling.

Now that Susan and I had kids and lived in Seattle, she pushed me to start calling my dad. Susan had a good relationship with both of her parents even though they, too, were divorced. With children of my own to think of, I couldn't afford the luxury of being a pissed-off son anymore. Relationships changed; earlier history was less relevant now. My dad's shortcomings in my early years didn't matter to Grace and Mae, and wouldn't affect them. I could see the value—even the importance—of his presence in my girls' lives.

The other thing I did was add running to my routine. There were plenty of dojos in Seattle that I could use—because of Benny's reputation, the doors were always open—but I had never found one to replace the House of Champions. Instead, I continued what Benny had taught me on my own. But I still wanted—no, needed—more pain, another challenge. So I joined a regular old gym in a tall building downtown and found myself running not on its treadmills but on the building's staircases. Then I decided to sign up for a marathon. I ran my first one the next year in three hours and forty-five minutes.

At the beginning of 2001, a letter from Seattle U arrived at the house. I opened it.

Dear Michael:

Congratulations on your outstanding academic achievement during the preceding quarter. Your grade point average of 4.0 should be a source of satisfaction and pride for you. It is evidence of your ability to focus your intellect and energy effectively to achieve academic excellence. It is also evidence of your continuing intellectual development. Your name is included on the President's List, a recognition for which only those who have completed twelve or more credits at Seattle University and who have earned a term grade point average of 3.90 or above qualify . . .

I had made the President's List! I went out and had the commendation framed and hung it proudly on the wall of our kitchen.

Near the end of that spring semester, Chloe, who had been slowing down for a few years, suddenly took a turn for the worse. I had to lift her from her latest guard post—by Mae's crib—and take her to the vet to see what was wrong. Chloe had developed liver cancer, it turned out, and the vet would have to operate.

That summer I devoted my attention to nursing Chloe, finally paying her back for all her love—especially for the time she'd stood by me as I'd been alone and recovering from my own organ failure. But several months after her surgery, she still hadn't rebounded. The old girl tried to hang in there for me despite the steady worsening of her pain. Finally I had to put Chloe down.

I took her to the vet on a Monday morning in the fall of 2001. It was one of the worst days of my life.

"I'll be okay," I told her as I gently petted her. "You don't have to worry about any of us now."

I miss her.

+ PART SEVEN +

FALL TO PIECES

CHAPTER FIFTY-FIVE

+ + +

I went back to L.A. every once in a while and one time in early 2002 I met Matt Sorum for lunch at Swinger's in Hollywood. We were joined that day by Randy Castillo, a drummer friend of Matt's. Of course, I knew who Randy was—he had played with Ozzy for years—and I had probably met him a few times in my using days. But it had become clear to me that meeting people sober was meeting them anew. Randy had throat cancer, though he told me and Matt that he'd gotten through the worst of it and was on the mend. A few months after that lunch, however, Randy's cancer returned and he died.

Randy had neither health insurance nor sufficient spare funds to cover everything out of pocket when this tragedy hit. After his death, the costs of his treatment trickled down to his parents and other family members. I guess they must have cosigned for a loan or a hospital stay, or both. Matt decided to put together a fund-raiser and memorial concert for Randy at the Key Club on Sunset Strip. His first calls were to me and Slash. We both agreed to do the gig, and the event—scheduled for the last Monday in April 2002—sold out in something like ten minutes. We were all rather surprised, but obviously happy to be able to help Randy's family in some small way.

Classes were still in session for me, so I flew in the weekend before the Monday-night gig. I had a statistics exam on the Tuesday after the show. Keith Nelson and Josh Todd from Buckcherry agreed to fill in on rhythm guitar and vocals. This was looking like a pretty kick-ass band.

All right! At rehearsal the day before the gig, Slash and Matt and I finally played our first notes together in almost nine years. It was like a 747 jet taking off in that room. Powerful yet familiar, comfortable, and friendly. There were no assumptions or ulterior motives. We were doing this for a friend's family in need. End of story.

Backstage at the Key Club, I had my business statistics textbook under my arm and tried to cram while the other acts played. The crowd lost it when we came out and started our set with "It's So Easy." By the end, Steven Tyler from Aerosmith got swept up in the excitement and hopped onstage with us to close out the benefit singing "Mama Kin" and "Paradise City." It was a great night of rock and roll that has stayed with me ever since. I let myself forget for a little while the early-morning flight and the exam awaiting me back in Seattle. That was tomorrow, and tonight we had just conquered. Everyone who was there said the same thing, and I believe it to be true: Randy Castillo was in the room smiling down on us that night.

My flight departed on time and I got through the exam, but now Slash, Matt, and I faced a bona fide dilemma. It felt too good together not to continue after that gig. We didn't have any new material yet, and had only the foggiest of ideas about what we might do, but the sheer power of us playing together was unmistakable and we knew that if we worked hard, the rest would somehow come. Same as it ever was, really.

Any lingering reluctance to continue had to do with a funny thing that happens after you've been in a popular band like GN'R—the personal stakes are higher for anything you do together with those same guys. It went unspoken, but I'm sure there was a tinge of fear about forming a band without Axl and having it fail. Then we might be dismissed as having been just the sidemen of a lead singer—sidemen who couldn't hack it on their own. Rumors that we were going to start a band without Axl had already circulated in 1996. We heard murmurs of "What do they think they're doing, trying to replace Axl?" One thing will always be certain, Axl is irreplaceable. Even now, in 2002, we figured we'd get slammed as GN'R–without–Axl. The difference now was that I didn't care. I'd been through way too much to let a few threads on Internet chat sites dictate the course of my life.

The search for a singer was on.

At that point, my band Loaded had been going for about two years and our latest lead guitar player was Dave Kushner. Not only had Dave played in the band Wasted Youth, but he and Slash had gone to high school together. Small world. I suggested to Slash and Matt that Dave might be a good fit as second guitar in our new band. He came down to rehearsal one day and got the gig. Just like that. Izzy was coming around a lot, too. I think he thought we could use a helping hand; plus he got to hang out with his old buddies. Whatever his motivation, Izzy gave us a nice spark from the get-go. I had watched and learned from Izzy from the moment we met in L.A. years prior—he was the quiet tough guy in a town that could have eaten me alive, and I learned to survive with his help. Izzy and I rarely ruminated about the past, but now that I was sober, I watched and learned from him again—now with a completely different perspective on survival. I found he was still a guy I looked up to. My sober friend. My old friend. It was something of a miracle that he had made it out of the darkness during all that madness, and he had become a guy who could see the humor in it all.

Dave Kushner was understandably a bit wary that Izzy was going to steal his gig, but I knew Izzy was just coming around to play some music and that a long-term band project complete with a lead singer was never again going to work for him. He already had a nice solo career that he could start and stop as he pleased and that suited him just fine, thanks. I totally got it. After the experience of Guns N' Roses, the prospect of doing something with so many moving parts could be daunting. And sure enough, once we started looking in earnest for a front man, Izzy just kind of faded from the scene, though ever since he's remained a close and treasured friend.

Ah, yes. This was going to be easy, right? We could find a singer at the drop of a hat. Just put out an ad and have singers send tapes to a PO box. Shouldn't take more than a couple months. Wrong. Oh, so wrong. As the months passed, we received hundreds of tapes and CDs from all over the world. We brought a few people in to audition live and a few were pretty interesting, but nobody quite fit.

We were writing a ton of songs, however, and that kept us going. We were also still hashing out our sound. Of course, we weren't seeking to completely reinvent ourselves as current or hip. But for my part, I hadn't been living in a musical vacuum. Playing with a bunch of different artists up in Seattle and forming Loaded had kept me in a good place as far as songwriting and seeing new bands. In fact, I seemed to be finding my way again as a player and songwriter, and it felt really, really good to continue doing so together with my old bandmates. We all brought good stuff to the table, and it showed.

I had known Scott Weiland for a while—Susan had introduced me to him and his wife, Mary, who was a friend of hers. Scott and Mary had kids, too, and our families had gotten together for dinner on a few occasions. Scott was having problems with his band, Stone Temple Pilots, and he had been through trouble with addiction—on those occasions when our families met up, we had a lot in common to talk about. But I didn't consider him for the new band because he had a band.

As 2002 turned into 2003 and we neared the one-thousandth demo tape of our search for a singer, a state of desperation nearly took hold. The project had gone from something none of us had even thought about to something we all really wanted to continue. But shit, were we ever going to find a damn singer?

Then one day I got a call from one of our managers.

"I just heard that Stone Temple Pilots broke up," he said. "You should call Scott."

I was reluctant at first because Scott and I were friends in a completely different context and I wasn't sure I wanted to cross that bridge. Besides, he still went through periods of pretty serious drug use and I hadn't spent big chunks of time with anyone in full-habit mode for about eight years. Still, I did have a lot of sober time under my belt and no harm could come from just asking Scott if he would be interested.

I called him.

He was into it.

Here we go.

CHAPTER FIFTY-SIX

✦ ✦ ✦

Scott came to our rehearsal studio and absolutely nailed it. He was head and shoulders above anybody else we had seen or heard. And he could hold his own on a stage with the big personalities in this band.

It was the first time that I had ever been in a situation where the band said, "Okay, we have all of this material—now go write your vocal parts." But Scott had a great ability to listen to something and concurrently hear a different arrangement of it in his head. He took demos we had recorded of "Fall to Pieces," "Set Me Free," and "Big Machine" and went into his studio in Burbank. He sang over the first two. Then, with "Big Machine," he twisted our arrangement into something he could really sink his teeth into and leave his mark on. He sort of turned the song upside down. It was clever. And it instilled confidence in us about Scott's ability, despite his being strung out on opiates and various other supporting drugs.

A movie producer who had heard rumors about the band approached us about using "Set Me Free" as the end-title song in Ang Lee's upcoming version of *The Hulk,* coming out in late June 2003. The deal gave us some breathing room. Everyone had some scratch, and we recouped some of the costs of our rehearsal space.

Things were really clicking. We settled on the name Velvet Revolver for the band. Matt and I were getting really tight as a rhythm section. Slash was pushing himself in new directions. Dave earned the nickname "Morphius" because of his wizardlike knowledge of cutting-edge guitar-effects technology. We had also cemented a team mentality: there were a lot of people just waiting for us to fail and, faced with all the naysayers and obstacles, we were determined to make the record of our collective lifetimes.

Then Scott just *disappeared.* His wife was down in San Diego taking care of their two small children and Scott, it turned out, had holed up alone in their apartment in L.A. and gone on a run for the ages. He was in the depths of heroin and crack addiction. Just months before, Scott, Mary, Susan, and I were having nice conversations at family picnics and Susan and I had even contemplated renting the apartment below theirs as a pied-à-terre in L.A. Now things had gone off the rails for Scott and for his relationship with Mary and his family. It was a mess.

I found myself dealing with a raging addict and all the drama that entailed. I thought I was strong enough to deal with it. In fact, at this point I thought of myself as bulletproof. That turned out to be a major mistake. All of us in the band had been through this crap before—rhythm guitarist Dave Kushner had been sober for about twelve years—so we figured we were the perfect group of dudes to get Scott through this. We tried hard to help. But he had been through rehab a dozen times already. Even we were tiring of his lack of progress as work on the rest of the songs ground to a halt for weeks on end. Finally he decided to go back into a drug rehab center one more time. Okay, this was a step in the right direction.

We all knew it wouldn't be easy for him. We had all been there. Even so, when I heard Scott had bailed on the rehab center to go down to see his family in San Diego, I was pissed. I knew he wasn't going there. I knew this was an excuse to go score and go on another run. I heard that he was back at his apartment in L.A. and I went there with the intention of telling him he'd worn out my patience—and maybe not in such measured words. I'm not sure how or why, but when I entered the apartment screaming and yelling Dave was already there. I tried to calm down, but I couldn't contain my anger. I threw off my coat and was ready for anything—even kind of hoping something would happen so that I could further vent my rage. I had seen how hard everyone had tried to help Scott. I had exposed my family to the dark side, too, and all of that boiled up inside me as I stood there yelling at Scott.

But he wasn't combative at all. Instead he asked me to help him one last time. He asked whether I would show him how I got sober through martial arts. He said traditional rehab techniques obviously weren't working for him. He needed a different way. He pleaded.

I regained my composure. *This guy's a dad,* I thought. In fact, I had originally become friends with Scott because we had that in common: we were fathers.

I agreed to help.

Immediately I had to come up with a plan.

Trying to accomplish anything in L.A. seemed like a bad idea. A few years prior, Susan and I had bought a cabin in the mountains about 150 miles east of Seattle—a getaway now that we had relocated full-time to the Northwest. I had found a dojo in a nearby town run by a kung fu teacher—or *sefu*—named Joseph. He was a completely different type of guy from Benny, but he knew Benny—everyone in the martial arts world seemed to know Benny—and let me work out in his dojo. Over the years I had learned that Joseph was a solid guy and a very respected martial artist. My first thought was to take Scott up to my cabin and have him go to Joseph's dojo every day, and also work out, hike in the mountains, go waterskiing. Just do normal shit while he detoxed. The cabin was pretty far off the beaten path and it would be hard for Scott to leave and find drugs.

I called Joseph about my plan. I didn't want to just show up one day at his facility with a raging drug addict.

"Joseph," I said, "I have a situation. I play music, I'm in a band, and the new singer wants to get clean."

"Oh, you play in a band?" Joseph said.

"Yeah, we're starting this new band."

I filled him in on some of the background.

"Oh fuck, I didn't know you were in Guns N' Roses," he said. He didn't know who Stone Temple Pilots were, but it didn't matter.

"I need to get this guy out of L.A.," I said. "Is there a time I can bring him in so we can work out every day? I don't want to spring some guy who's jonesing on your dojo."

"Tell you what," Joseph said. "It does sound like you have a situation. I can help. Until you are ready to go back to L.A. and start with Benny."

"Great," I said.

"Listen," said Joseph. "I live on top of a mountain. I live in a place where there's no way out. If you guys stay at your place, he can get on a bus, go to an airport, and get out. Up here, there is no way out. Why don't you just stay with me?"

Joseph had never faced the challenge of detoxing someone, but as soon as I had told him Scott had two kids, he wanted to do anything he could.

Dave Kushner was a big part of the plan, too. He actually had the most sober time of all of us and his calm, steady mind would help out immensely. He saw this as his band, too, and wanted to help Scott any way he could. Dave took me and Scott to a doctor in L.A. who specialized in helping addicts get off opiates. The doctor supplied us with detox drugs to take up to the mountain.

Honestly, this was probably the point when I first got a little cocky in my sobriety. Here I was with a backpack full of Buprenex, Soma, Xanax, and syringes, left totally in my care with a doctor's note to get me through airport security. A year earlier, my life had been so damn normal and far removed from all of this kind of nonsense.

It's okay. Just focus on the mission: to get Scott sober, productive, and reliable—and to help a friend be a father to his kids again.

Scott, Dave, and I flew from Burbank to Seattle and stayed the first night in my house there in the city. I got my first lesson on how to shoot up another person in the thick of their ass muscle that first night. Sexy. Scott was a trouper. He was in the throes of a brutal jones but did not waver in his determination. Before we left the next morning, I took him through a meditation that Sensei Benny had taken me through many times before. It felt good to be able to pass on to someone else something that had helped me so much, and it allayed—rightly or wrongly—some of the doubts I harbored about my ability to play the role of teacher.

During the car ride out to the mountains, Dave and I listened to music and talked and joked while Scott slept in a drug stupor in the backseat.

We met Sefu Joseph in a Safeway parking lot about twenty miles from his mountaintop retreat. In Safeway, we bought healthy food, razors, soap, and little else. This was not going to be a pleasure cruise and the bare essentials would suffice.

Sefu Joseph may have been a little surprised at first about Scott's state, but he did not show it. Tailing Joseph and his girlfriend Addy and their big black Lab named Blue, we drove toward what would serve as our home for the next month. I had no idea what to expect. I had been to Joseph's dojo many times, but never to his house. The steep road wound through switchback after switchback and just kept going up. A beautiful lake appeared and then receded, smaller and smaller as we climbed even higher. Then we turned off the main road and onto a dirt road that burrowed farther into the wilderness.

The brake lights on Joseph's pickup indicated we had finally arrived. I was stunned by the scenery. The setting was like a hidden Chinese monastery in an old kung fu movie—there were meditation pagodas, wooden dummies, fighting platforms, and a covered area with heavy bags. A man-made waterfall disappeared into a well-kept Zen garden. Beyond that was a tree-lined path. And to top it all off, there was an impressive wrap-around view of the surrounding Cascade Mountains and Lake Chelan far below. I suddenly had high hopes—and not just for Scott. I was here to learn and grow as well. If there was one thing that the ardent study of martial arts had taught me, it was to continue to try to learn and grow until the day you died: never get set in your ways.

As we climbed out of the car, I noticed stairs ascending a huge grassy mound. There, at the back of a deck, a glass door was set into the mound. The house appeared to be underground. My jaw dropped. Scott must have been shitting his pants at this point. When Joseph had first tossed out the idea of us staying with him, he had mentioned something about his home being an "earth berm" house, but having no idea what that meant, I hadn't given it a second thought. Now, as we climbed the stairs to the deck in front of the mound, that conversation came back to me. From the outside, his place looked way too small for five adults and a large dog, and I thought I had made a mistake committing sight unseen to stay here.

When we entered the house, though, I could see I was completely wrong about the size. It was amazing inside. Flat-screen TV, fireplace, phone, full kitchen, three bedrooms, and two bathrooms.

As we unpacked the groceries, I made a mental checklist of the meals that would hopefully help to cleanse Scott's drug-ravaged bloodstream of its nasty toxins. Fresh fish and free-range chicken. Lots of green vegetables and corn on the cob. Irish steel-cut oatmeal. Pineapples, bananas, melons, and apples. Tons of espresso roast coffee. And my trade secret, baked beans. I'm not really sure whether beans have any cleansing properties, but they sure do get out a lot of hot air.

I put Scott on the diet that had done me so well during my first year of sobriety: fruit for breakfast, grilled fish over greens for lunch, and barbecued chicken with corn and beans for dinner. I added oatmeal to Scott's diet because I supposed with all the exercise we'd be doing, he could use the extra carbs. He did not have fifty pounds of booze weight to lose—he was a rail. The larder was filled to the brim and there was nothing left to do now except what lay directly in front of us: getting Scott detoxed and keeping his body too exhausted and confused to do anything more than sleep.

At this point, I should have taken a step back and assessed the situation. Never before had I felt I had so many people depending on me. I was now juggling being a good father and husband with trying to get a guy sober so that he could do the same. But I was also doing this because I saw real possibilities for this new band with Scott as our singer. Other people recognized the potential there, too, and I was fielding phone call after phone call saying I had to make this happen. *The Hulk* had come out, and even though the movie did only so-so, it seemed like every rock radio station in America had picked up "Set Me Free." With the national exposure there was a lot of interest in Velvet Revolver. Of course, everything hinged on the band actually existing. For the first time ever, I was mixing the spiritual healing of martial arts with commerce.

Seeing Scott nodding and jonesing up there reminded me of some not-so-pleasant memories. In hindsight I see this was the moment I swerved away from the path I'd been on, a path that shielded me from the dark parts of my past. Each of us makes a handful of decisions in life that can have a drastic impact on subsequent events. By getting involved with Scott, I had made one of those potentially life-altering decisions. We did start to have some fun up there after about a week, though. Scott had gotten through the worst of his withdrawal by that point and could start to do some of the physical stuff.

A typical day up there:

Breakfast
Meditate outdoors
Jump rope
Stretch
Work the punching bags
Train on technique
Lunch
Run and lift weights
Work on the wooden dummies
Practice tai chi
Write
Dinner
Talk with Sefu Joseph and write more
Read
Bed

This rigid regime we dubbed "Man Camp." The idea was not only to test physical strength and endurance, but, through the talks and writing, to foster honesty and responsibility. Once in a while Sefu Joseph brought in someone from the community to pitch in. We went mountain biking with friends of his. We went fishing with other friends. A local SWAT guy even came up with an arsenal of guns and taught us how to clean, load, hold, aim, and shoot everything from riot shotguns to large-caliber handguns. It seemed as though the whole town was pitching in and pulling for us to succeed.

After about two weeks of this, Susan and the girls came up to our

cabin, which was about forty miles away from Joseph's mountain re-
doubt. It was Susan's birthday and I was more than happy to see them all.
During the six years I had been with Susan, we lived in a safe bubble that
we controlled. We now found ourselves in uncharted territory. Susan had
my back and even felt some responsibility—after all, she was the one who
had introduced me to Scott. Yet she and I had never had a conversation
about the possible consequences of working with him. Suddenly her man
was gone and she had to take care of our kids on her own—and shit, this
was even before recording and touring started.

I continued to get daily calls from L.A.

"Do we have a singer?"

"Should we book studio time?"

I started to see glimpses of hope with Scott up on top of that mountain. Scott became so enamored of the area that he asked Joseph if he
knew any local real-estate brokers. This from a guy who just weeks earlier
was on a drug run for the ages. Crack houses in L.A. now seemed the last
thing on his mind. Looking back, we made progress fast.

Slash and Matt were relieved to hear Scott was getting better, but I'm
sure they were also still suspicious. I couldn't blame them. But when we
arrived back in L.A., they saw with their own eyes the results of our Man
Camp. Here we were at the rehearsal space with an ass-kicking mountain man, practicing martial arts and meditating before band practices.
Scott seemed inspired and focused now. He started to listen to more of
the music that Slash, Matt, Dave, and I had written over the past year.
We would sort of spoon-feed him two or three songs at a time; to throw
everything at him at once would have been overwhelming given the fact
that we had something like fifty-five songs by this point.

With the band lineup finally solidified and "Set Me Free" still on the
radio, every major record label now wanted a piece of us. One of the
people who wanted to schedule a meeting with us was the same executive
who had dropped me from Geffen without so much as a phone call back
in 1999. He was president of another company now and apparently didn't
remember the incident. But I did. I told the guys the story. At first, they

said we should just cancel the meeting. Then they decided it would be more fun to have him in and fuck with him. He arrived at our rehearsal space and went through his routine, using all the standard industry buzz-words: *artistic freedom, artist-focused, personal touch, like a family,* blah, blah, blah. Then Scott asked him to talk more about the way he would personally take an interest in the project. Scott listened thoughtfully and then started talking—seemingly off-the-cuff—about a friend who had been dropped one time without a call from the label.

"Look, we know the industry is changing," Scott said, "but we don't want to work with people like that."

The guy took the bait: "No way, I treat my artists like family. That would never happen with me."

Then Scott dropped the bomb: "That friend was this guy here," he said, pointing to me, "and you're the asshole who didn't have the decency to make the courtesy call. Get the fuck out of here."

We also flew to New York to meet the legendary Clive Davis. He had helped develop everyone from Janis Joplin to Bruce Springsteen to Beyoncé. When Clive Davis said he believed in our band, I was sold. Even guys like us, who had been through it all in this industry, respected Clive. After that, the process was just an exercise as far as I was concerned. I knew we would go with Clive from the very beginning of that summer. Done deal.

Another interesting aspect of these meetings was that I found I did in fact understand the lion's share of what was going on financially with the band. I also learned that word had gotten around about my studies. People took me more seriously in business meetings. Cool shit. Sometimes I looked into the eyes of industry types and saw a flash of panic: *Shit, I wonder if Duff knows more than I do.*

I also started to get requests to make media appearances as an expert on the business of music. It was nice to be thought of as an intellectual equal at least. After I did interviews on PBS's *Frontline* and in the *Wall Street Journal,* I started to get calls from other artists with questions on how to manage their personal wealth and anticipated earnings. I had been in the exact place these people were in: I hadn't known a damn thing about money, I'd been scared of who might be trying to rip me off. After getting at least a dozen different calls from peers about their dough, I started to think about perhaps one day starting a financial consulting firm of my own.

But that could wait. My new band was on a roll.

CHAPTER FIFTY-SEVEN

✦ ✦ ✦

Susan and I decided to rent a house back down in L.A. and I took a leave of absence from Seattle University. Our first priority was to find a good school for Grace, who was about to start kindergarten. We found one we loved in Studio City and then worked backward from there to find a place to live with easy access to the school.

In Seattle, Susan and I had built up quite a nice circle of friends, a lot of whom had kids the same age as ours. Now back in L.A., we reconnected with one of the few couples we knew with a growing family—Richard and Laurie Stark. Back in 1993, I had hosted a shower for their first baby up at my house on Edwin Drive. (I'd had the place cleaned and made sure none of my knucklehead buddies stopped by during the baby shower.) I had met Richard in 1988, when he was peddling jewelry and leather he designed from the back of his Harley. In the interim, his little business had grown into a full-fledged company called Chrome Hearts, with hundreds of employees and stores all over the world. I'd been among his early customers and we'd become friends. Richard and Laurie now had three kids and were glad to have me and Susan back in L.A.

This period was really good for us. We were facing different challenges from the ones we were used to as a family, but Susan trusted my judgment and supported my every move. What more could a guy hope for?

Then I started to get sick a lot. At first, I chalked it up to Grace's being in school—she must have been bringing home new kid colds all the time. Hard physical activity was still the key to my ability to meditate, and the endorphin spill into my system also helped stave off drug and alcohol cravings. I was getting sick so much by this point that it was hindering my ability to go to the gym. Not a good thing for a guy like me. And sometimes I skipped a workout or a morning meditation even when I wasn't feeling sick. Hey, I was busy. After so many years of sobriety, I had convinced myself I would never use again, even if I let my routine slip. Though I didn't realize it at the time, this attitude would come back to haunt me.

Eventually I got sick so often that I began to worry. I shuddered to think what might be wrong. Some strange immunity deficiency? Cancer? HIV? I asked my doctor to run some tests on me. The tests all came back negative, however, and he said he thought it was just a recurring sinus infection. Even after he mentioned that, it never dawned on me that my coke-damaged sinuses might not function very effectively as a filter against germs.

At least I had plenty of work to do through the end of 2003 and the first part of 2004. Velvet Revolver decided to record our album at NRG Studios, the same place where I had done basic tracks for the Neurotic Outsiders record. I'd had a great experience there before and so, all in good spirits, we began work on our debut record, *Contraband*.

I don't think any band can survive without at least one person who helps to fuse the personalities and defuse the inevitable problems. It's just like any job in that regard, except in a band there is no formal boss. Just four or five outcasts who, in our case, had always used shitloads of drugs and alcohol to deal with life and its conflicts. So much drama started to swirl in and around the band that someone had to sort of take charge. It fell to me. This was, I believe, the first time any of us had entered a band partnership while married. Not that the wives posed any real problems, but there were twice as many opinions—and at times very, very strong ones. It was fine for now, just different.

We kicked off our first tour in May 2004, in St. Louis. *Contraband* entered the charts at number one upon its release in June.

Touring made it difficult to be rigorous about my workouts and meditation.

I'll get to it tomorrow.

Then the same thing would happen the next day.

And I continued to get sick on tour, further limiting my time in the gym. I was tired and I was beat-up mentally—not from the shows themselves but from the constant background shit. We had a few weeks off in July after the U.S. leg before we were due in Europe. One night as I was trying to figure something out, Susan asked, "Why are you always the one who has to fix all the problems?"

The first week of August we flew to Denmark to begin a five-week leg through Scandinavia, Germany, Spain, and the UK, with some additional festival dates in Switzerland, Austria, Belgium, Italy, and Holland. At first, I made sure to get in a workout and meditation every morning. Sometimes I'd hit the gym several times a day just to clear my mind. But then I started getting to it less and less frequently.

Just too busy, I told myself. *And besides, you're strong now.*

If so many people can depend on me—my family, the band—I must be dependable, I must be strong. Hell, I'm even keeping Scott's shit together— I'm the man!

By the time we finished that leg, I was lucky to manage ten seconds of meditation at some point during the day.

The same pattern accompanied subsequent legs. We had been out on tour—with breaks here and there—for thirteen months by the time we arrived in Germany in June 2005, for a second European leg. Workouts and meditations dwindled again. Then I stopped altogether. Meanwhile the band started to show cracks. Being around drugs and booze had proved manageable; handling band business amid increasingly rancorous interpersonal drama, however, *drove me fucking nuts.*

I had a stash of Xanax pills for panic attacks. I had them in my backpack all the time for emergency use on flights. Though I had been able to really get a handle on my attacks in everyday life, I did still get uncomfortable when flying. It wasn't the plane-could-go-down part of flying that freaked me out, it was the being-stuck-in-a-metal-tube-with-no-way-to-get-out part. For the most part, just knowing I had Xanax with me was sufficient to ward off any potential attack. I knew the drug worked quickly, so having that little bottle in my carry-on bag was enough to keep me panic-free on plane rides. Between 1994 and 2004, I had taken a quarter pill—you could cut them to avoid taking a full dose—on three occasions, always on an airplane. Except for those three occasions, I had always been able to go to my place, the calm safe house I knew from martial arts training.

One day in Essen, Germany, my shoulders and back were tense and my head was throbbing. I felt trapped. Trapped, like on a plane. As I sat in my hotel room, I reached into my backpack and took the Xanax bottle out of the side pocket of my bag.

I looked at the bottle for a few minutes, then opened it and shook one of the pills out onto the palm of my hand. I swallowed a Xanax pill sitting in a hotel room because everything seemed to be coming down on my shoulders.

Fuck.

It wasn't for a flight. It was for "stress."

This is shady.

I was worried.

Then the pill kicked in.

Mmmm.

Everything is fine.

I had a solution to the chaos I felt encroaching on me.

The next day, I took two pills. My high tolerance for drugs came right back.

By the third day, I was figuring out how to get hold of more pills. Lots more pills. I called the promoters in the cities we would be visiting next and had them arrange prescriptions from local doctors. I told them I had panic attacks and needed this and that. I had a cocktail going real fast— Xanax and Soma, a muscle relaxer.

I had forgotten I was an addict.

Wait, was I an addict?

Nah.

Lie.

Dave Kushner suspected something was wrong with me.

"Duff, man, you all right?"

"I'm fine," I said. "Just tired."

Lie.

My workouts actually picked up steam. I would go to the gym and fool myself into thinking it wasn't so bad. I was still on track. After all, I was still working out. Lie.

Susan called me one afternoon.

"You sound funny," she said.

"I'm fine."

"You're slurring your words. Are you sick?"

"Maybe a little stuffed up, but I'm fine. I'm just really, really tired."

I'm fine.

I *am* fine.

It's not like I'm drinking or doing coke. This shit was probably developed in a lab at fucking Harvard Med School.

Doctors gave it to me.

Lie.

I thought about my wife and kids all the time and felt guilty for letting them down. That just compounded things.

I'll deal with this soon.

I've got what it takes.

I'll go cold turkey as soon as I'm home.

Soon.

I arrived back in early July 2005, with a few weeks off before another American leg. Susan and the kids were in Seattle. It was warm—eighty-five degrees, which in Seattle feels like 100—and they were all playing in the backyard when I got home.

I was shivering.

"I'm tired," I said. "I'm going upstairs to bed."

I was too fucked up to play with the kids. Susan had never known me fucked up, so she didn't recognize it.

Every bone ached, and when I went inside I threw up secretly in the downstairs bathroom.

I went upstairs to our bedroom and called Ed.

"Hey, man, I'm having some big problems."

"Oh yeah?" he said. "What's going on?"

"I'm strung out. I'm fucking strung out."

"Okay, do you want me to come get you? I can come right over," said Ed.

"Yeah, I need to go to a support group or something."

Ed said he knew a group.

"Ed, there's one other thing."

"Yeah?"

"Susan doesn't know."

Ed drove into the driveway less than an hour later. I was still shivering, freaking out. Together we attended a meeting of drug addicts. Afterward a friend of Ed's came over to talk to us.

"What's your buddy coming off of?" he asked.

I answered, even though the question was only indirectly posed to me.

"Xanax, Soma," I said.

He asked me how much I was doing. I told him the story: started with a single pill and two weeks later I hit twenty-two pills a day.

"Oh, man, you can't fucking cold-turkey that. You could have a seizure."

I had no idea.

"You have to go see a doctor. You have to taper it down. You should go to rehab."

I went home.

Still I didn't tell Susan.

With my stash of pills I figured I would just taper down my intake on my own. I took a few pills.

In the middle of the night, I woke up, ran to the bathroom, and threw up.

I began to cry. I was so disappointed in myself.

Susan woke up, too, and came into the bathroom, where I was slumped next to the toilet.

"I'm strung out on prescription pills," I said, bawling my eyes out.

CHAPTER FIFTY-EIGHT

+ + +

Once I'd told Susan, the first thing I did the next morning was to call my Uncle John, who was both sober and a doctor.

It's hard to imagine he wasn't worried, but he calmly reassured me that I would be okay. He said he would call some doctor friends to find out what I needed to do. Soon he called me back and explained the basics of tapering down the cocktail of pills I was using. He offered to set up a meeting with one of the specialists he knew.

I declined.

I needed to get down to L.A. quickly. For one thing, I felt I should get back into the House of Champions. For another, Velvet Revolver had obligations to honor, including a string of Ozzfest dates.

I tried all sorts of Chinese herbs to help with the withdrawal. I was jonesing so bad I would take anything to feel better. I was also emaciated—down to 145 pounds. As my drug intake had risen, I had just ceased to eat.

I just wanted to get to the dojo.

Can I beat this?

Yes.

Benny the Jet, it turned out, had flown to Europe. He was out of town for a few weeks.

Another sensei, Majit, volunteered to help me.

"Don't worry, man, we're going to get you better," he said.

Majit was straight-up martial arts. He didn't understand drug addiction. But I knew that if I asked him not to let me leave the dojo all day, he wouldn't let me leave. I needed pain.

Up to this point, I had never gone to see a doctor who specialized in addiction. I never delved that deep. Besides, it wasn't as if I was white-knuckling it. I'd been on a high from martial arts for so long. Now, back in L.A., I went to see a specialist. Dave Kushner from VR went with me.

The doctor explained the process of tapering down and assembled a kit. He also prescribed an anti-seizure medication.

"I'd really like to see you go to rehab," he said.

"I'm not going to rehab. I have to go on tour."

"It's not a good idea for you to have all of these," he said, motioning to the drug supplies meant to be used to taper down my usage.

Dave stepped in and agreed to hold the supplies and taper me down himself. The whole thing would take a month.

The first week of August 2005, Velvet Revolver hit the road again for the final month of full-time touring. Dave doled out my taper-down drugs. Susan came out to see me at several stops along the way. It was a group effort and it worked.

When the tour ended I found myself doing a lot of thinking. In hindsight, I could see a number of missteps. But the key mistake was succumbing to a smug sort of complacency about my sobriety. I had overstepped self-assuredness. I had gotten to the point of thinking I was no longer an addict. Relapsing really woke me up.

I am a fucking addict and always will be.

In all the time I had been sober, I had never gone to a support group for alcoholics or to a rehab facility to find out about the biochemical side of addiction. I weighed the idea of trying rehab. I talked to Susan and to Benny. They both thought it would be useful.

Benny revealed that he, too, had faced a drug problem in the past. I had never known. He told me some other guys in the dojo had been through treatment programs, too. I had no idea.

Yes, confidence was knowing I could do anything. But, I realized, confidence must always be rooted in work. In sweat. In pain—*good* pain. And in honesty.

Right now that meant facing reality, and it meant taking advantage of a new level of self-awareness I might be able to get from rehab. I decided to check into a monthlong program. But before I cloistered myself away for a month at rehab, I flew up to Seattle to see Uncle John, who had been diagnosed with cancer and was not doing well.

"Stay sober, Duff," he said.

Those would be the last words he ever said to me.

In the middle of the monthlong rehab program, Uncle John died. The administrators let me leave to fly up for his funeral—I think they figured it might help in my recovery. I think they also realized I would have just walked out if they had tried to hinder me.

Uncle John had the same knack that my mom had: he could make you feel like you were the most important person in the world. In the first years after Mom's death, I had felt sorry for everyone else in the family, as I was sure that Uncle John spent an inordinate amount of time talking with me on the phone. I soon realized, though, that he made each of us feel that same way—and all told, there were about fifty or sixty of us by this point.

Remembrances of Uncle John had broad significance in his community in eastern Washington, as he had delivered 15,000 babies over the decades of his medical practice. But despite the crowds at the wake, my uncle once again seemed to be speaking directly to me—now through his eldest son, Tim, who read an Irish prayer John had picked out in advance for the occasion:

> Life is not a journey to the grave
> With the intention of arriving safely in a well-preserved body,
> But rather to skid in sideways
> Thoroughly used up, totally worn out, and loudly proclaiming:
> "Wow, what a ride!"

+ PART EIGHT +

YOU CAN'T PUT YOUR ARMS AROUND A MEMORY

CHAPTER FIFTY-NINE

+ + +

When my daughter Grace was in the third grade, she came up to me one day and said, "Dad, how come you don't drink wine when all of the other grown-ups do?"

This was a really good question. She had realized that when guests came over or when we all went out to dinner, other people—including Susan, of course—had drinks. People had asked me how I was going to tell my kids about my past drug and alcohol use. Grace's question gave me an opportunity to tell her a little bit.

"Well, honey, that is a very good question and I am glad you asked. You see, I have an allergic reaction to that stuff. If I were to have just one glass, I would then have to have another. Two glasses would turn into four, and my allergy would make me want to drink all of the stuff that we have in the house. I would then have to go to the grocery store to buy everything that they had there, and I would drink all of that. I would probably start to get really crazy, and I wouldn't be like your dad for a while."

"Oh," she said. "You'd better not have a glass of wine, then!"

"That is what I am thinking, too, honey."

Back home in late 2005, I found that two little girls put a rather pink hue on my world. Three exclamations dominated our household:

"Cute!"

"OMG!"

"Awwww!"

I had given up my hopes of them becoming die-hard Mariners fans or backcountry hiking enthusiasts. And so far they showed no interest in the guitar. But I loved that they always seemed to need something from me, even if it was just a simple cuddle. Looking around, I realized I was living the life I had always dreamed of—the life I had given up on as unattainable while in the throes of addiction. Here I was, white picket fence and all. Well, okay, it was actually black wrought iron. But still.

The girls had been asking for a new dog for several years, and up to now Susan and I had always shaken our heads no. We decided the time might finally be right that Christmas. Still, we traveled a ton as a family, and split time between L.A. and Seattle. I had crated Chloe on flights enough times to know that flying was no fun for a pet. If we were to get our kids a dog, we would have to get one that could fly with us in the cabin. Of course, this brought with it another dilemma—I am not the biggest fan of little yip-yap dogs.

We started to pore through dog breed books, feeling ourselves getting excited again about the prospect of a new little guy in the house. (We decided we would get a boy dog to even out the estrogen/testosterone ratio in Casa McKagan.) Every small breed we ran across, however, carried a warning about the way the breed interacted with small children. That is, until we found a picture of a breed that we fell instantly in love with: the Cavalier King Charles spaniel. They were reportedly great with kids—and they didn't yip. Sold.

The next step was to go online and find some breeders up near where Santa lived. I quickly realized breeders of small dogs were a freaky lot. I received, for instance, a picture of a prospective puppy dressed in a pink dress that matched its owner's. One breeder didn't have a computer and didn't know anybody who did, but said I was more than welcome to meet her at the Kmart just outside of some dinky eastern Washington town and follow her sixty miles back to her farm.

Listen, lady, I saw *Deliverance.*

Luckily for us, Santa came through on Christmas morning. The girls went wild with excitement. They quickly agreed on a name for the new dog. The day before, they had gone to NORAD's Santa Tracker Web site and ended up trading emails with an "elf" named Buckley. So Buckley it was. (And yes, the site really exists.)

I still wanted to address the chronic sinus infections that had kept me under the weather for much of the last few years. I had a CT scan done at an ear, nose, and throat specialist in L.A. It turned out my sinuses were totally fucked up—completely closed in some areas, burned through elsewhere, and in no shape to rid themselves of infection. That would explain the constant prescriptions for antibiotics I'd gotten over the last few years when I came down sick time and time again. The doctor proposed laser surgery to cut out the scar tissue in my head, the remnants of all that coke use a lifetime ago. I was ready to try anything that might help me avoid getting sick and having to miss workouts. And the one thing that *might* have given me pause—getting addicted to whatever medication they gave me—actually did not. At one time or another, I had tried virtually every kind of drug, and, somewhat miraculously, there was a type I disliked: painkillers.

The surgery itself took only about two hours—though I was knocked out for it, of course, and it took me an hour or so to come out of the fog of general anesthesia. They had packed cotton all the way back inside my head to stanch the bleeding. For three days I had long strings hanging out of my nose—the only means of pulling the cotton plugs back out. There was simply no way to breathe comfortably through my nose. This was something I had not figured on, and it triggered my claustrophobia. I nearly had a panic attack.

When the day came to pull the cotton out, I was relieved.

Then the doctor attempted his first pull.

FUCK!

I jumped so high I nearly hit my head on the ceiling. That first tug at all the scabbing inside my head felt like a knife being jabbed into my brain. I nearly shit myself. Literally. Poo.

Not long after I finished surgery, I received a call from Jerry Cantrell of Alice in Chains to see whether I would be interested in playing rhythm guitar for a few reunion shows. I had remained good friends with the guys in the band since they partied at my place after their first L.A. concert in

1990. I knew firsthand the utter heartbreak these men had gone through (and continue to feel) at the loss of their singer and brother, Layne Staley, to an overdose. Layne had been a lion of a man with a gentle soul and a wicked sense of humor—like Andy Wood, like Big Jim, like Todd Crew, like West Arkeen.

The band was struggling with self-doubt about going forward after Layne's death. The remaining members were hyperconscious that some longtime fans thought continuing without Layne would be somehow sacrilegious. While his death was sad and needless, I for one did not think it meant the door should be shut on a band that had changed the landscape of modern rock. My opinion may not have been a popular one, especially in Seattle. But for me, the choice was clear: these guys had to move on because they still had way too much to offer the rock-and-roll world. In an age of paint-by-numbers corporate rock, we fucking needed Alice in Chains.

I dove headfirst into the Alice in Chains catalogue. My critical peek inside these songs, riff by riff, opened my eyes to what truly amazing song craftsmanship went into them. I began to feel truly honored to be connected in any way to this musical history. Playing the songs live with them that spring of 2006 ranks as one of the most treasured moments I have experienced as an artist, period. As the band's confidence grew with permanent new member William DuVall, I could almost see the new life being breathed into the music. This minitour settled any questions about why or how. It was a truly moving sight to see, gig after gig.

Jerry summed up his thoughts in an interview a few years later: "Here's what I believe. Shit fucking happens. That's rule one. Everybody walking the planet knows that. Rule two: things rarely turn out the way you planned. Three: everybody gets knocked down. Four, and most important of all: after you take those shots, it's time to stand up and walk on—to continue to live."

Around the same time, I decided I needed another source of physical suffering, of good pain. I had run a marathon. Where could I push things from there? Well, books about exploration and mountain climbing had become a real passion of late—I'd read Into Thin Air, of course, but also *Touching the Void* by Joe Simpson, and Alfred Lansing's classic *Endurance: Shackleton's Incredible Voyage.* Suddenly a natural next step occurred to me: to test myself against mountains. Richard and Laurie Stark—our family friends who ran Chrome Hearts—had become friends with an aspiring high-altitude climber named Tim Medvetz, who had already summited Mount Everest. One night at a party, they introduced me to him and an unlikely climbing duo was born. Tim—better known as "Biker Tim" from the Discovery Channel's *Everest* series—became my mentor, and we soon climbed some of the local peaks in Southern California, starting with 10,500-foot Mount Baldy and 11,500-foot Alta Peak. Seattle's Mount Rainier became a long-term goal for me as I started to learn how to use crampons and ropes, practiced high-altitude survival methods, and grew accustomed to cuddling with Tim in a tiny high-camp tent.

Then, in the middle of 2006, Velvet Revolver regrouped to start writing songs for our second album. Even though Scott didn't tell me or any of the other guys directly, I knew there'd been murmurs of a Stone Temple Pilots reunion tour at some point in the future. On the face of it, I didn't have a problem with that, though it annoyed me that it was all kept hush-hush. His sneaky behavior created suspicion and tension. In the tight space of a band, that stuff can get unhealthy fast.

As we created songs for the record, new rumblings began. First, Scott demanded to write all the lyrics this time around. We reluctantly agreed. I thought it was a waste of everyone else's talents. Plus it made me write music differently; up to now, lyrical ideas had always informed the way I conceived of songs. But fine, this was a concession I could make to keep my bandmate happy. Then Scott decided he wanted a bigger share of the publishing rights—because he'd written all the lyrics. Oh, boy. This was typical stuff where I'd come from: success bred greed and megalomania. Still, I figured if we could just talk about it, we could come to a workable solution. I knew Scott was a smart guy and would listen to reason. I kept calling him, leaving him messages: *Let's have coffee, let's talk it over, face-to-face.* Finally, when I didn't hear back from him, I sent Scott an email, using an analogy to express my problem with his demand: "A group of guys build houses together, but suddenly one of them insists on building the roof by himself even though they had previously constructed first-class roofs all together. So the rest of the team agrees to concentrate on the foundation and walls while the other guy builds the roof. The day comes when the house is complete and the man who built the roof asks for more money. The roof is the most important part, he says, because it keeps the rain out. Would you describe that as fair, Scott? A large part of business is dialogue and compromise, and I suggest that we, as a band, try a little of both."

No reply.

The issues were left unresolved, but the album—eventually called *Libertad*—got finished. As we prepared for its release in July 2007, we booked an appearance on Jimmy Kimmel's TV show. After the performance, we were finally going to sort out the rot at a band meeting at a suite at the Roosevelt Hotel, a short walk from Kimmel's studio on Hollywood Boulevard. My hope still was that we'd be able to sit down calmly, put everything on the table, and discuss it like businessmen. Yelling and screaming was no longer my preferred method of negotiation. Unfortunately, Scott was drunk and a levelheaded discussion was not in the cards. Nothing was accomplished before the meeting devolved into yelling and screaming—and then Scott and Matt squared off as if they were going to fight. I walked out. That's when management stepped in to avert disaster. They probably saw the value in VR going back out on tour, and knew that if Scott started swinging at Matt, their gig might be up. They basically took cuts in their own commissions to get Scott close to what he wanted. It seemed as if Scott was chuckling through the rest of the talks. If you asked me, the managers should have held their ground. But at least they were actually *doing* something, which was a new experience for me.

The same week we appeared on Kimmel, in July 2007, my dad died. I was glad we had made our peace in the last few years of his life; we'd had some good times and many laughs. He'd been a good grandpa, and Grace and Mae definitely benefited from knowing him.

Now I had the honorable duty of being a strong male figure to my own daughters. Being a dad was a daily learning process—a lot of things

I supposed would be simple common sense got thrown out the window. I really never had any idea what was in store for me next. I had to be a "man's man" at times and at other moments I needed to be sensitive and soft. Earlier in life, I had gauged masculinity by how tough someone was in a threatening situation. More recently I'd come to understand that such bravado was usually a mask for fear. My biggest challenge, and the core of what I now saw as true manliness, was being honest with my-self and others and being forthright and true in my actions and dealings with my family, friends, and business associates. I didn't have this shit fig-ured out—and still don't—but for me, especially after my relapse offered another glimpse of failure, the true essence of manhood was now clear: being a caring husband and father.

CHAPTER SIXTY

✦ ✦ ✦

Velvet Revolver headed out on tour for the rest of the summer—first through South America with Aerosmith, then across the United States with Alice in Chains. Slash and I had regained our footholds on sobriety, and Alice in Chains guitarist Jerry Cantrell had also been sober for a couple years by that point. We would meet every day to support one another. It was a perfect situation for Scott to turns things around.

Instead, things fell apart. Scott went back to dabbling in crack and pills. I felt bad for him in a lot of ways. He was a shell of the cool guy I'd gotten to know quite well, and his marriage was falling apart—again. He traveled separately from us and began to show up late and make our crowds wait around, often drawing boos from our fans. Hadn't I been through this all before? His performances started to suffer; one time he even nodded off right in the middle of a song only to come to again singing the wrong part of the song. The crowd realized and started to heckle him.

Matt Sorum fell off the wagon at this time, too, before eventually regaining sobriety. The backstage areas of the tour quickly became as debauched as they'd been in the old days. This time, however, none of it affected me. I made sure to keep up my routine. And I got the fuck out of there. I had become the proud owner of a black 2006 Harley-Davidson Road King motorcycle and took it with me on the tour. During downtime, I revved it up and roared out of the vicinity of the band, the crew, the entourage—all the craziness.

Alice in Chains drummer Sean Kinney had gotten sober two weeks before the tour started. Over the years, he and I had become good friends and rode our bikes together a lot in Seattle. In fact, he had taught me to ride my big Harley. He and his drum tech, Tavis, also brought their motorcycles along on that tour. When the strippers arrived and the crack rocks were torched at the latest venue, Sean, Tavis, and I just cruised off into another beautiful landscape. As a result, I never felt trapped.

Riding in a state park instead of listening to drums getting tuned all day over a PA system was a good thing indeed. Sometimes we would ride off to have lunch and browse bookstores. It staved off loneliness while also offering new perspectives on places I had been before but never really seen.

During my teens and twenties, I would say that it was a great and genius thing that I did not have a motorcycle. The one time I did get on a bike during that time was at a video shoot for "Don't Cry." I asked a cop to let me try his bike. The poor cop was just working the shoot, but he let me take it for a spin. I crashed it. I owed my later epiphany about the pleasures of the motorcycle to Martin Feveyear, a producer who helmed a lot of Loaded recording sessions over the years. When we made the first Loaded record with him in 2001, he had laid out photos of a 1951 Sunbeam SX he was putting together from parts. The bike had been in Martin's family from the day he was born in the south of England. For a time it was his family's lone mode of transportation. Or so the story went. Martin's dad had shipped the old family bike in pieces to Martin in Seattle, and by trial and many errors, he eventually fixed the broken bits and put that 'Beam back in working order. Martin's studio was in the heart of the Wallingford section of Seattle, and the area was a crossroads for bikers. Each year, come springtime—which in Seattle meant anytime the thermometer topped forty and it wasn't raining—I'd see other friends who'd gotten their bikes out of their garages, fired them up, and were gallivanting around town, too. Eventually I started to ask myself why I wasn't riding now that I was sober, and I decided to buy my own bike. I realized now, on tour in 2007, that the timing had been perfect.

The other way I maintained my sanity on that second VR tour was by taking online college courses. For a long time I had remained steadfastly unwilling to finish my degree anyplace but Seattle U. I had worked so hard to get into that school. I had the family connection to that school. I had learned to learn at that school. But I had to concede that I would no longer be able to attend a full slate of classes in Seattle with ongoing band obligations and with Grace and Mae happily ensconced in their school in L.A. Eventually I decided to fill in missing credits with online courses.

A number of the online courses involved group projects, and I got to know people in my class—via computer. The students came from disparate backgrounds and from all over the country; for one class, my project team included an army sergeant, a woman who managed the office of a construction company, and a bank executive. Touring with VR allowed me to meet some of my classmates in person. I would put them on the guest list or meet them for coffee—I remember the office manager came to our show in Minneapolis. Somewhat surprisingly, the workload for these courses proved every bit as rigorous as at Seattle University, and the teachers often had distinguished backgrounds. One of my first online professors had taught at Berkeley for years. Even so, I still had mixed feelings about having to transfer my credits from Seattle U to an online university. I just had to hope Seattle would let me transfer the credits back and allow me to fulfill my dream of hanging a diploma on my wall to match my uncle's and to honor my mom's memory.

While I was maintaining my sanity by riding and studying, Slash, Matt, and Dave were getting more and more upset about Scott. We held a band meeting—without Scott—just before heading out on the last leg of the tour, which started in Dubai and then hit Europe and the UK. Our conclusion: there really was no other choice than to fire Scott at the end of the run. A funny thing happened. Once we came to this conclusion, it was as if a huge weight had been lifted from our shoulders. We went onstage every night on time, whether Scott was in the building or not. Once this started happening, Scott began to show up on time. With everything resolved, the band played better than it ever had, and we just plain forgot that Scott was even there. His drug-induced antics no longer had any impact on us, and we blazed right through any garbled rant that we might earlier have given him time to indulge. By the last gig, in Amsterdam, we were bordering on giddy about ridding ourselves of Scott. I wished him luck and I think he knows that he can always reach out to me. But I was happy to be done with the drama.

I arrived home to find my daughters starting to act almost like teenagers. Suddenly Grace couldn't wait to drive, to have an apartment and a job, to go off to college and not be walked to school in the morning by her mom and dad. Naturally Mae wanted to be just like her older sibling. When I suggested to them that they should enjoy their youth and not rush everything, they gave me a look like I was the oldest and nerdiest coot ever to walk the face of the earth.

I'd been warned about this stage—it's a stage at which daughters suddenly depart emotionally from their fathers. I knew it was just a phase, but it still entailed a profound sense of loss for me right then. As a typical guy, I wanted to "fix" the situation, but that only made my daughters think I was even dorkier and less cool than I had been the day before.

Still, I craved some serious dad time with my girls. I held out hope that in the right scenario they would somehow respond to the soothsayer-like genius with which I dealt with life and the universe. So I was thrilled when Susan asked whether she could take a weeklong trip with her mom, aunt, and sister.

"Of course, honey!"

The way I pictured it, once it was just me taking care of the girls, I could wait patiently in my easy chair—or, better yet, wait cross-legged in a yoga position to offer visual reinforcement of my mystic wisdom—until Mae or Grace inevitably clamored to be the first to pose all her life questions to me. *Perfect.*

On day one of Susan's absence, the girls came home after school and both went to their rooms with nothing more than a cursory "Hi, Dad."

That's okay, I thought. I knew they had a lot of tests to study for and homework to do.

Day two went the same way. As did day three.

But kids can't live on schoolbooks alone. I was still a strong believer in the power of things like playing catch with a baseball in the backyard.

That kind of thing could fix any and all problems. I decided to take my daughters on a hike after school that Friday.

They were *delighted.*

Actually, they both groaned.

"Come on!" I said.

I thought surely a little fresh air and exercise would loosen their tongues, and finally they would talk to me about life and ask for my insight and knowledge. I had decided we would walk a fire road in a park not too far from our house. But first I had to convince my girls to put on tennis shoes in place of their fancy sandals.

They both gave me a look.

"Oh, my god—what if a *boy* sees us?"

As we were climbing the first hill, I noticed that Grace had her purse with her. I didn't understand why a young girl needed a purse at all, much less out here in the park. When I asked her why she had brought it along on a wooded and not-so-easy hike, she replied, "Lip gloss! Duh!"

Duh indeed. Sometimes it was best just to keep my mouth shut and trudge on. And sometimes I just had to run up the white flag of surrender. I just wasn't going to understand it all.

CHAPTER SIXTY-ONE

✦ ✦ ✦

With Velvet Revolver on ice, I spent the rest of 2008 playing rhythm guitar with Loaded—lead guitarist Mike Squires, bassist Jeff Rouse, and on drums first Geoff Redding and then Isaac Carpenter. While we were in the studio one day recording some demos, I counted in a song we were working on. Later that afternoon, we were listening to some of the songs. That one came on.

"One . . . two . . . one, two, three, four . . ."

The other guys all looked at one another.

"What?" I said.

"That sounds just like the beginning of 'Patience.' That's you counting in 'Patience,' right?"

"Yeah. So?"

"Dude," said Squires, "you could walk into the trendiest restaurant in the world, a place with a six-month waiting list for a reservation, and when the snooty maître d' came up, dripping with disdain, and said, 'May I help you, sir?,' all you'd have to do is go, 'Uh, yes, my good man, actually you can help me: one . . . two . . . one, two, three, four,' and he would escort your ass straight to the best table in the house. That can open *any* door."

This became a running joke in Loaded, and I was expected to magically whisk us through any sticky situations with that incantation.

We released our album *Sick* in early 2009 and spent much of the year touring. We launched the U.S. tour at the legendary Crocodile Café in

Seattle's Belltown neighborhood. The Croc had folded a few years prior and had just been reopened by a group of people including Sean Kinney from Alice in Chains. My old friend Kurt Bloch, from the Fastbacks, got up and played a few songs with us, including "Purple Rain." It almost felt as though the punk-rock commune I'd wished for long ago had come together—at least for a night.

I spent much of the *Sick* tour actually sick. I even came down with pneumonia at one stage. The success of my sinus surgery was a thing of the past. This time, however, I refused to let the recurring infections hinder my training, and, if anything, continuing to work out helped subdue the aches and pains and throbbing ear infections. Another reason my renewed sinus problems didn't bother me too much was because being on the road with Loaded was totally devoid of drama. When you toured with nine guys—band plus crew—on a bus, playing night after night, all expectations of space and privacy were left at the curb. There was literally no room for bullshit. We washed our laundry in the backstage sink at whatever venue we played that night and hung it to dry in the bus; we only booked one night per week in a hotel—and even then we all crammed into just two rooms at the cheapest place around.

The way we dealt with close quarters was with humor. Tons of it. There was the warning call we used when two of us approached each other in the narrow aisle between the onboard bunk beds: *ass to ass.* The call had entered our lexicon a few years back when a huge security guy got ruffled after a band member passed him crotch to ass in a space about the same width as the aisle on a budget airline. This security guy did not exactly dig the fact that his manhood might have been compromised in that fleeting instant. He dressed down the young rocker right then and there: "Man, it's always ass to ass, dog . . . *ass to ass!*"

The incident became part of Loaded folklore and we practiced the ass-to-ass program on our bus—unless someone felt a bit frisky. In that case, you could surprise your fellow band member with a "junk drag," a quick spin just as you met your bandmate in the aisle to create a crotch-to-ass passage. I had a college education at this point and was a responsible father and husband, but, hey, you just can't beat juvenile fun sometimes.

A tour diet is never very wholesome. In fact, it's often downright gross. We ate dinner after we played, and at 1 a.m. we were lucky to find pizza or schawarma. In the UK, we lapped up cheap, spicy Indian food. Nine guys, one bus, mutton vindaloo, few rest stops—it was a recipe for a lot of flatulence. One of our guitar techs, the hilarious "Evil" Dave, from Sheffield, England, suggested we start a contest: who could come up with a word that most sounded like any given burst of gas. Some sounded like, say, "teapot." A more throaty one might become "streeeetpost." This not only passed the time, but also broadened our vocabularies; racking our brains for a winning word was almost like playing Scrabble.

When I returned from the various tour legs—in addition to dates here and in Europe, we crisscrossed South America and hit the festival circuit—I didn't have anyone to play Name That Fart with. My daughters ran from me when I so much as brought it up. And anyway, my diet also returned to normal.

The new words in my quiver came in handy, however, as during the same time period I kicked off a writing career with a column in the *Seattle Weekly* and a series of pieces on finance for *Playboy*. One . . . two . . . one, two, three, four: doors really were opening for me now.

A decade prior, I'd been unsure how to begin an admissions essay and now I was writing on a regular basis in a public forum. Of course, I was always looking for new hurdles, the more difficult or seemingly incongruous, the better. These latest seemingly monumental challenges didn't elicit any physical pain (well, maybe just a little—I'm still a crap typist). But I found them taxing in a different—and equally thrilling—way. I also loved the interactivity permitted by new media. When my pieces were posted online, I was able to engage in a genuine and substantive back-and-forth with readers. It may sound like a bit of a stretch, but it struck me as very punk rock—breaking down the barrier between artist and audience; bringing me and the readers face-to-face, if only virtually; turning readers into writers by allowing comments. I even made sure to invite my harshest critics (at least those brave enough to post their whereabouts) to come shake hands whenever I passed through their towns with Loaded.

Writing about financial strategies in the midst of a recession made

me reconsider some of the implicit lessons I was teaching at home. I remember telling Mae a bedtime story one night. Usually these consisted
of made-up tales about Buckley, the family dog—he was a superhero at
night, which explained why he slept all day. But this night, I decided to
tell her one of the stories my mother had told me about growing up during the Depression. My mom's stories haunted every major financial decision I made in adulthood. It dawned on me that maybe it was time for
me to teach my girls more of the values I was taught growing up in a large
family with working-class parents.

I maintained an idealized Norman Rockwell–like picture in my mind
of how our home life should look. Ah, but things seldom happen accord-
ing to plan when you have kids. I tried to teach my daughters to play
guitar many times over the years. Or at least to get them interested in
it. It seemed logical. I'm a musician, and my girls would probably take
after their old dad, right? Wrong. The reality was that they thought I was
a dork, and that all the things I did were somewhat dorky—including
playing in a rock band. Okay, I got it: my girls would never start the new
Runaways or L7. Fine. I had let that dream fade years ago. My girls would
blaze their own trails.

But then my wife and I took the girls to see Taylor Swift. Before anyone chastises me for my taste in music, let me just say that I completely
backed my girls' enthusiasm about Taylor Swift. Raising kids was hard
enough—if my kids happened to be into an artist with a sweet and innocent message, well, more power to them. And maybe, just maybe, it
showed they weren't in such a rush to grow up after all.

The day after the Taylor Swift concert, my wife asked me if I could
show her a few chords on the acoustic guitar.

"Yeah, sure," I said.

I muttered that I was a crappy teacher, but that I would do my best.

To my surprise, Susan locked right into it and played the chords I
showed her for the rest of the day.

The next morning, Grace asked me if I could show *her* a few chords
on the guitar, and if I could teach her an MGMT song.

"Um . . . sure!"

Grace and Susan ended up playing all that day. The next two days after that, Grace went straight to the guitar when she got home from school. Susan stuck with it, too.

Then, on the day after that, Mae came into the living room—where I have DirecTV's baseball package so I can watch my Mariners when I am down in L.A.—and asked if she, too, could learn a few chords.

"I want to play with my sister," she said.

There I was with all three of my girls asking me guitar questions. They were all playing different chords at the same time. Buckley the dog was snoring something fierce. Ken Griffey Jr. was at the plate, and we had a chance to go up by two in the eighth inning.

"Why do you have such an old guitar?" asked Grace.

The guitar in question was a Sears-made Buck Owens American acoustic that I treasure. I started to get flustered, until I suddenly realized that right there, right then, I had everything I'd always wanted. A family that needed me. Kids who were excited about something I could actually help them with. Two dumb dogs (we had added an unruly pug somewhere along the way) who were finally semi-house-trained. And my baseball team on the TV.

If only Norman Rockwell had been there to paint the scene.

CHAPTER SIXTY-TWO

✦ ✦ ✦

In the summer of 2010, I had to be in L.A. for a few weeks to work on the next Loaded record while my wife and kids were in Seattle for summer vacation. But that was okay. It was cool to be a lone wolf once in a while, to range free and howl at the moon—as long as I was home by 11:30 so I could call my wife before she went to bed. And yes, uh, well, my dogs got lonely when I was gone too long.

Once while Susan and the girls were gone, I was invited to a friend's birthday party at an ultrachic Hollywood lounge. I was too afraid of blowing my cover to ask for the address. Cool people were just expected to know where this place was. If you didn't know, you didn't belong anyway. There I was, the guy calling 411 to ask for an address. I had to try about four different spellings of the name—*is it French?*—before I got it right.

As I walked up to the doorman, my phone rang. It was my wife making sure I had fed the dogs and was wearing a coat and had taken my vitamins and drunk enough water. She loved me. I told her I had to get off the phone. I didn't want to look like *that guy*: the douche bag on his phone heading to the door of a cool club.

"Yes, you are my monkey," I whispered. "Yes, dear, the girls are our monkey babies. Yes, okay . . . I love you, too."

In October, Susan and I took a trip to London. For about a year, I had been working on starting a wealth management company—called Meridian Rock—together with a British finance partner named Andy Bottomley. And now we had reached a key moment: hiring a fund manager.

We planned to spend a week taking meetings with the final candidates and then making some company decisions. This was serious stuff. But it was also the final hurdle of another challenge I'd set for myself, to create a company of my own to help others with the nuts and bolts of finance and investing.

Our British Airways flight touched down at Heathrow Airport on the morning of October 14 at about quarter to noon. My meeting schedule that day was fierce, and kicked off only two hours after we landed. We collected our bags, went through customs, met our car at the curb, and drove to the Metropolitan Hotel in central London for a quick shower before the first of three meetings, staggered at two-hour intervals until dinnertime.

As we walked into the hotel lobby, the manager met us to ask how our trip had gone. *Exceptional service is one of the reasons I stay at this hotel whenever I come to London,* I thought to myself, *but they've really outdone themselves this time.* But then I remembered: Susan and I were staying in an unusually big room, a suite—in fact, the hotel's biggest suite. I'm by no means in the habit of staying in extravagant hotel rooms, however, and there was a simple explanation behind our staying in one now. My financial partner had booked the suite, which would also serve as headquarters and conference room for the week's business and was being paid for accordingly. Since it was such a lavish space, it seemed perfectly normal when the manager offered to personally escort us up to the room.

As we glided upward in the elevator, the manager said to me, "So, sir, you are playing a concert this evening?"

"No, no, I'm not here for a concert this time. I'm here on other business."

"Are you quite sure you're not playing this evening, sir?"

"Yes," I said. "I'm not playing at all this entire trip."

A slightly pained look flashed across his face.

"Well, sir, in that case I feel compelled to tell you that a Mr. Axl Rose is staying in the room adjoining yours. But I'm sure you are already aware."

"Uh, no . . . I can't say that I was aware of that. But thanks."

Though it wasn't something that gnawed at me over the years, I realized as soon as the hotel manager said Axl's name that I did have this one last unresolved connection to the past. Thirteen years is a long time not to talk to someone with whom you went through a formative phase of your life. And if I'm completely honest with myself, there was an element of personal doubt involved in it—I guess I wondered whether lingering resentment or just plain anger would emerge from somewhere deep inside of me when I finally, inevitably, saw Axl again.

Time was a luxury I was short on that day, however, so I didn't have a chance to dwell on this strange coincidence or mull the situation over just then. I had to shower fast and have a final brushup with Andy before we started our interview sessions—Andy and I had worked for a year solid to get us to this point. The first two meetings went great. I was getting my feet underneath me and sort of hitting my stride. During the third meeting, shortly after 6 p.m., the phone rang in what was serving as our conference room. I apologized to the gentlemen in the room, then answered.

"Duff McKagan!" I heard.

It was Axl's manager.

Okay, I guess the word was out that I was staying in the same hotel. I told him that I was in the middle of a meeting and asked him what room he was in; I would call him back.

After finishing that last interview of the day, Andy and I went over our notes and had a discussion about the three candidates we had met. Only after that did I start to think about my neighbor on the other side of the wall.

Though it had been thirteen years since we'd last spoken, I had always assumed Axl and I would one day meet again. I didn't know how it would happen, I just held out hope of perhaps rekindling a relationship of some sort, at some time. These days our only relationship, if you could call it that, consisted of being CC'd on the same emails about various business and legal affairs. Often vitriolic, caustic, or unpleasant emails. This type of language, I've found, keeps the clients angry and the lawyers employed.

Now here I was, a forty-six-year-old father of two girls Axl had never met. Grace provided a real-time gauge of how long it had been since Axl and I had spoken, since my departure from GN'R coincided with her birth.

In the end I just went to the door of his hotel room. People from his entourage stopped me in the hallway.

"You can't go in right now, man," said one. "He's about to get in the shower to get ready for the show tonight."

"I've seen him naked before," I said.

The door to Axl's room opened a crack.

"I thought I heard your voice out here," said Axl.

He wasn't naked.

He motioned with his head and said, "Come on in."

And so, for the first time in much too long. Axl and I finally met again face-to-face. Any doubts I had about what might happen melted instantly.

We hugged.

From then on, there was no awkwardness at all. It turned out it wasn't a big deal for either one of us, I don't think. It was just cool. After so much time gone and lost, we both seemed eager to mend a personal fence, to bridge a gap between us that had felt wider the longer we had gone without meeting. Time apart had done some damage in the form of the aforementioned legal wrangling, but time had also allowed me to figure out some major shit that had happened in my life. With Axl, or really anyone from my past, I tend to look at how I might handle a similar relationship now. What I did back then remains in the past. I don't necessarily forget those things, but I only bring them out of my memory from time to time to help me better deal with things today. So was I still harboring resentment or anger? To my relief, the answer, I now knew, was a resounding no.

The O2 Arena, where Axl's gig was that night, sits at the tip of a thumb of land at a bend in the Thames River. Rather than go there by limo, Axl had a boat ferry him to the venue, and he invited me and Susan to go along. He and I told jokes and old war stories as we cruised through central London on the river. He reminded me that I once tried to burn down Gorilla Gardens in Seattle when the club owner withheld our payment.

And now Susan knew I had once tried to burn down Gorilla Gardens, too. That must have been one from the vault that I'd forgotten to tell her.

Susan just laughed.

I showed him pictures of my daughters and he had a chance to get to know Susan a little bit, now that he had helped her learn something about me.

When we arrived at the O2 Arena, everyone there made us feel welcome, and that went a long way toward making it an enjoyable experience. I had always wondered what it would be like to see this band called Guns N' Roses from anywhere but the stage. The guys in Axl's current band are great players and good fucking guys. I'd had a chance to hang out with a few of them in other contexts over the years. And I'd been a fan of the guy who replaced me on bass—Tommy Stinson—for decades. He was an original member of the legendary Replacements, underground heroes of the 1980s. I must say I had a blast watching them all at the O2 Arena—and the band played awesome.

Then, during the encore, they hauled me out to play "You Could Be Mine," a song I hadn't played since the *Use Your Illusion* tour. I heard the crowd of 14,000 gasp and then go crazy when I emerged from the side of the stage and Tommy handed me his bass. Then I kind of forgot about one of the bridges in the song. *Oops.* At least Axl sounded good.

A little later I had a chance to go back out onstage and play along with "Patience." And though I didn't count the song in, it still felt as if doors were opening. Or perhaps reopening. Given this serendipitous chance to reunite with my old friend, I didn't want to let it be a one-and-done chance meeting and leave it at that. I decided I would make an effort to remain a friend now.

Axl invited me and Susan to dinner a few nights later, which timed well with my meetings. This was a much more leisurely evening, and one without questions hanging in the air. Axl and I could let down our guard. We both now knew: things were fine.

When the waiter came to take our drink orders, Axl looked up at him, paused, glanced at me, and then said, "I'll have a *virgin* mojito, please."

CHAPTER SIXTY-THREE

+ + +

When Susan and I returned to the States, I was surprised to learn the Seattle Seahawks had started to blast a new Loaded song, called "We Win," during their home games. It turned out a sports radio broadcaster had played the song and urged Seattle teams to get behind a local band. The whole thing sort of took off, and soon I received a call from the Seahawks organization to ask whether Loaded would play a halftime show on November 10, 2010.

Killer!

Seattle sports teams have always meant a lot to me. I'll never forget being at game seven of the Western Conference finals in 1996 when the Sonics beat Utah to reach the NBA Finals. The crowd went nuts, confetti fell from the air, and "Paradise City" blared from the rafters. That was a dream come true. This halftime show had the chance to be another.

As the show approached, though, I came down with a bad sinus infection. My whole body ached. Once we took the stage it was fine. But afterward I thought to myself, *No more.* No more of this bullshit. I need to fix the inside of my head once and for all. Dr. Thomas suggested a local specialist and I went to see him for a new batch of tests and another CT scan.

The doctor had me back to his office and showed me a huge poster of a healthy sinus system. Then he put my scan up next to it. Hello, surgery number two.

Ah, cocaine seemed like such a good idea once upon a time.

Watching my kids grow up has made me realize just how young I was when I did some of the things I did. Sometimes I cringe when I look at Grace and Mae. I really try to have an open and nonjudgmental relationship with my daughters, and my goal is for them always to feel safe coming to me with any problems or ordeals. The McKagans do honesty these days, and I probably learned that in part from my own father *not* doing it.

Of course, I knew the day would eventually come when I would have to face the realities that accompany growing up. Recently it had gotten back to Susan that the kids in our girls' middle school had started joking around about sex.

"Joking around?" I said. "What the hell does that mean?"

The time, alas, had come for me and my wife to sit down and speak somewhat candidly about the birds and bees with our daughters. I started to sweat.

We have a standard way to start our team meetings.

"McKagan family conference!"

The girls always got excited at what might be in store. Sometimes we called a family conference to plan a vacation together, for instance. This time, however, a look of dread started to spread across their faces as I began talking.

"You know that you girls can tell us anything," I began.

When I said the word *sex,* Mae started to bawl.

Oh shit, this isn't going to be easy.

Things settled down once it was clear that no one was in trouble and that this wouldn't be an inquisition. Grace soon stepped up and put everyone at ease with her candor.

"Yes, Dad," she said, "the older girls do talk about all of that stuff, but I think that it's pretty silly—they are just trying to act grown-up."

The mood of the talk became lighter and our family bond became a little tighter that afternoon.

Our house and its contents are always in constant motion. Girls are so different from boys—well, a lot different from me, at least. I can't wrap my head around the fact that in that ever-growing pile of debris on the floor someone could actually find something to wear, or, in at least one case I witnessed, something to eat. I have learned the hard way to stash my important stuff in a backpack and hide it. Yes, that's right. The king of this domain and alpha male of this wolf pack must tuck things like his passport, phone charger, laptop, and headphones in a bag in the trunk of his car to keep them from disappearing into those growing piles on the floor.

Still, when I am riding my big, rumbling Harley—swathed in black leather, my skin covered in yards of tattoos, the toughest and baddest man ever to ride two wheels—I can finally feel my testosterone return when the loud tailpipes set off car alarms as I roll menacingly down the bad streets of wherever I am. If, however, I get home after everyone is in bed, I shut the bike down a good block away from our house. I don't want to wake my sleeping angels. Just don't tell any of my biker friends, okay? As I walk through the door, Buckley rolls over on his back for me to scratch his belly before he leaves on another secret mission. He waits for me to change into my superhero costume. The launching spot for our crime-fighting forays is always the bed in the master bedroom, right next to Susan.

Listen, Buckley, maybe we should rest up and cuddle before we go. Or just go to sleep.

Ah, yes. But when I go out and rock, when I play live shows, I am still that glass-chewing, fire-breathing man among men. I spit and swear and lose myself in the moment. That is my time, and my family understands and gives it to me freely, with their full support. Susan and my girls are often dancing and cheering me on from the side of the stage.

When I come off, Mae invariably says, "Daddy, you cuss too much."

I'm proud to say that's one of the only vestiges left of what you might call a typical rock-and-roll lifestyle. In fact, I would go so far as to say I now have contempt for the term *rock star.* You may be saying to yourself, *Yeah, right, the dude from Guns N' Roses has a beef with a term that probably describes him to a T.* Let me tell you something: I cringe whenever that term is directed anywhere near me. Here's why.

I was fortunate enough in my teens to see the Clash on their first U.S. theater tour. This was before they received broader recognition on the

London Calling record and long before songs from *Combat Rock* landed them on MTV, but they were already larger than life to me. And they seemed truly exotic to me, too, somehow different and removed from me and my world. If the term *rock star* could have been used at any time in my experience, it would have been then and it would have described these guys who inspired true awe in me.

About two hundred people showed up at the Paramount in Seattle to see this gig and it was, simply put, mind-blowing. During the show, a big yellow-shirted security guy up front punched a fan and broke his nose. Blood was everywhere. The Clash stopped the show. Bassist Paul Simonon appeared from the wings of stage right wielding a firefighter's axe that he must have plucked from the wall. He jumped down in the pit and proceeded to chop down the wooden barrier separating the fans from the band while guitarist Joe Strummer dressed down the security goon and went on to say that there was no difference between the fans and the bands: "We are all in this together! There is no such thing as a rock star, just musicians and listeners!" That moment remains crystal clear in my mind to this day.

I also have a strong dislike for the term *rock star* because I do actually know some people in the biz who refer to themselves as rock stars. These people really think they're better than their fans. I, for one, find that kind of behavior embarrassing. Don't get me wrong. I get why the term is used and I was myself easily smitten with rock stars as a little kid—I was mes-merized by the likes of Jimi Hendrix and Led Zeppelin. Over the years, though, I have had the distinct honor of meeting some of the artists who occupied my classroom daydreams and have been pleasantly surprised at the regular-dude quality of these older rock musicians. I guess the ass-holes get weeded out and longevity tends to happen for those who see themselves as serving the music. I like that.

The term seems to have evolved a lot, too—from a noun into a much overused adjective, as in, "he sure has on some *rock-star* clothes." Fami-lies of touring musicians can attest to the fact that rocking is just a job, really, one that allows, at times, for the clan to see some cool places together. At other times, it brings forth almost desperate loneliness for all. Those times aren't very "rock star."

A moment of great humility came for me a few years ago after I played a huge stadium in Buenos Aires, Argentina, with Velvet Revolver. I was in the midst of finishing an online course at the time and had a question for the professor of the course. I told my wife that I had to call him when we got back to the hotel—we were getting a police escort back because the fans there can get a little, um, overzealous. When we got back to the room, fans had surrounded the hotel, singing soccer chants modified for the occasion. I had timed my call to catch this professor during his office hours.

When he picked up the phone, I said, "Hi, Professor Greene, this is Duff McKagan in your Business 330 class and I want to ask you a question about this week's assignment. I am calling from out of the country, so I was hoping to make this quick."

I had just played a stadium, been given a police escort, and now people were chanting my name on the street outside.

"Duff who?" he replied.

I came back down to earth in a hurry. And somewhere Joe Strummer was probably laughing his ass off.

ACKNOWLEDGMENTS

✤   ✤   ✤

The idea of writing a book would never have occurred to me if I hadn't already started to write in public forums where others could read my work. For that I must thank Chris Kornelis at the *Seattle Weekly* and Tim Mohr, then at *Playboy*, for believing in me enough to give me a chance as a weekly columnist in their respective publications back in 2008. These two editors gave me fruitful ideas, helpful advice, and ample room to grow.

It was through those columns that I learned I could actually get my ideas across much more clearly in written form. Talking or doing interviews was one thing, but committing my thoughts to paper became—and remains—a passion. I also have to thank and give props to my readership at the *Seattle Weekly*. I have been honored to receive your comments, and the constant exchange has given my writing more depth, insight, and color. My fellow writers at the *Weekly* also set a high bar for me to aspire to—especially Krist Novoselic and John Roderick.

When I approached my erstwhile *Playboy* editor Tim Mohr with the idea of writing a book, he gave me the confidence and energy to give it a proper go. Tim has been with me every step of the way on this book, and was my daily editor and consigliere. *It's So Easy (and Other Lies)* is as much his baby as mine.

Long before I ever thought of writing professionally, back when I first tried to enroll at Seattle University in 1999, I had to compose an admissions essay. I hadn't written an essay since sometime in the *very* early

1980s. My good friend Dave Dederer—Brown graduate and Presidents of the United States of America alum—walked me through those first scary steps of writing again. I still have his gift of Strunk and White's *Elements of Style* proudly displayed on my library shelf.

My wife, Susan, showed me the tricks of typing back then, as well as how to punctuate correctly. The typing is going strong, but she cringes now at some of the "creative" punctuation that's slipped into my writing in the meantime. She is as smart a wife as anyone could ask for, especially when it comes to writing and grammar. (All of this, *and* she is smoking hot!) Thank you, baby. I love you.

Writing is a solitary undertaking. Whenever I feel all alone, though, my dog Buckley is always there, snoring right by my side. Thanks, pal.

My literary agent, Dan Mandel at Sanford J. Greenburger, eased me through the process of securing my book deal. This could and should have been a pain in the ass. Dan, you made it all understandable and actually fairly enjoyable.

I wish to thank my band Loaded: Jeff Rouse, Mike Squires, and Isaac Carpenter. Thanks, fellas, for putting up with me burying my face in a damn laptop for countless hours in the studio, on the bus, on flights, and wherever else.

Thanks also to my business manager, Beth Sabbagh, the rock and voice of reason in my often chaotic life; to my lawyer Glen Miskel— we've come a long and eventful way together and I'll miss you; to Andy Bottomley, for being the smartest business partner a guy could ever ask for as well as a good friend; and to Jim Wilkie for letting me continue to hone my craft with a column on ESPN.com.

My editor, Stacy Creamer, Touchstone's publisher, believed in this project from day one, a fact that still floors me. When a professional of her caliber shows such unabashed excitement, it shames the rest of us who are jaded and gray. Thank you, Stacy. We are fellows cut from the same cloth; threadbare, sliced open, and constantly looking for the sun breaks to warm the calluses and cold away.

Words, of course, are the ammunition with which we writers fight. *New York Times* crossword guru Will Shortz has over the years helped add crafty and smart vocabulary words to my arsenal. Jon Krakauer and Thomas Friedman write stunning and readable nonfiction that constantly inspires me. Cormac McCarthy and the late, great Upton Sinclair craft the most wonderful and dark prose ever written. Period.

To Axl: thanks for putting up with my shit and being my friend in those dark hours.

To Izzy: thanks for leading the way and being a mentor.

To Slash: thanks for being such a musical inspiration.

To Steven Adler: I will always love you like a brother.

To Matt Sorum: you're a lion of a man.

To Dave Kushner: you are the *real* hero of Velvet Revolver.

To Scott Weiland: keep on, my friend.

To Sensei Benny Urquidez and Sensei Sarah "Eagle Woman" Urquidez: simply put, I learned to live again through the two of you.

To the Seattleheads worldwide: you guys fucking kick *ass!*

To Marybeth: thanks for being an *awesome* friend and for getting a whole mess of photos for this tome. You are one of a kind, sister.

Thanks also to Iggy Pop, who provides the ethical compass I use to point my way. You keep it real. I try to.

To my siblings Jon, Mark, Carol, Bruce, Claudia, Joan, Matt—for starters, let's just get this out of the way: Mom loved me best. You probably overheard her whispering this to me from time to time. What's that? You say she loved *you* best? God, we were lucky to have that woman as our mother. But I also feel lucky to have had you all as sisters and brothers. I appreciate all the inspiration, support, and guidance you have provided—and your low tolerance for bullshit.

And to Grace and Mae: I know that someday you may both be curious to read this book. You have asked me questions about my youth and I have done my best to responsibly answer your questions without terrifying you guys too much. This is the whole story—the good, the bad, and the ugly—and these pages are an attempt to make some sense of the crazier times in my life. Writing this book has made me realize just how lucky I am to have two daughters at all, and I hope that I don't embarrass either of you with any of these stories. In fact, I hope you guys can learn a thing or two from them, and I hope that going through so much hell allowed me to learn lessons that I can apply now as your father. You guys and your mom have provided me with a new life and light, and I will always treasure and protect you and do my best to steer you clear of some of the deep and dark chasms I fell into.

ABOUT THE AUTHOR

Duff McKagan played drums, guitar, and bass in punk bands in Seattle before taking his bass and moving to Los Angeles at the age of twenty. There, he and four new friends soon cofounded Guns N' Roses, whose *Appetite for Destruction* became the best-selling debut album in history. In 1994, McKagan barely survived when his pancreas burst as a result of drug and alcohol abuse. After thirteen years in GN'R, he left to start a family and study business at Seattle University. He went on to form the bands Loaded and Velvet Revolver, as well as to play stints in Alice in Chains and Jane's Addiction.

ABOUT THE COLLABORATOR

Tim Mohr is an award-winning translator of German novels, whose own writing has appeared in *The New York Times*, *The Daily Beast*, and *The eXile*, among other publications. He also spent several years as a staff editor at *Playboy* magazine, where he worked with writers including Hunter S. Thompson, Matt Taibbi, and Harvey Pekar. Prior to joining *Playboy*, he made his living as a club DJ in Berlin. He is currently at work on a history of East German punk rock.

INDEX

AC/DC 118
Adamson, Barry 84
Adler, Steven: first meets DM 30–2; joins GN'R 69–70; first GN'R tour 70–80; and DM 83–5; musical tastes 96; scrounging 99; drug abuse 116, 117, 148, 151, 154, 155–6, 162, 172; drum kit 118, 133; and Drunk Fux 122; in Chicago 150, 151–2; and Axl 151–2; and DM's marriage to Mandy 159–60; kicked out of GN'R 171–2; lawsuit 195
Aerosmith 103–4, 135, 138–9, 143, 161, 342
Affuso, Rob 203
AIDS 51, 95, 100, 145
Alice in Chains 128, 167–8, 337–8, 342, 343
Alpine Valley Amphitheatre, Wisconsin, 183
Alternative Tentacles 62
Ament, Jeff 128
Amsterdam 128, 345
Andreadis, Teddy 14
Andy (friend) 16–18, 40–2, 43–4, 272
Anthony (Sensei) 272, 288
Anvil 30
"Anything Goes" 59
Appetite for Destruction 96, 97, 121, 122, 125, 127, 129, 133, 135–6, 143–5
Argentina 222–3
Arkeen, West 86–7, 104, 122, 271–2, 288
Aronoff, Kenny 161
Art to Choke Hearts (Rollins) 120
Asian tour, 1988 145–6
Australia 145, 146, 225
Avery, Eric 84

Bach, Sebastian 203
Back in Black (AC/DC) 118
Barcelona 221–2
Bators, Stiv 119
Beaman, Rick "Truck" 13
Beat, Nicky 83
Beatles, The 33, 34
Beautiful Disease 296–7
Beck, Jeff 203–4
Believe in Me 12–13, 224
Believe in Me tour 12–13
Bennett, Tony 167
Biafra, Jello 62
Big Bear mountain-bike race 236, 237, 241, 244–6
"Birthday" 34
Biscuits, Chuck 38–9
Black Angus, The 27, 36, 45–6
Black Flag 29, 38, 62, 66, 120
Black Randy 100
Black Sheep 69
Bloch, Kurt 44, 48, 78, 348
Body Count 169
Bogotá, Colombia 214–16
Bottomley, Andy 352–3, 354
Brian (friend) 16
Brick by Brick (Iggy Pop) 162
Buckley (dog) 336–7, 350, 359
Burnett, T.Bone 66

Canter, Marc 70, 83, 89–90, 104

Canter's Deli 29–30, 83
Cantrell, Jerry 128, 203, 337–8, 342
Carpenter, Isaac 347
Carson, Johnny 55
Castillo, Randy 309–10
Castle Donington, Monsters of Rock festival 136–8
Cheap Trick 119
Chicago 149, 150–4, 188, 203
Chile 216
Chloe (dog) 166, 170, 197, 231–2, 240, 280, 294, 306, 336
Chrysalis 112
Circle Jerks, The 38
"Civil War" 149, 151, 163
Clarke, Gilby 197–8, 217–18, 220
Clash, The 84, 128, 359–60
Clink, Mike 120, 121, 171
Cobain, Kurt 15–16, 225
Colombia 214–16
"Coma" 172
Combat Rock (The Clash) 360
Connick, Harry, Jr. 205
Contraband 324
Coolies, the 223
Cooper, Alice 119–20, 129, 143
"Crack Pipe" (The Coolies) 223
Crass, Chris 41–2, 44
Crazy Horse 257, 281
Crew, Todd 98, 121, 122, 125–6
Cullinan, Dave 245–8, 249, 267–8, 268–9, 280
Culprit 62
Cult, The 125, 126–7
Cunningham, Petey "Sugarfoot" 273–4
curfews 184
Czech Republic 201

Dancing Waters club 59
Danny (friend) 70–1, 74, 78, 80
Dave, "Evil" 349
Davis, Clive 321
Day, Adam 162, 235, 244, 247–8
Dead Kennedys, The 29, 62
Dederer, Dave 300–1, 304–5
Del (friend) 85, 104, 108–9, 122
Dexter (brother-in-law) 145
Dick, Alan 137–8
Dickies, The 120
Dizzy 217–19
D.O.A. 38, 54, 62
Donner 65, 66, 70–1, 75–7
"Don't Cry" 59, 343
"Double Talkin' Jive" 163
Dr. Dre 169
drug abuse 3–4, 9, 48, 50, 64, 96, 117, 148, 172, 184, 195, 197–8, 199–200, 205; cocaine 10–11, 13, 138–9, 151, 154, 160, 180, 216; heroin 51, 54, 56, 63, 65, 85–6, 95, 128, 216–17; crack cocaine 106–9, 116
Drunk Fux 122
Duffy, Billy 127
Duran Duran 277
DuVall, William 338
Dylan, Bob 125

Earl, Big 152–3, 197
Eazy-E 169
Ed, Red 85
Eddy (friend) 16, 54–6, 85–6, 123, 127, 168, 234, 237,